LIFETIME EFFECTS

HIGH/SCOPE
EDUCATIONAL RESEARCH FOUNDATION
Ypsilanti, Michigan

Monographs of the
High/Scope Educational Research Foundation
Number Fourteen

LIFETIME EFFECTS:

The High/Scope Perry Preschool Study Through Age 40

Lawrence J. Schweinhart, Jeanne Montie, Zongping Xiang
High/Scope Educational Research Foundation

W. Steven Barnett
National Institute for Early Education Research
Rutgers University

Clive R. Belfield, Milagros Nores
Teachers College, Columbia University

Commentaries by

James J. Heckman
University of Chicago

Diana T. Slaughter-Defoe
University of Pennsylvania

Ypsilanti, Michigan

Published by
High/Scope® Press

A division of the
High/Scope® Educational Research Foundation
600 North River Street
Ypsilanti, Michigan 48198-2898
(734)485-2000, FAX (734)485-0704
press@highscope.org

Lynn Taylor, *Editor*
Kazuko Sacks, Profit Makers LLC, *Cover design, text design, and production*

Library of Congress Cataloging-in-Publication Data

Schweinhart, L. J. (Lawrence J.), 1947-
  Lifetime effects : the High/Scope Perry preschool study through age 40
/ Lawrence J. Schweinhart, Jeanne Montie, Zongping Xiang.
     p. cm.
  Includes bibliographical references.
  ISBN 1-57379-252-7 (pbk. : alk. paper)
  1. Children with social disabilities—Education
(Preschool)—Michigan—Ypsilanti—Longitudinal studies. 2. Education, Preschool—Michigan—Ypsilanti—History. I. Montie, Jeanne, 1947- II. Xiang, Zongping, 1953- III. Title.
  LC4093.Y67S35 2005
  372.21'0977'435—dc22

                                    2004028785

ISBN 1-57379-252-7

Printed in the United States of America

10 9 8 7 6 5 4 3 2 1

Contents

Tables and Figures

Tables

Figures

Acknowledgments

We thank the many persons who have contributed to the eighth comprehensive report of the High/Scope Perry Preschool study. High/Scope President Larry Schweinhart designed and secured funding for the age 40 study and wrote seven of the chapters. High/Scope researcher Jeanne Montie supervised the data collection, contributed to Chapter 2, and wrote Chapters 6 and 9. Researcher Zongping Xiang conducted the data analyses. The three of us collaborated on countless decisions relating to this report—regarding instrument development, data collection, data analysis, and writing. Coauthors Steve Barnett, Clive Belfield, and Milagros Nores conducted the cost-benefit analysis and wrote Chapter 7.

We especially wish to recognize the enormous contributions of the late David P. Weikart, who designed and directed the original Perry Preschool study as well as the preschool program that was the object of the study. Dave continued to provide ideas and motivation until his death on December 9, 2003. Although he did not live to see the completion of the study he began in 1962, he was able to see the many results of his labors along the way, and he joined in authoring well-regarded reports when study participants were 10, 15, 19, and 27.

We also wish to extend special thanks to the study participants who willingly opened their lives to our scrutiny, and to Van Loggins, tracker and interviewer of the study participants at age 40, who matched his extraordinary success in completing interviews with participants at ages 19 and 27 by interviewing all but 4 living study participants at age 40. Thanks to Lyn Griffin for entering the data and to Deb Dixon and Annie Balck for transcribing the audiotapes; to Nicole Gardner for cleaning the data and conducting preliminary analyses and literature reviews; to Kenneth Lindow for collecting the crime data from courts throughout southeastern Michigan; to Jill Claxton for cleaning the crime data and conducting preliminary analyses; to Charles Overby, Jim Davis, and Charles Sheffer of the Policy Analysis and Program Evaluation Division of the Michigan Family Independence Agency for providing social services data; and to John Henige of the Unemployment Agency in the Michigan Department of Consumer and Industry Services for providing unemployment data. We thank Laura Klem of the University of Michigan Center for Statistical Consultation and Research for her timely assistance with constructing a structural-equation model for the study. Finally, we wish to thank the High/Scope editors and others on staff who reviewed and edited the manuscript, and Jim Heckman and Diana Slaughter-Defoe for their thoughtful commentaries.

The board and staff of the McCormick Tribune Foundation deserve a special thanks, particularly our contact people—Ellen Collins-Bush, Alicia Menchaca de Cerda, Denise Carter-Blank, Wanda Newell, and Nicholas Goodban—for providing funds to complete this report. We thank their board for encouraging us a few years ago to conduct the age 40 study and the staff for their patience as we did so.

Executive Summary

The High/Scope Perry Preschool Study Through Age 40

The High/Scope Perry Preschool study is a scientific experiment that has identified both the short- and long-term effects of a high-quality preschool education program on young children living in poverty. From 1962 through 1967, David Weikart and his colleagues in the Ypsilanti, Michigan, school district operated the High/Scope Perry Preschool Project for 3- and 4-year-old children to help them avoid school failure and related problems. They identified a sample of 123 low-income African American children who were assessed to be at high risk of school failure and randomly assigned 58 of them to a group that received a high-quality preschool program at ages 3 and 4 and 65 to a group that received no preschool program. Because of the random assignment strategy, children's preschool experience remains the best explanation for subsequent group differences in their performance over the years. Project staff collected data annually on both groups from ages 3 through 11 and again at ages 14, 15, 19, 27, and 40, with a missing data rate of only 6% across all measures.

As shown in Figure E.1, the study found evidence of positive effects on program-group children's intellectual performance, school experiences, lifetime earnings, and crime rates: Their school achievement was at a higher level, they were more committed to school, and more of them graduated from high school than members of the no-program group. In

Figure E.1

MAJOR FINDINGS: HIGH/SCOPE PERRY PRESCHOOL STUDY AT 40

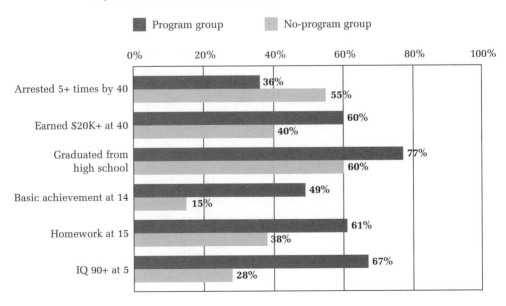

their adult lives, program participants have achieved higher earnings and committed fewer crimes than members of the no-program group.

The program group significantly outperformed the no-program group on highest level of schooling completed (77% vs. 60% graduating from high school). Specifically, a much larger percentage of program than no-program females graduated from high school (88% vs. 46%). (Each group difference reported in this summary is statistically significant with $p < .05$, one-tailed.) In the early years of the study, fewer program than no-program females required treatment for mental impairment (8% vs. 36%) or had to repeat a grade (21% vs. 41%). Overall, the entire program group, on average, outperformed the entire no-program group on various intellectual and language tests from their early childhood years up to age 7; on school achievement tests at ages 9, 10, and 14; and on literacy tests at ages 19 and 27. At ages 15 and 19, the program group also had better attitudes toward school than the no-program group, and program-group parents had better attitudes toward their 15-year-old children's schooling than did no-program-group parents.

At ages 27 and 40, more of the program group than the no-program group were employed (76% vs. 62% at age 40; 69% vs. 56% at age 27), and the program group had higher median annual earnings than the no-program group ($20,800 vs. $15,300 at age 40; $12,000 vs. $10,000 at age 27). Also at ages 27 and 40, more of the program group than the no-program group owned their own homes (37% vs. 28% at age 40; 27% vs. 5% at age 27) and cars (82% vs. 60% at age 40; 73% vs. 59% at age 27). At age 40, more of the program group than the no-program group had savings accounts (76% vs. 50%).

Through age 40, fewer of the program group than the no-program group were arrested 5 or more times (36% vs. 55%), and fewer were arrested for violent crimes (32% vs. 48%), property crimes (36% vs. 58%), or drug crimes (14% vs. 34%). By age 40, the biggest differences between the program and no-program groups in specific types of crimes cited at arrest were dangerous drugs (3% vs. 20%), assault and/or battery (19% vs. 37%), and larceny under $100 (9% vs. 22%). Fewer of the program group than the no-program group were sentenced to prison or jail by age 40 (28% vs. 52%), particularly from ages 28 to 40 (19% vs. 43%).

Other significant findings are that more program than no-program males took responsibility for raising their children (57% vs. 30%). More program than no-program males married (71% vs. 54%), and more had second and third marriages (29% vs. 8%). Fewer program than no-program males reported using sedatives, sleeping pills, or tranquilizers (17% vs. 43%); marijuana or hashish (48% vs. 71%); or heroin (0% vs. 9%). From ages 26 to 40, fewer members of the program than the no-program group reported health problems that stopped them from working for at least 1 week (43% vs. 55%). At age 40, more of the program group than the no-program group said they were getting along very well with their families (75% vs. 64%).

In constant 2000 dollars discounted at 3%, the return to society was $258,888 per participant on an investment of $15,166 per participant—$17.07 per dollar invested. Of that return, 76% went to the general public—$12.90 per dollar invested (as compared to $7.16 in the age 27 benefit-cost analysis of this program), and 24% went to each participant—$4.17 per dollar invested. Of the public return, as shown in Figure

E.2, 88% came from crime savings, and the rest came from education and welfare savings and increased taxes due to higher earnings. A full 93% of the public return was due to the large program effect of reduced crime rates for program males. Male program participants cost the public 41% less in crime costs per person, $732,894 less in undiscounted 2000 dollars over their lifetimes. Preschool program participants earned 14% more per person than those who did not attend the preschool program—$156,490 more over their lifetimes in undiscounted 2000 dollars.

Figure E.2

HIGH/SCOPE PERRY PRESCHOOL PROGRAM PUBLIC COSTS AND BENEFITS

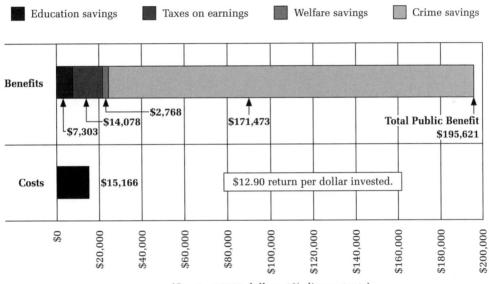

(Constant 2000 dollars, 3% discount rate)

A path model of the study suggests how the preschool experience positively affected the program group's age 40 successes. Beginning with their initial preschool experience and their preprogram intellectual performance, the model traces cause-effect paths to the program children's improved postprogram intellectual performance, then to their school achievement and commitment to schooling, then to their actual educational attainment, then to their greater adult earnings and fewer lifetime arrests in comparison with the no-program group.

Such positive outcomes are possible for any preschool education program that is based on the High/Scope model of participatory education and run by teachers with bachelor's degrees and certification in education, each serving up to 8 children living in low-income families. Success is also predicated on having teachers visit families (or arranging for parent meetings) at least every 2 weeks and having children participate in the program for 2 school years at ages 3 and 4, with daily classes of 2½ hours or more. Head Start, state preschool, and child care programs in the U.S. and other countries that emulate this model can achieve these results.

LIFETIME EFFECTS

I The High/Scope Perry Preschool Study Through Age 40

David Weikart and his colleagues in the Ypsilanti, Michigan, school district developed the idea of the High/Scope Perry Preschool Project in the early 1960s (Hohmann & Weikart, 2002). While he was the district's director of special education, Weikart worked with two committees looking for a better way of dealing with failing students—one committee composed of 3 elementary school principals, the other composed of members of the district's special services staff. The committees focused on preschool education for 3- and 4-year-olds as a way to address the problem of school failure while avoiding the complexity of districtwide school reform. As a result of these deliberations, Weikart proceeded to operate the state's first publicly funded preschool program, which was financed through the Michigan Department of Education. To meet the state's requirements, Weikart hired 4 teachers certified in both elementary and special education (difficult to do in a time of teacher shortage). He found space for a classroom in a community center for the first year of the project, then in Ypsilanti's Perry Elementary School for the rest of the project.

To provide program structure, the special services committee considered using the standard nursery school approach of the day, which focused on children's social and emotional development (Sears & Dowley, 1963), but subsequently decided that they must focus more squarely on children's intellectual development to prevent school failure. Then several outside experts advised the committee to abandon the project altogether because they believed 3- and 4-year-old children lacked the maturity to function in a school setting. Instead of abandoning the project, however, Weikart decided to set up an experimental study to assess the effects of the program, randomly assigning children to either a program group, whose members were enrolled in the preschool program, or a no-program group, whose members were not enrolled in the preschool program. The special services committee set three criteria for the preschool curriculum they would select. First, it had to be based on a coherent theory of teaching and learning. Second, it had to support each child's capacity to develop individual talents and abilities through ongoing opportunities for active learning. Third, researchers and teachers had to be able to work as partners so that theory and practice received equal consideration.

The curriculum development team's interest in children's active learning drew them to the work of Jean Piaget, initially as summarized by Hunt's *Intelligence and Experience* (1961), and the team developed a model using processes, goals, and content areas derived from Piaget's ideas. As time went by, however, the team experienced tension between the researchers—who insisted on strict interpretation of Piaget's ideas—and the teachers—who sought to integrate these ideas into their daily classroom experience. Under Weikart's guidance, the researchers continued their pursuit of knowledge, while the teachers' struggles to integrate theory and practice led to the development of the High/Scope participatory education model. Although development of the model has continued over the years, it has nevertheless maintained its basic orientation toward children's active learning and development.

The Cyclical History of the Study

This monograph reporting the High/Scope Perry Preschool study through age 40 is the eighth comprehensive report of its findings. The preschool program that is the subject of study served 3- and 4-year-olds in Ypsilanti, Michigan, from 1962 through 1967. As the preschool program ended, Weikart (1967) reported the initial findings. Comprehensive monographs have followed study participants from their preschool years up to various ages, several with economic cost-benefit analyses:

- Ages 5–9 (Weikart, Deloria, Lawser, & Wiegerink, 1970)

- Age 10 (Weikart, Bond, & McNeil, 1978), with the study's first economic cost-benefit analysis (Weber, Foster, & Weikart, 1978)

- Ages 14–15 (Schweinhart & Weikart, 1980)

- Age 19 (Berrueta-Clement, Schweinhart, Barnett, Epstein, & Weikart, 1984), with cost-benefit analysis (Barnett, 1985b)

- Age 27 (Schweinhart, Barnes, & Weikart, 1993), with cost-benefit analysis (Barnett, 1996)

Professional education and social sciences journals have published summaries of the study (Barnett, 1985a, 1992, 1993; Farnworth, Schweinhart, & Berrueta-Clement, 1985; Schweinhart, 2002a, 2002b, 2002c; Schweinhart, Berrueta-Clement, Barnett, Epstein, & Weikart, 1985a, 1985b; Schweinhart & Weikart, 1981a, 1988a, 1988b, 1993, 1998; Weikart, 1967, 1988, 1989, 1998). Books edited by social scientists and educators have included chapters summarizing the study (Berrueta-Clement, Schweinhart, & Weikart, 1983; Schweinhart & Weikart, 1981b, 1983, 1989, 1992, 1995; Schweinhart, 1987, 1988c, 1992, 2001; Weikart, 1996, 2002; Weikart & Schweinhart, 1992). In the work leading to publication of two of these chapters, the Consortium for Longitudinal Studies and the American Psychological Association Task Force on Prevention provided unusually intense scrutiny of the study.

Cycles

A longitudinal study is a cyclical, recurrent accounting of people's lives. The Perry Preschool study provides an accounting of its participants' lives at birth, then annually from ages 3 to 11, again at ages 14 and 15, 19, 27, and now age 40—14 periods of measurement over 40 years of life. The stability of recurrent measurement casts into relief changes over time. The changes have occurred in everyone involved—the study participants and the researchers—and in the social contexts that surround them. As people move from childhood to adolescence to adulthood, the explanations for their patterns of behavior and accomplishment shift from psychology to sociology to economics, and expand from a unified developmental focus into the study of the impact of various social problems, such as poverty, crime, teen pregnancy, and high school dropout rates. The presentation of the High/Scope Perry Preschool study to various audiences has also shifted from one emphasis to another—academic performance and educational attainment for educational psychologists, crime for criminologists, earnings and economic return for economists.

Changes in research staff and other project staff are not supposed to affect the consistent, objective, scientific perspective of a longitudinal study, but they do, of course. We set the standards a little higher for each monograph, not only because of the need to respond to criticisms or perceived shortcomings of previous monographs but also because of the development of, and our learning of, new techniques and knowledge. In addition, while a longitudinal study by definition has no new study participants in later data collections, some researchers remain while others come and go. David Weikart was with the High/Scope Perry Preschool study throughout its 41-year history. Lawrence Schweinhart has been involved in the study for 29 years, and High/Scope's Ann Epstein has been engaged in writing case studies from time to time over the years. Van Loggins has served as the study's principal interviewer for 25 years. Steve Barnett has conducted several editions of the cost-benefit analysis over 20 years. Other researchers have been involved in either the beginning of the project through the early 1970s or at one of the data collections at ages 19, 27, or 40. Indeed, well over 100 researchers have been involved in conducting the study in some capacity—providing one type of confirmation on the study's objectivity and the validity of its findings.

It is also important to note that this study has developed in the changing social contexts of poverty and early childhood programs.

The Changing Context of Poverty

U.S. poverty today resembles U.S. poverty in 1962 in some ways and differs from it in others. The definition of poverty remains the same: lack of money and material possessions. Also, the federal poverty threshold has existed with modest modifications since 1965, increasing primarily with inflation (Fisher, 1992). Nevertheless, some government welfare programs exist today that did not exist in 1962, and the welfare reforms of recent years have transformed programs such as Aid to Families With Dependent Children into the streamlined Temporary Assistance to Needy Families program.

The U.S. Census Bureau defines the poverty level for a person or family as an income before taxes that equals the cost of a minimum diet multiplied by 3 to allow for other basic needs. This level is adjusted annually by the Consumer Price Index. In 2002, the poverty threshold for a family of 3 persons including 2 related children was $14,494, and 12% of the U.S. population lived in poverty. This percentage fluctuated between 17% and 22% from 1959 to 1965, and between 11% and 15% from 1966 to 2002. U.S. poverty rates in 2002 were 8% for non-Hispanic white Americans, 22% for Hispanic Americans, and 24% for African Americans. Poverty rates for U.S. children under 18 in 2002 were even higher—9% for non-Hispanic white American children, 29% for Hispanic American children, and 32% for African American children. Family configuration plays an important role in determining the U.S. poverty rate: The 2002 poverty rates were 6% for married couples and 29% for families headed by females (Proctor & Dalaker, 2003).

The cycle of poverty concept makes a recurring connection from inadequate schooling to adult poverty within lifetimes that then becomes an intergenerational connection from families' poverty to children's inadequate schooling (Solon, 1992, 1999). In other words, children born in poverty do not perform well in school and attain less schooling, and then their inadequate level of schooling negatively affects their degree of economic success. This cycle is clear when considering that the educational attainment of the U.S. population has grown steadily over the years, but not for the poor. The percentage of American adults aged 25 and over who graduated from high school was 63% in 1975 and 84% in 2000; the percentage who graduated from college was 14% in 1975 and 26% in 2000. Average annual earnings in the U.S. in 1999 were $18,894 for high school dropouts, $25,909 for high school graduates, and $45,394 for college graduates (Day & Newburger, 2002). Similarly, 1997 U.S. poverty rates were 22% for high school dropouts, 9% for high school graduates, and 2% for college graduates (U.S. Census Bureau, 2003a). The Progress in International Reading Literacy Study of 2001 (PIRLS) found that the higher the percentage of poor children (eligible for free or reduced-price lunch) in a public elementary school, the lower were fourth-graders' reading literacy scores (Ogle et al., 2003).

A worldwide trend of the past half-century has been the feminization of poverty—the increasingly greater percentage of poor people who are women (and children). One reason for this shift in the U.S. has been the increasing percentage of children living in single-parent families—rising from 10% in 1965 to peak at 29% in 1997, then slightly declining to 27% in 2001; the rate for African American children rose from 26% in 1965 to 63% in 1995 and dropped to 57% in 2001 (Ellwood & Jencks, 2004). Ellwood and Jencks (2004) attribute the increase in these rates to rising divorce rates in the 1960s and 1970s and rising out-of-wedlock births in the 1980s and 1990s, and the slight decrease in the last few years to the combination of welfare reform and low unemployment.

The U.S. crime rate in general has doubled since the time of the High/Scope Perry Preschool Project, even though it has dropped in the last 2 decades. According to the Federal Bureau of Investigation's Uniform Crime Reports of arrests throughout the U.S., the crime index rate per 100,000 inhabitants was 2,020 in 1962, peaked at 5,950 in 1980, and was 4,124 in 2000 (The Disaster Center, 2004). The violent crime rate was 162 in 1962, peaked at 758 in 1991, and was 506 in 2000. The much higher crime rate has changed U.S. society in general and poor neighborhoods in particular—increasing the numbers of both criminals and victims, coarsening lives, forcing security considerations into daily experience, making prison a growth industry.

The Changing Context of Early Childhood Programs

During the past half century, preschool programs for young children living in poverty have grown substantially. Head Start began in 1965 as a summer program, serving 561,000 children at a cost of $96.4 million—$172 per child. In 1971, when it had become a full-school-year program, Head Start served 397,500 children at a cost of $360 million—$906 per child. In 2002, Head Start served 912,345 children at a cost of $6.5 billion—$6,934 per child (Head Start Bureau, 2003). Corrected for inflation and using FY 2002 dollar value, Head Start's cost per child was $794 in 1965 and $3,266 in 1971 (*Economagic.com,* 2004). Clearly, the lightly funded project of 1965 was growing significantly 6 years later, and the cost per child today ($6,934) is about four fifths of U.S. public school cost per pupil ($8,745 in 2001–2002; National Center for Education Statistics, 2002a).

Virtually unknown in 1965, state prekindergarten programs in 2003 served an estimated 718,926 children, at an estimated cost of $2.6 billion (Education Commission of the States, 2003). A recent survey of U.S. public elementary schools found that 35% of them—19,900 schools—had prekindergarten classes (58,500 in all) serving 822,000 children with federal, state, and local funding (Smith, Kleiner, Parsad, Ferris, & Greene, 2003). Most of these schools included children with disabilities; for this specific purpose, 80% of the schools used state and local funds, and 51% used federal and local funds.

Maternal employment and the resultant need for nonmaternal child care have also grown enormously in the last half-century. The U.S. labor force participation rate of women with infants up to 12 months old was 31% in 1976 (the first time it was recorded), 59% in 1998 (its peak to date), and 55% in 2000 (Bachu & O'Connell, 2001). Of women with infants in 2000, 34% were employed full-time, 17% were employed part-time, 5% were unemployed, and 44% were not in the labor force. As the maternal employment rate has increased, more child care has moved from other people's homes into organized facilities. Comparing primary arrangements for children under 5 with employed mothers from 1977 to 1994, care in organized child care facilities rose from 13% to 29%, while care in other people's homes dropped from 41% to 31%, and care by working mothers themselves dropped from 11% to 6%; care in children's own homes remained steady at about 33% (U.S. Census Bureau, 1998).

Generalizations of the effects found in the High/Scope Perry Preschool study and similar studies require that the programs compared have similar characteristics and that the children served also are similar in important characteristics. Key variables concerning children are whether they live in poverty or are otherwise at risk of school failure. Some key program variables are structural, such as group size and number of teaching staff per group, academic credentials and pay of teaching staff, type of program used, program-specific training of teaching staff, and scope of the parent outreach aspect of the program. Other key program variables involve program objectives and practices, such as whether a program focuses narrowly on children learning reading and arithmetic or broadly on children developing intellectually, socially, and physically; and whether a program encourages children to take initiative or expects them to follow adult directions at all times.

The various forms of governance of these programs set policies and practices that determine the extent to which these conditions are met. Teaching and caregiving staff define and deliver programs to children and families. Center directors and school principals provide onsite governance. Agency directors, school superintendents, and state, regional, federal, and central-office early childhood administrators provide various levels of off-site governance. Governance also varies from expecting teaching staff to comply strictly with directives to encouraging them to exercise some or much flexibility and autonomy in the interpretation of directives.

Although Head Start programs have always been centralized under federal administration, they have varied in the strictness of their governance and how it applies to structure, objectives, and practices. The advent of the Head Start Program Performance Standards in the 1970s gave structural guidance to Head Start programs. In recent years, the federal Administration has moved toward specifying the program's objectives in greater detail. In 2000, Presidential Candidate George W. Bush indicated his desire to make literacy learning a major focus of Head Start, and Head Start has indeed intensified its focus on literacy during his tenure. Also, the Head Start federal reauthorization of 1998 identified certain features of Head Start child outcomes in literacy and mathematics. Then the Head Start Bureau (2003) developed the Head Start Child Outcomes Framework to capture both the breadth and the specificity of Head Start objectives. At this writing, the next Head Start federal reauthorization is pending in Congress, and the federal government has initiated a national reporting system based on testing children in literacy and mathematics.

Thus, Head Start finds itself at the center of a great debate on the purpose of early childhood education. Traditionally, the program has focused on the broad array of objectives in the Head Start Child Outcomes Framework and has espoused a child-centered approach to education. The current Administration, however, is more focused on literacy and mathematics learning, and there is pressure to shift the focus of the program to the lesson-centered approach to education that is common in the public schools.

The Preschool Program Research Tradition

In the 1950s, the conventional wisdom was that schooling did not begin before ages 5 or 6. Kindergarten, Froebel's (1826, 2004) early childhood innovation of the nineteenth century, focused on 3- to 5-year-old children, but came to America as a program for 5-year-olds. Nursery schools did exist at this time to provide an enrichment experience for young children in families that could afford them. But educational programs for 3- and 4-year-olds were not a matter of public policy.

In preschool program research, 1962 was a seminal year. In the summer of 1962, Susan Gray and her colleagues started the Early Training Project in Murfreesboro, Tennessee. In the fall of 1962, David Weikart and his colleagues started the High/Scope Perry Preschool Project in Ypsilanti, Michigan. Martin and Cynthia Deutsch's Institute for Developmental Studies at New York University was also running a preschool enrichment program and a study of its effects. Theoretical work and basic research suggested the potential effectiveness of such programs in improving young children's intellectual performance (Bloom, 1964; Hunt, 1961), and several studies suggested the efficacy of early childhood education programs with mentally impaired children (Kirk, 1958; Skeels & Dye, 1939; Skeels, 1966). But the 1962 studies were the first of a new tradition of studies designed to examine the potential effectiveness of preschool programs for young children living in poverty.

The federal Head Start program was first authorized by the Economic Opportunity Act of 1964. Sargent Shriver, first head of the Office of Economic Opportunity, got the idea of a preschool program for poor children from Susan Gray's Early Training Project (Stossel, 2004). These were also years when the federal government started to evaluate its programs. A couple years after it began, Head Start was the subject of a post-test-only national evaluation (Westinghouse Learning Corporation, 1969) that claimed that the summer programs had no effects and the school-year programs had short-lived ones. These results were heavily contested (summarized by Datta, 1976). However, this situation did not lead to better designed national evaluations of Head Start in the 1970s, but rather to a general wariness of evaluation by practitioners and policymakers concerned with Head Start.

Nonetheless, the preschool research tradition flourished through the 1960s and 1970s, with additional studies conducted of local preschool and parent education programs, comparing them to no-program groups and also comparing various types of programs. In the late 1970s, the principal investigators brought a dozen of the best of these studies together to form the Consortium for Longitudinal Studies (1983). Collaborating in data collection and analysis, the Consortium found robust evidence of preschool program effects on children's intellectual performance at school entry, reduced need for placements in special education, and reduced need for retention in grade. Several of the studies found that a greater percentage of preschool program graduates became high school graduates.

While most of the preschool studies have relied on quasi-experimental designs determined by which children and families chose to enroll in the program, the High/Scope Perry Preschool study and the Abecedarian study—which began in 1972, a decade after the High/Scope study—randomly assigned children and families to program and no-program groups (Campbell, Ramey, Pungello, Sparling, & Miller-Johnson, 2002). As the number of these studies increased, so did reviews of them, from early ones commissioned by the federal government (Bronfenbrenner, 1974; White, Day, Freeman, Hantman, & Messenger, 1973) to more recent ones (Barnett, 1995, 2004; Currie, 2000; Karoly et al., 1998; McKey et al., 1985; Yoshikawa, 1995). Studies have also moved beyond innovative programs at single sites to focus on service programs at multiple sites (Reynolds, Temple, Robertson, & Mann, 2001; Gilliam & Zigler, 2000).

Recent Evidence on Preschool Programs

Growing evidence indicates that high-quality preschool child develop-ment programs contribute to the short- and long-term development of children living in poverty. Some recent studies have been experimen-tal, involving random assignment of children and families to program and no-program groups and providing the most unequivocal evidence regarding program effects. Other recent studies have been quasi-experi-mental, involving either a nonrandomly assigned no-program group or no comparison group at all; these do not completely rule out alternative explanations, but permit examination of evidence in situations in which experimental design is impossible.

Recently Reported Experimental Studies

An evaluation of the Head Start Comprehensive Child Development Program (Goodson, Layzer, St. Pierre, Bernstein, & Lopez, 2000) randomly assigned 4,410 children and families living in poverty at 21 sites either to this pro-gram or no program and followed them for 5 years. Although the program's comprehensive services centered on the assignment to each family of a case manager to help them meet their needs, only 58% of the program group actually met with a case manager, as did 18% of the control group due to other programs. The study found no statistically significant, positive group differences on either child or parent outcomes, suggesting that families do not really profit from case management associated with early childhood pro-grams. However, the difference between groups in case management use was only 40% (58% minus 18%) rather than the 100% that might be expected. On a key measure of achievement at age 5, the difference was 1.7 points, which could have been 4.3 points and statistically significant if the case management difference had been 100% (Angrist, Imbens, & Rubin, 1996).

An evaluation of some 3,000 infants and toddlers and their low-income families in the Early Head Start program, the federal program that began in 1995, found program effects through age 2 (Love et al., 2002). When compared to a randomly assigned control group, Early Head Start children did modestly but statistically significantly better on measures of cognitive, language, and social-emotional development, and their parents scored significantly better than control-group parents on measures of par-enting behavior and knowledge of infant-toddler development.

Two evaluations of the Even Start Family Literacy program (Planning and Evaluation Service, 1998) randomly assigned children and families to Even Start or not. Somewhat greater percentages of the Even Start group than the control group received various services, 95% versus 60% participating in early childhood education, for example. Consequently, both groups experienced gains, with the Even Start group experiencing some greater gains—the pattern for adult literacy, adult GED attainment (22% vs. 6% in one of the studies), cognitive stimulation and emotional support by the family, and children's vocabulary. Even Start children improved their basic school readiness skills (e.g., recognition of colors, shapes, and sizes), but their non-Even Start peers caught up with them a year later, a common finding for intellectual achievement in preschool programs. Again, the lack of compliance with group assignment may have led to underestimation of program effects.

A few years ago, the U.S. General Accounting Office (1997) observed that no studies had evaluated effects of typical (rather than model) Head Start programs using experimental designs that randomly assigned children to program and no-program groups. Head Start's 1998 reauthorization included an Advisory Committee on Head Start Research and Evaluation (1999) that recommended a framework for studying the impact of Head Start. The National Head Start Impact study, now under way, should soon provide useful results.

Recently Reported Quasi-Experimental Studies

The IEA Preprimary Project (Olmsted & Montie, 2001; Weikart, Olmsted, & Montie, 2003) is a multinational study of preprimary care and education sponsored by the International Association for the Evaluation of Educational Achievement (IEA). High/Scope served as the international coordinating center for this study. Working collaboratively with researchers in 15 countries, High/Scope staff were responsible for sampling, instrument development, data analysis, and the writing of six published reports (including one in press). The major purpose of the study is to identify how process and structural characteristics of community preprimary settings affect children's language and cognitive development at age 7. The study is unique because many diverse countries participated, using common instruments to measure family background, teachers' characteristics, structural characteristics of the settings, experiences of children, and children's developmental status. The age 4 sample included over 5,000 children in more than 1,800 settings in 15 countries. Ten of the initial 15 countries collected language and cognitive outcome measures, developed by an international team, on children at age 7, when all had entered primary school. The median retention rate across country samples of children was 86%.

Four findings emerged that were consistent across all of the country samples of children included in the data analysis:

- Children's language performance at age 7 improves as the predominant types of children's activities that teachers propose are free rather than personal/social. From greatest to least contribution, activity types were as follows:

  - Free activities, which teachers let children choose.

  - Physical/expressive activities—gross- and fine-motor physical activity, dramatic play, arts, crafts, and music.

  - Preacademic activities—reading, writing, numbers, mathematics, physical science, and social science.

  - Personal/social activities—personal care, group social activities, and discipline

- Children's language performance at age 7 improves as teachers' years of full-time schooling increase.

- Children's cognitive performance at age 7 improves as they spend *less* time in whole group activities—times when the teacher proposes the same activity for all the children in the class, such as songs, games, listening to a story, working on a craft, or a preacademic activity.

- Children's cognitive performance at age 7 improves as the number and variety of equipment and materials available to children in preschool settings increase.

Across diverse countries, child-initiated activities and teachers' education appear to contribute to children's later language performance; and minimization of whole group activities and a greater number and variety of materials in preschool settings appear to contribute to their later cognitive performance.

The Family and Child Experiences Survey (FACES; Zill et al., 2003) is a study of a representative national sample of Head Start programs in the U.S. The first cohort of 3,200 children entered Head Start in fall 1997; the second cohort of 2,800 children entered Head Start in fall 2000. In Head Start, children improved on important aspects of school readiness, narrowing the gap between them and the general population, but still lagging behind. Relative to national norms, children made significant gains during the Head Start year, particularly in vocabulary and early writing skills. Children in Head Start grew in social skills and reduced hyperactive behavior, especially if they started out more shy, aggressive, or hyperactive. The study found that Head Start classrooms were of good quality. Most programs used a specific integrated curriculum, particularly Creative Curriculum and High/Scope. Use of these curricula and higher teacher salaries were predictive of positive child outcomes. Teachers' educational credentials were linked to greater gains in early writing skills. In addition, provision of preschool services for a longer period each day was tied to greater cognitive gains by children. Based on follow-up of the 1997 cohort, Head Start graduates showed further progress toward national averages during kindergarten, with substantial gains in vocabulary, early mathematics, and early writing skills. Most Head Start graduates could identify most or all of the letters of the alphabet by the end of kindergarten and more than half could recognize beginning sounds of words.

Gilliam and Zigler (2001) report that as of 1998, evaluations had been conducted of 13 of the 33 state preschool programs. They summarize these evaluations as finding modest support for positive program effects on children's developmental performance, school performance and attendance, and reduced percentages of children held back a grade. Similarly, an evaluation of North Carolina's Smart Start programs, not included in their review, found evidence of modest improvements in children's skills as rated by teachers at kindergarten entry (Smart Start Evaluation Team, 1999).

Oden, Schweinhart, and Weikart (2000) studied 622 22-year-olds born in poverty who had or had not attended Head Start years before. Of the females at the site that permitted such comparisons, more of the

Head Start graduates graduated from high school or obtained a GED (95% vs. 81%), and only one third as many had been arrested for a crime (5% vs. 15%). At the same site, the study compared children who had participated in regular Head Start classes to children in Head Start classes using the High/Scope participatory education model, in which teachers systematically supported children's intentional learning activities. Both males and females who had experienced High/Scope rather than regular classes achieved a higher elementary grade point average (3.2 vs. 2.4 on a 4-point scale) and had only 38% as many criminal convictions by age 22 (0.54 vs. 1.41 convictions per person). Independent analyses suggested that these program effects were probably underestimated.

Currie and Thomas (1999) examined the effects of Head Start in the representative National Longitudinal Survey of Youth by comparing Head Start children to their siblings who did not attend Head Start. The survey had identified who had attended Head Start by asking the children's mothers. Focusing on 750 Latino children, they found that relative to their siblings, Head Start children had higher vocabulary and mathematics test scores and were less likely to repeat a grade. Applying the same method to the nationally representative Panel Study of Income Dynamics data, Garces, Thomas, and Currie (2000) found long-term effects of Head Start programs in a sample of 255 young adults on the high school completion and college attendance of whites and the crime convictions of African Americans.

Three Long-Term Preschool Studies

Three long-term preschool program follow-up studies stand out for their duration and methodological quality—the Carolina Abecedarian Project study, the Chicago Child-Parent Centers study, and the High/Scope Perry Preschool study. These three studies offer the best evidence of the long-term effects of good preschool programs. It is useful to examine their similarities and differences in greater detail. Another study by David Olds and his colleagues in Elmira, New York (Olds et al., 1997, 1998), was similar to these studies in employing random assignment of study participants, follow-up 15 years after the program, and cost-benefit analysis, but examined a different type of program—prenatal and infancy home visitation by nurses (Olds, Henderson, Phelps, Kitzman, & Hanks, 1993).

The Carolina Abecedarian Project

Craig Ramey and his colleagues at the University of North Carolina at Chapel Hill began the Carolina Abecedarian Project in 1972 (Campbell, Pungello, Miller-Johnson, Burchinal & Ramey, 2001). They randomly assigned 111 infants averaging 4.4 months of age from poor families to a special program group ($n = 57$) or a typical child care group ($n = 54$) that used the child care arrangements in homes and centers that were typical in the 1970s. The special program was a full-day, full-year day care program for children that lasted 5 years, from birth to elementary school. Some of the study participants also received follow-up support during kindergarten to grade 3. The special program's goal was to enhance children's cognitive and personal characteristics so they would achieve greater school success. It offered infants and toddlers good physical care, the optimal stimulation of adult-child interaction, and a variety of playthings and opportunities to explore them. It offered preschoolers a developmentally appropriate preschool learning environment. The curriculum, called Learningames (Sparling & Lewis, 2000–2003), was a series of 16–18 games for each 6-month period of development, designed to enhance the overall development of infants and toddlers and the language, problem-solving skills, and emergent literacy of preschoolers. Adults learned the significance of each game for children's development. They were taught how to play each game in a playful, back-and-forth exchange with the child, praising and encouraging the child to engage in the expected behavior.

This is the first such study to find preschool program benefits *throughout* participants' schooling on their intellectual performance and academic achievement. Mean IQs of program and no-program groups were 101 versus 84 at age 3, 101 versus 91 at age 4½, 96 versus 90 at age 15, and 89 versus 85 at age 21; achievement scores at age 15 were 94 versus 88 in reading and 94 versus 87 in mathematics. When children were 4½, more teen mothers of program-group children than teen mothers of no-program group children were self-supporting. By age 15, 31% of the program group versus 55% of the no-program group had been retained in grade, and 25% versus 48% had received special services. At age 21, 70% of the program group versus 67% of the no-program group had graduated from high school or received a GED certificate. By age 21, 35% of the program group versus 14% of the no-program group had attended a 4-year college. As teens, 26% of the program group and 43% of the no-program group became parents; of those who were parents at age 21, the average age at the birth of the first child was 19.1 for the program group and 17.7 for the no-program group (Campbell, Breitmayer, & Ramey, 1986; Campbell & Ramey, 1995; Ramey & Campbell, 1984; Campbell et al., 2002). The program and no-program groups did not differ significantly in arrests by age 19 (Clarke & Campbell, 1998). Analysis of the costs and benefits of the Abecedarian program indicates that, in 2000 dollars discounted at 3% annually (converted from the 2002 dollars reported), the program cost $34,476 per child ($13,362 per child per year) and yielded benefits to society of $130,300, $3.78 return per dollar invested (Massé & Barnett, 2002). Most of the benefits came from mothers' earnings (54%), participants' earnings (28%), and health improvement due to less smoking (13%).

The Chicago Parent-Child Centers study

Beginning in 1985, Arthur Reynolds and his colleagues examined the effects of the Chicago Child-Parent Centers (CPC) program offered by one of the nation's largest public school systems. This program was citywide—much larger in scale than the research programs of the High/ Scope Perry Preschool and Abecedarian studies. The study sample was also larger, with 1,539 low-income children (93% African American, 7% Hispanic) enrolled in 25 schools, 989 who had been in the CPC program and 550 who had not. Families in this study went to their neighborhood schools, and children were not randomly assigned to groups. Preschool-program group members attended a part-day preschool program when they were 3 and 4 years old, while the no-preschool-program group did not. At age 5, some members of both groups attended part-day kindergarten programs, while others attended full-day kindergarten programs (Reynolds et al., 2001). The CPC program involved the agency's traditional family-support services and preschool education. Parent outreach was provided by a family-support coordinator and a parent-resource teacher. The classroom program emphasized attainment of academic skills through relatively structured learning experiences presented by the teacher, making it somewhat similar to the Abecedarian approach, but decidedly different from the child development-centered instruction in the High/Scope Perry Preschool Project. For example, the teacher would say, "Today we are going to play a shopping game. Each one of these boxes will be a store." She would then point to the picture on each box and have a child name it. Then she would ask related questions, such as "Where do we buy milk? Do we buy milk at the grocery store or at the toy store?" This format was used to teach language, literacy, and mathematics skills (Reynolds, 2000).

The preschool-program group did significantly better than the no-preschool-program group in educational performance and social behavior, with lower rates of grade retention (23% vs. 38%) and special education placement (14% vs. 25%) followed by higher rates of high school completion (50% vs. 39%), more years of education (10.6 vs. 10.2), and lower rates of juvenile arrests (17% vs. 25%)—both violent (9% vs. 15%) and nonviolent (14% vs. 19%)—and school dropout (47% vs. 55%; Reynolds et al., 2001). High school completion rates were 43% for program males versus 29% for no-program males (a 14% difference), but 57% for program females versus 48% for no-program females (a 9% difference); this was the reverse of the preschool experience by gender pattern of the High/Scope Perry Preschool study. Analysis of the costs and benefits of the Chicago Child-Parent Centers program indicates that, in 2000 dollars discounted at 3% annually (converted from the 1998 dollars reported), the program cost $6,956 per child participating 1½ years and yielded benefits of $49,564 per participant, $7.10 return per dollar invested (Reynolds, Temple, Robertson, & Mann, 2002). Benefits to the general public were $26,637 per participant, $3.83 per dollar invested, with the largest benefits coming from more taxes paid on higher earnings (28%), reduced crime victim costs (18%), and reduced costs of school remedial services (18%).

Study comparisons

Table 1.1 compares the principal characteristics and outcomes of the three long-term studies, anticipating the age 40 High/Scope Perry Preschool study findings presented later in this report. On most characteristics, one of the studies can be contrasted with the other two, but not always the same two versus the other one.

The Abecedarian, Chicago, and High/Scope Perry Preschool studies differed in time and place. The High/Scope Perry Preschool Project began first, in 1962; the Abecedarian Project came second, beginning in 1972; and

Table 1.1

CHARACTERISTICS OF THREE LONG-TERM PRESCHOOL STUDIES

Characteristic	Carolina Abecedarian	Chicago Child-Parent Centers	High/Scope Perry Preschool
Design			
Beginning year	1972	1985	1962
Type of setting	College town	Major city	College town
Sample size	111	1,539	123
Assignment to groups	Random	Existing classes	Random
Scale	Research	Service	Research
Program entry and exit age	0.4–5	3–4	3–4
Program hours a day, days a week	8, 5	2½, 5	2½, 5
Program weeks a year, years	50, 5	35, 2	35, 2
Parent program	—	Family and health services	Weekly home visits
School-age services	Yes	Yes	No
Control group experience	Some child care arrangements	Some child care arrangements	No preschool program
Common outcomes			
Intellectual performance tests	Ages 3–21	—	Ages 4–7
School achievement tests	Age 15	Ages 14–15	Ages 7–27
Placed in special education	25% vs. 48%	14% vs. 25%	65% vs. 60%
Retained in grade	31% vs. 55%	23% vs. 38%	35% vs. 40%
High school graduates	67% vs. 51%	50% vs. 39%	65% vs. 45%
– Males		43% vs. 29%	50% vs. 54%
– Females		57% vs. 48%	84% vs. 32%
Arrested by 21	45% vs. 41%	17% vs. 25%	15% vs. 25%
Age at birth of first child	19.1 vs. 17.7	—	20 vs. 21
Cost-benefit analysis[a]			
Program cost	$34,476	$6,956	$15,166
Program cost per year	13,362	4,637	8,540
Public return, total	—	26,637	195,621
Public return, per dollar invested	—	3.83	12.90
Societal return, total	130,300	49,364	258,888
Societal return, per dollar invested	3.78	7.10	17.07

[a] Per participant in 2000 dollars discounted at 3% annually

the Chicago CPC study is the most recent, beginning in 1985. These temporal differences represent differences in the programs' context. The High/Scope program operated in the 1960s when there were few if any other services offered in the community that the no-program group children might receive. The other two programs operated in the 1970s and 1980s, when families made a variety of child care arrangements, such as relative care, family day care, and center care. The Abecedarian and High/Scope Perry Preschool studies focused on poor people in college towns, while the Chicago study focused on poor people in one of the nation's largest cities. Similarly, the Abecedarian and High/Scope Perry Preschool studies involved random assignment of samples of 100-plus children, while the Chicago study involved a sample size of 1,500-plus children in preexisting classes with no scientific intervention in the enrollment process. Indeed, the Abecedarian and High/Scope Perry Preschool studies were intentional studies from the beginning, while the Chicago study was an evaluation of an existing program that was not set up for the purpose of the study.

The Abecedarian program was a full-day child care program serving children from shortly after birth to kindergarten entry, while the High/Scope Perry Preschool and Chicago programs provided part-day preschool education to children 3 and 4 years old and related services to them and their families. The High/Scope Perry Preschool Project provided weekly home visits to parents and their participating children, while the Chicago program provided a range of family and health services. The High/Scope Perry Preschool Project provided no follow-up program in elementary school, while both the Abecedarian and Chicago programs did provide school-age programs, although the Abecedarian study did not find these school-age programs to contribute to children's success as did the preschool child care program in the same study.

The meaning of group differences in the three studies is determined not only by the nature of the program experience but also by the nature of the control group's experience. The High/Scope Perry Preschool Project's control group children lived at home and had virtually no extensive child care experience away from home. The Abecedarian study and Chicago study control groups, however, had a good bit of child care experience away from home.

While the Chicago study did not assess children's intellectual performance, both the Abecedarian study and the High/Scope Perry Preschool study found evidence of a program effect on children's intellectual performance. The evidence suggests that this effect lasted to age 7 in the High/Scope Perry Preschool study and into adulthood in the Abecedarian study. All three studies found evidence of a program effect on school achievement in adolescence; the High/Scope Perry Preschool study found evidence that this effect lasted throughout schooling and into early adulthood. The Abecedarian and Chicago studies found evidence that the program reduced placements in special education; the High/Scope Perry Preschool study found evidence that the program reduced special education placements specifically for mental impairment. The Abecedarian and Chicago studies found evidence that the program reduced retentions in grade; the High/Scope Perry Preschool study found evidence of a reduction in retentions in grade for females only. All three studies found evidence that the program improved the high school graduation rate of participants. This improvement was due to females in the High/Scope Perry Preschool study, but to both males and females in the Chicago study. The Chicago study found evidence that the program significantly reduced juvenile arrests. The High/Scope Perry Preschool study found a group difference in juvenile arrests of comparable size that was not significant perhaps because of smaller sample size, then went on to find substantial evidence of reduced adult arrests and prison sentences by age 40. The Abecedarian study found that program females were on average 1.4 years older than no-program females at the age of their first child; the High/Scope Perry Preschool study found that program females were on average 2.8 years older than no-program females at the age of their first child.

The Abecedarian program was the most expensive, overall and per year, followed by the High/Scope Preschool Perry program, and then the Chicago program. The High/Scope Perry Preschool program had the highest return, followed by the Abecedarian program, then the Chicago program. The Chicago program, however, had a higher rate of return on investment than the Abecedarian program because of the higher cost of the latter program.

The High/Scope Perry Preschool study was the only one of the three studies that found the program group to exceed the no-program group in better attitudes toward school in adolescence, a higher adult employment rate and higher earnings, more adult home and car ownership, and receipt of more social services in early adulthood. The Carolina Abecedarian study was the only one of the three studies that found that more teen mothers were employed during the program and more participants attended a 4-year college.

The Job of the High/Scope Perry Preschool Midlife Study

The High/Scope Perry Preschool study has already discovered much. It and the Early Training Project (Gray, Ramsey, & Klaus, 1982) were the first of the evaluative studies of preschool programs for young children living in poverty and the first to identify the large effects of these programs on children's intellectual performance lasting a few years. These two studies and the Carolina Abecedarian Project (Campbell et al., 2002) are among the very few existing long-term studies of preschool programs based on random assignment of children to program and no-program groups. The High/Scope Perry Preschool study was the first of these studies to identify lasting effects on many outcome variables, any one of them disproving the hypothesis that preschool program effects fade out over the years: reduced need for special education placement by age 10; higher achievement test scores at age 14; a higher rate of high school graduation; less teen pregnancy; greater adult earnings, wealth, and reduced need for social services; fewer criminal arrests; and a positive and substantial economic return on taxpayers' investment.

The midlife study was not conducted to rediscover what this study and those that followed it had already discovered. Nor was it conducted to tightly generalize findings to existing large-scale programs like Head Start or state preschool programs. Other studies, such as the Family and Child Experiences Survey (Zill et al., 2003) and the Michigan School Readiness Program Evaluation (Xiang & Schweinhart, 2001) better serve these purposes.

Rather, its job is now what it has always been: To discover the possible—just how much a good child development-centered preschool program can accomplish throughout the lives of young children born in poverty. *Its job is to give us all a reasonable fix on a defensible position of legitimate hope for what good preschool programs can accomplish.* On the basis of such evidence, these programs continue to occupy a pivotal position in America's great political debate about the proper role of government in the lives of its citizens.

II Experimental Design

When the High/Scope Perry Preschool Project was conceptualized in the early 1960s, the first idea was to deliver a service program to those children and families who met the necessary standards for state funding of the project. When some members of the program's advisory committee and state special education officials challenged the concept of such service, the response was to develop the program within a carefully controlled research project to answer the questions raised. High standards for a field-based study were maintained.

To conduct the High/Scope Perry Preschool study, staff identified 123 young African American children in Ypsilanti, Michigan, living in poverty and assessed to be at high risk of school failure; randomly assigned them to a program group and a no-program group; operated a high-quality preschool program for the program group at ages 3 and 4; collected data on both groups annually from ages 3 through 11 and at ages 14, 15, 19, 27, and now at age 40; and, after each period of data collection, analyzed the data and wrote a report of the study to date.

The Study Participants

This study has followed the lives of persons who originally lived in the attendance area of the Ypsilanti, Michigan, school district's Perry Elementary School, a predominantly low-income, African American neighborhood. The study was conducted in Ypsilanti, Michigan, because David Weikart, the principal investigator, was the district's director of special education services, as well as a doctoral candidate at the University of Michigan in Ann Arbor. In 1970, Weikart and all his special education staff resigned from the Ypsilanti school district and formed the High/Scope Educational Research Foundation, an independent nonprofit organization, to house their burgeoning work in research, staff development, and publishing in early childhood education and other innovative programs. Perry Elementary School was the site of the study because of its high rates of poverty and school failure and because Eugene Beatty, the school's principal, was active in school reform and willing to support the effort.

Ypsilanti, Michigan

Founded in 1823, Ypsilanti in the twentieth century became a center for the automotive industry and higher education, with Ford and General Motors automotive plants and Eastern Michigan University. In the 1960 U.S. Census, the city of Ypsilanti had 29,538 residents, 20% of them African American, and 27% of its residents living in poverty. In the 2000 U.S. Census, the city had 22,403 residents, 30% of them African American, and 26% of its residents living in poverty (U.S. Census Bureau, 2000).

The years of the High/Scope Perry Preschool study have been times of significant change for African Americans in Ypsilanti and throughout the nation, with the reduction of segregation in education, business, housing, and politics by federal laws such as the Civil Rights Act of 1965 and the Fair Housing Act of 1968. However, in the 1960s and 1970s African Americans also experienced increasing numbers of poor, single-parent families and unemployed males. African Americans have lived in Ypsilanti since the 1850s, when the city was a stop on the "underground railroad," a means of escape for African Americans who had been slaves in the South (Berrueta-Clement et al., 1984; Tobias, Baker, & Fairfield, 1973). During World War II and the boom of the 1950s, automotive jobs attracted additional workers and their families, including African Americans, to the area. An indicator of the heavy African American migration to Ypsilanti in the late 1940s and the 1950s is the fact that, of the 277 mothers with children at the all-African American Perry School in 1962, 77% had been born in the South and 53% had been educated there (Weikart et al., 1970). Almost all African Americans in Ypsilanti in the 1960s lived on its south side.

The Ypsilanti school district has nine elementary schools, two middle schools, and one high school. Through the 1960s, the elementary schools were racially segregated as was the housing. At the elementary school level, the district's only African American teachers were at Perry School and in special education services. The Ypsilanti school district has a long history of concern about the low achievement and high school completion rate of its African American students.

Formerly named Harriet School, Perry School was renamed to honor Lawrence Perry, a dentist and the first African American to serve on the school board, from 1953 to 1956. The late Eugene Beatty, another African American educator, was the first principal of the school from 1940 to 1967 and made it available as a community center for sports and meetings and for the Perry Preschool Project. Under Beatty's leadership, over 85% of parents attended parent-teacher conferences (Howe, 1953). To meet desegregation requirements, beginning in the 1970s the district bused the African American students living in the Perry School attendance area to other schools in the district and replaced Perry School itself with a citywide kindergarten facility known as the Perry Child Development Center.

Selecting Children With the Odds Against Them

Project staff identified a pool of children for the study sample from a census of the families of students then attending Perry School, referrals by neighborhood groups, and door-to-door canvassing. They selected families of low socioeconomic status and children with low intellectual performance at study entry who showed no evidence of organic handicap. The only self-selection in the study sample was that 3 families with children identified for the study refused to participate in it (Schweinhart & Weikart, 1988a).

Project staff identified families of **low socioeconomic status,** defined by their low scores for parents' years of schooling, parents' occupational levels, and rooms per person in their households (Deutsch, 1962). These scores were computed as follows:

- Half of either the average of the highest years of schooling of both parents or the highest year of schooling of the single mother

- 2 times the father's or single mother's occupational level (1 = unskilled or unemployed, 2 = semiskilled, 3 = skilled)

- 2 times the rooms per person in the household (Weikart et al., 1970, p. 133).

The factors (½ for schooling, 2 for occupational level, and 2 for rooms per person) divide each component by its approximate standard deviation for this sample (2 for schooling, ½ for occupational level, and ¼ for rooms per person), then double the weight of rooms per person (¼ × 2 = ½).

Because of these selection criteria, families whose children participated in the study were considerably worse off in most ways than the U.S. population at the time and slightly worse off in most ways than the African American population at the time (Schweinhart & Weikart, 1980). As shown in Table 2.1, half of the mothers in the study had left school by the end of ninth grade, and half of the fathers had left school by the end of eighth grade, educational levels that were just a few months below the median of U.S. African Americans, but several years below the median of the U.S. population. Only about one fifth of the mothers and one tenth of the fathers in the study had completed high school, compared with one third of African American adults and one half of all adults in the U.S. in 1970. Nearly half of the children participating in the study lived in single-parent families in the 1960s, rising to nearly three fifths in the 1970s, as compared to one third of African American families and one seventh of all families in the U.S. in 1970. About half of the fathers in the study were employed, somewhat lower than the 60% national rate for African American men and only about two thirds of the 74% rate for all men nationally in 1970. Although only one fifth of the mothers were employed at study entry, 45% of them were employed when study participants were 15 years old, about the same as the percentage of all African American women and a little higher than the percentage of all women in the U.S. in 1970. Half of the study children lived in families receiving welfare assistance, as compared to less than one fifth of African American families and one twentieth of all families in the U.S. Although residences were of typical size for urban areas, families in this study were over twice as large and their households were twice as crowded as those of either the African American population or the total population. Also, the mothers of 79% of the study participants were born in the South, and 36% of the study participants lived in public housing projects at study entry.

It is interesting to compare families with children in the High/Scope Perry Preschool study to families with children in current Head Start programs. With minor exceptions, children qualify for Head Start if their families have incomes below the federal poverty line ($28,850 for a fam-

Table 2.1

DEMOGRAPHIC STATUS OF STUDY PARENTS AND U.S. FAMILIES

Variable	Study Parents in 1962-65[a]	African Americans in 1970[b]	U.S. Population in 1970[b]
Schooling of mothers/women			
Median years of school	9.7	10.0	12.1
Completed high school	21%	33%	53%
Schooling of fathers/men			
Median years of school	8.0	9.6	11.8
Completed high school	11%	32%	54%
Family composition			
Husband-wife families	53%	69%	86%
Husband-wife families in 1973-77	46%		
Single-head families	47%	33%	14%
Single-head families in 1973-77	54%		
Employment of parents/adults			
Not employed or looking for work	40%[c]	25%	17%
Mothers/Women employed	20%	47%	38%
Mothers employed in 1973-77	45%[d]		
Men employed[e]	47%	60%	74%
Unskilled	81%	35%	16%
Semiskilled	14%	30%	20%
Skilled	5%	25%	39%
Professional	0%	9%	25%
Family on welfare	49%	18%	5%
Household density			
Median persons	6.7	3.1	2.7
Median rooms	4.8	4.7	4.8
Persons per room.	1.40	0.66	0.56

Note. Data sources are the initial parent interview and the U.S. Bureau of the Census (1970).

[a] Except as noted, study statistics report the status at study entry of the parents of the 101 families of the 123 Perry study participants, when mothers were 18–48 years old and fathers were 22–52 years old.

[b] U.S. statistics for males and females 25 and over come from the 1970 U.S. Census as reported by Schweinhart and Weikart (1980).

[c] Combines study mothers and fathers.

[d] Study mothers' employment levels were either unskilled or, in 10 cases, unreported.

[e] Percentages of men employed at each employment level.

ily of 4 in 2004) or are eligible for public assistance (U. S. Administration for Children and Families, 2004a; Federal Register, 2004). A family survey of Head Start parents in 1997 (O'Brien et al., 2002) permits the following comparisons:

- 73% of Head Start parents today have graduated from high school, as compared to only 17% of the Perry Preschool study parents.

- 42% of Head Start children today live with 2 parents, as compared to 53% of the Perry Preschool study children.

- 52% of Head Start children today have an employed parent, as compared to 53% of the Perry study children.

Project staff used the Stanford-Binet Intelligence Test (Terman & Merrill, 1960) to assess the **intellectual performance** of the young children of families of low socioeconomic status. They selected for the study those children whose intellectual performance scores (IQs) at this initial testing qualified them as "borderline educable mentally impaired" by the State of Michigan, following the American Association on Mental Deficiency (AAMD; Weikart, 1967), that is, in the range of 70 to 85. (In fact, of the 123 children in the longitudinal sample, 14 had entry IQs between 61 and 69; 90 had entry IQs between 70 and 85; and 19 had entry IQs between 86 and 89.) Between 1959 and 1973, the AAMD placed the upper IQ limit for mental impairment at 85, although placing it at 70 before and after that time (Grossman, 1973). Zigler (1987) observed that the IQs of Perry Preschool children at study entry were lower than those of most African American children living in poverty; indeed, a few children were screened out of the sample pool because their IQs were above the cutoff point. However, the IQs of the Perry study's no-program group increased to medians between 80 and 86 over the years of the study, similar to the median IQ of all African American children in the 1960s (Kennedy, Van de Riet, & White, 1963). So there is little reason to see low intellectual performance as an absolute limit on generalization from this sample of children.

Although 128 children were originally selected for the study, 4 children did not complete the preschool program because they moved away, and 1 child died shortly after the study began, so that the longitudinal study had 123 participants. Children entered the study in five successive classes annually from the fall of 1962 to the fall of 1965. Table 2.2 presents the numbers of longitudinal study participants at entry and the calendar years of their ages at times of data collection. In October of 1962, the first class of 28 children entered the study at age 4 along with the second class of 17 children who entered at age 3. When the second class of children turned 4, in October of 1963, the third class of 26 children joined them. The fourth class of 27 children entered the study in 1964, and a fifth class of 25 children entered in 1965. Staff randomly divided the children in each class into those enrolled in the preschool program and those not enrolled in any preschool program. Of the 58 program-group children, 45 attended the preschool program at ages 3 and 4, except for the 13 of them in the first class, who attended only at age 4.

This report adds the findings at the age 40 follow-up, with interviews collected at a mean age of 40.8, with class ages averaging from 39.3

Table 2.2

NUMBER OF STUDY PARTICIPANTS AND YEARS OF DATA COLLECTION BY AGE

Variable	First Class	Second Class	Third Class	Fourth Class	Fifth Class	All Classes
Number of participants						
Total sample	28	17	26	27	25	123
Program group	13	8	12	13	12	58
No-program group	15	9	14	14	13	65
Years of data collection by age						
Birth	1958	1959	1960	1961	1962	1958–62
Age 3	1961	**1962**	**1963**	**1964**	**1965**	1961–65
Age 4	**1962**	**1963**	**1964**	**1965**	**1966**	1962–66
Age 5	**1963**	**1964**	**1965**	**1966**	**1967**	1963–67
Age 6	1964	1965	1966	1967	1968	1964–68
Age 7	1965	1966	1967	1968	1969	1965–69
Age 8	1966	1967	1968	1969	1970	1966–70
Age 9	1967	1968	1969	1970	1971	1967–71
Age 10	1968	1969	1970	1971	1972	1968–72
Age 11	1969	1970	1971	1972	1973	1969–73
Age 14	1972	1973	1974	1975	1976	1972–76
Age 15	1973	1974	1975	1976	1977	1973–77
Age 19	1977	1978	1979	1980	1981	1977–81
Age 27	1985	1986	1987	1988	1989	1985–89
Age 40	1998	1999	2000	2001	2002	1998–2002

Note. The years presented are when the study participants in a class reached the various ages, with eligibility extending to December 1 of the preceding year (7 study participants were born in December). The years during which the program groups attended the preschool program are boldfaced.

to 42.5. The assumption was that a greater age spread at midlife would not affect the findings, and following this assumption, data collection was compressed from 5 to 2½ years.

All study participants were African American, as was everyone in the Perry School neighborhood at the time they attended. Limiting the sample to African American children removed racial differences from the design, but raises a question about generalizing findings to other races, including the 78% of poor children in the U.S. who are white (Zigler, 1987; updated statistic from Dalaker, 2001). Obviously, poor African American children and poor white children differ in many important ways. But because the program addressed intellectual, social, and physical abilities common to all races rather than racially specific characteristics, it is reasonable to believe that it would have had similar effects on poor children of any race. Indeed, having positive effects on African American children may have been even harder to achieve, since they and their families also faced racial prejudice and discrimination in schooling, housing, and employment.

Most of the parents of study participants had come from the southern U.S.: the mothers of 79% of the children ($n = 108$) reported being born in the South (33% in Alabama; 32% in Georgia, Mississippi, or Tennessee; only 11% in Michigan; and 9% in other states); the mothers of 47% of the children reported being educated in the South; and a few had even graduated from high school, married, and had some of their older children in the South. Proportions were similar for the fathers of the study participants. Because these people were recent immigrants into the area, they tended to have the last choices of available jobs and were the first to be laid off (Scanzoni, 1971).

Assignment to Groups

The scientific strength of this study, its ability to assess preschool program effects even many years later, is largely due to an experimental design in which study participants were **randomly assigned** to one of two groups: a program group enrolled in the preschool program or a no-program group not enrolled in any preschool program. Neither parents, teachers, nor the psychologists testing the children influenced children's group assignments, so there is no reason to think that any of them influenced group differences in children's or parents' abilities or dispositions before the preschool program began.

The High/Scope Perry Preschool study used randomizing techniques at several steps in the assignment of study participants to groups. After selecting children for a class in the study sample each fall from 1962 to 1965, project staff assigned them to program and no-program groups as follows:

- They identified pairs of study participants matched on initial Stanford-Binet intellectual performance scores (IQ; Terman & Merrill, 1960) and assigned pair members to either of two undesignated groups.

- As part of the initial assignment procedure, they exchanged 1 or 2 pair members per class to insure that the groups were matched on mean socioeconomic status, mean intellectual performance, and percentages of boys and girls.

- By flipping a coin, they randomly assigned one group to the program condition and the other to the no-program condition.

In addition, as part of the initial assignment procedure in later classes, they exchanged 1 or 2 pair members per class to reduce the number of children of employed mothers in the program group, because it was difficult to arrange home visits with them. We have reported the total number of exchanges for all classes as 2 or 5 elsewhere, based on investigator recall (e.g., Schweinhart et al., 1993). Based on a probability estimate, the number of exchanges could have been as many as 8, in that the program group ended up with 5 children of employed mothers, as compared to 20 in the no-program group (5 + 7 or 8 = 12 or 13; 20 − 7 or 8 = 12 or 13).

Also, they assigned younger siblings to the same group as their older siblings, to prevent the preschool program from affecting siblings in the no-program group. This procedure in effect made the sampling unit the family rather than the child. The 123 study participants came from 101 families—82 with 1 child in the sample, 17 with 2, 1 with 3, and 1 with 4. The 58 program-group members came from 48 families, and the 65 no-program group members came from 53 families.

To assess whether the inclusion of additional siblings in the sample and their assignment to the same group as the first sibling distorted the findings of the study, we compared key findings for the full sample to those for two subsamples with only 1 of the siblings present from families with more than 1 sibling in the sample. All three samples included the 82 study participants with no siblings in the sample.

- The full sample added in all 41 study participants with siblings in the sample ($n = 123$).

- The "oldest sibling" subsample added in only the 19 study participants who were the oldest siblings in the sample ($n = 101$).

- The "next oldest sibling" subsample added in only the 19 study participants who were the second oldest siblings ($n = 101$).

Findings for almost all major outcome variables that were statistically significant in the full sample—IQ after 1 preschool year, school achievement at 14, years retained in grade up to 19, monthly earnings at 27 and at 40, lifetime educational attainment, and lifetime arrests—were also statistically significant in both subsamples. The only exception was literacy at 19, which had a statistically significant group difference in the full sample and the oldest sibling sample, but not in the next oldest sibling sample—a difference presumably due to chance.

Initially, 64 children were assigned to the program group and 64 children were assigned to the no-program group. Because 2 children were transferred from the program group to the no-program group after initial assignment, the program group had 62 children and the no-program group had 66 children. Then 4 children in the program group moved out of the area before completing the preschool program, and 1 child in the no-program group died, leaving the program group with 58 members and the no-program group with 65 members, which constituted the final sample for the longitudinal study.

Similarity of Preschool Experience Groups on Background Characteristics

The assignment procedures make it highly probable that group differences found after 1 or 2 years of the preschool program represent the effects of the preschool program. Comparisons indicating that groups were not significantly different on various background characteristics make it even more likely. As shown in Table 2.3 for the continuous background variables, the two groups did not differ significantly (with a two-tailed probability of less than .05) at study entry on Stanford-Binet IQ (Terman & Merrill, 1960), family socioeconomic status, mother's or father's highest year of schooling, number of children in the family, number of siblings older or younger than the study participant, child's age, mother's or father's age, rooms in home, or persons per rooms in home.

As shown in Table 2.4 for the categorical background variables, at study entry the two groups did not differ significantly on participants' gender, family configuration (single-parent vs. 2-parent, nuclear vs. extended), father's employment level, family welfare status, family in public housing, mother born in the South or elsewhere, population of mother's birthplace, or family religion. In the longitudinal sample, there were 33 program-group males, 25 program-group females, 39 no-program-group males, and 26 no-program-group females. Most of the fathers of the study participants had unskilled jobs—janitors, construction laborers, and a few automotive assembly-line workers; the two with managerial jobs were a laundry supervisor and a local union president. All of the employed mothers had unskilled jobs—maids, laundry workers, domes-

Table 2.3

CONTINUOUS BACKGROUND VARIABLES AT STUDY ENTRY,
BY PRESCHOOL EXPERIENCE

Variable	Program Group		No-Program Group		
	Mean	SD	Mean	SD	Effect Size
Stanford-Binet IQ at study entry	79.6	5.9	78.5	6.9	0.16
Family socioeconomic status	8.0	1.2	7.9	1.1	0.36
Mother's years of schooling	9.5	2.4	9.4	2.0	0.05
Father's years of schooling[a]	8.4	2.3	8.8	2.5	−0.02
Children in family	4.9	2.5	4.8	2.8	0.06
Older siblings	2.8	2.4	3.0	2.8	0.08
Younger siblings at study entry	1.1	1.0	0.8	1.6	0.10
Child's age in months at study entry	42.7	6.2	41.9	5.9	0.14
Mother's age in years at study entry	29.6	6.2	28.7	6.9	0.13
Father's age in years at study entry[b]	31.5	5.0	34.0	8.2	−0.31
Rooms in home at study entry	5.2	1.2	5.2	1.6	0.01
Persons per room at study entry	1.2	0.3	1.4	0.6	−0.33

Note. Program group $n = 58$, no-program group $n = 65$, except as noted; data source is the initial parent interview; the *p*-values (none indicated) are based on *t*-tests.

[a] Program group $n = 34$, no-program group $n = 34$.

[b] Program group $n = 55$, no-program group $n = 59$.

*p (two-tailed) < .05.

Table 2.4

NOMINAL BACKGROUND VARIABLES AT STUDY ENTRY, BY PRESCHOOL EXPERIENCE

Variable	Program Group %	No-Program Group %	Effect Size
Participant's gender			
Male	57%	60%	0.06
Female	43%	40%	
Family configuration at study entry			
Two-parent	55%	51%	0.09
Single-mother	45%	49%	
Nuclear	15%	20%	0.14
Extended	85%	80%	
Employment of parents			
Father and mother employed	5%	9%	0.44*
Father alone employed	44%	35%	
Single mother employed	4%	22%	
No parent employed	47%	34%	
Father's employment level[a]			
Managerial or skilled	3%	2%	0.29
Semiskilled	9%	3%	
Unskilled	28%	40%	
Family welfare status at study entry			
On welfare	58%	45%	−0.25
Not on welfare	42%	55%	
Family in public housing	40%	32%	−0.15
Mother's birthplace region[b]			
Southern U.S.	83%	75%	0.19
Elsewhere in the U.S.	17%	25%	
Mother's birthplace population[c]			
Population under 10,000	38%	39%	0.16
Population 10,000–100,000	33%	43%	
Population over 100,000	29%	18%	
Family religion			
Baptist	80%	72%	−0.20
Other Protestant	18%	21%	
Catholic	0%	4%	
None claimed	2%	4%	

Note. Program group $n = 56$–58, no-program group $n = 63$–65, except as indicated; data source is the initial parent interview; the p-values are based on chi-square statistics.

[a] All employed mothers reporting were at the unskilled level.

[b] Program-group $n = 48$, no-program group $n = 55$.

[c] Program-group $n = 42$, no-program group $n = 56$.

*p (two-tailed) < .05.

tics, and a few store clerks, uncertified nurses' aides, cooks, waitresses, and dishwashers.

As shown in Table 2.5, when study participants were 15 years old, the two groups did not differ significantly in family configuration (2-parent vs. single-parent), parental employment status, parent rating of the neighborhood, number of times the family moved since the study participant began school, or number of persons per room in the households.

Significantly fewer of the program-group members than the no-program-group members had mothers who were employed (9% vs. 31%), particularly single mothers (4% vs. 22%) at study entry, due to the exchanges that moved them from the program group to the no-program group. However, as shown in Table 2.5, program and no-program

Table 2.5

BACKGROUND VARIABLES AT AGE 15, BY PRESCHOOL EXPERIENCE

Variable	Program Group Mean (SD)/%	No-Program Group Mean (SD)/%	Effect Size
Family configuration			
Two-parent	43%	47%	0.08
Single-parent	57%	53%	
Parental employment			
Father and mother employed	15%	24%	0.16
Father only employed	17%	14%	
Single mother employed	27%	24%	
No parent employed	42%	38%	
Neighborhood rating by parent			
Excellent	21%	15%	0.12
Good	45%	46%	
Fair	13%	19%	
Not so good	13%	7%	
Poor	9%	13%	
Times family moved, from school entry to age 15	1.3	1.3	
0	15%	17%	0.01
1	58%	54%	
2–4	27%	30%	
Persons per room at youth age 15	0.84 (0.32)	0.86 (0.32)	0.07

Note. Program group $n = 48$, no-program group $n = 54$; the data source is the parent questionnaire at youth age 15; significance testing was conducted by binary logistic regression analysis, ordinal regression analysis, or ordinary least-squares regression analysis, but groups did not differ significantly at p (two-tailed) $< .05$ on any of these variables.

groups did not differ significantly in their percentages of single mothers employed when study participants were 15 years old. In short, the difference between groups at entry was limited to a temporary difference in maternal employment rates. Further, as shown in Table 2.7, p. 47, **maternal employment at study entry was not significantly correlated, indeed not correlated more than .13, with any of the major outcome variables.** Nevertheless, it was used as a covariate in the outcome analyses.

Similarity of Preschool-Experience-by-Gender Subgroups on Background Characteristics

While the program and no-program groups were intentionally matched on certain initial characteristics, this was not the case for program and no-program males or program and no-program females. However, because differences attributable to their preschool experience emerged later for males and females, it is important to know if these subgroups differed from each other at study entry. As might be expected from the overall group differences in maternal employment, program males differed significantly from no-program males in percent of mothers employed, as did program females from no-program females. On other background variables, no significant differences were found either at study entry or at age 15 for program males versus no-program males or for program females versus no-program females on the background variables listed in Tables 2.3 to 2.5. Nonetheless, because gender is an important variable, it was included as a covariate in the outcome analyses.

Aggregation Across Classes

The analyses in this report combine the five classes to achieve a larger sample size. Given the small sample size, we decided not to include these classes as covariates: the five classes would have required four dummy variables as covariates and four degrees of freedom. Instead, we compared the effect sizes or odds ratios of the study's major findings as presented throughout this report with those found in parallel analyses that used classes as covariates. The effect sizes were virtually the same in both analyses for Stanford-Binet IQ after 1 preschool year, school achievement at age 14, and literacy at age 19; and the odds ratios were virtually the same for years retained in grade up to age 19, monthly earnings at age 27, monthly earnings at age 40, and lifetime arrests.

Differing Experience of Groups

Participation or nonparticipation in the preschool education program was the only categorically different experience of study participants. Regardless of which group they were in, all study participants received the same schedule of tests and interviews. Except during the preschool years, neither testers nor interviewers knew which group study participants belonged to. If school teachers independently learned who attended the preschool program, such knowledge was a natural extension of the preschool program experience. While the data collection program has been considerable over study participants' lifetimes, the program group and no-program group received this same special attention, so it cannot account for any group differences found.

The Preschool Program

High/Scope Perry Preschool Project teachers conducted daily 2½-hour classes for children on 5 weekday mornings and made weekly 1½-hour home visits to each mother and child on weekday afternoons. The 30-week school year began in mid-October and ended in May. Of the 58 children in the program group, the 13 in the first class participated in the program for 1 school year at age 4 and the 45 in subsequent classes participated in the program for 2 school years at ages 3 and 4. Successive program group classes—first and second, second and third, third and fourth, and fourth and fifth—attended the program together, the older class at age 4, the younger at age 3. In 1966–67, the final year of the program, a sixth class of 11 3-year-olds who were not included in the longitudinal sample joined the 12 4-year-olds in the fifth class. Thus, the 4 teachers in the program served 20 to 25 children each school year, forming a child-teacher ratio varying from 5.00 to 6.25 children per teacher. This ratio was set to accommodate the demands of the weekly home visits—that is, a visit to 1 or 2 families per weekday afternoon. Friday afternoons, however, were generally used for staff training and project meetings.

Between 1962 and 1967, 10 teachers certified to teach in elementary and special education served in the program's 4 teaching positions. Over the years, 7 white and 3 African American women served as teachers, and at least 1 African American teacher was always on staff. One of the teachers stayed throughout the project, from 1962 to 1967; 3 stayed 2 to 3 years, and 6 stayed 1 to 2 years. In addition to project director David Weikart, 9 researchers worked on the study while the program was in operation, 2 or 3 at a time between 1962 and 1967.

The High/Scope Perry Preschool Project cost about $1,500 per child per school year in the dollars of the 1960s (Berrueta-Clement et al., 1984), the equivalent of about $7,000 in 2003 dollars. This cost includes **all** program costs, even school-district administration and building overhead costs. The cost was principally due to having 4 public school teachers, paid 10% above the district's standard pay scale, for every 5.7 children (overall project average). These were years of severe teacher shortages, and qualified teachers were very difficult to locate and employ. Since this program was experimental, the district did not demand high economic efficiency. It is reasonable to assume that the quality of the program could have been maintained if the number of children per staff member had been increased to 8 or 10. The High/Scope Preschool Curriculum Comparison study (Schweinhart & Weikart, 1997a, 1997b) found that preschool programs could be highly effective with 8 children per staff member; and the National Day Care study (Ruopp, Travers, Glantz, & Coelen, 1979) provided evidence that program effectiveness does not decline substantially until the number of children per staff member exceeds 10. Increasing the number of children per staff member to 10 and making no other changes, the program cost would have been reduced to about $4,138 per child in 2003 dollars (based on conversion by the gross domestic product price deflator, *Economagic.com,* 2003).

Head Start cost per child in FY 2002 averaged $6,934, about the same as the per-child spending on the High/Scope Perry Preschool Project after correcting for inflation. Contrary to what is commonly believed, the Perry Preschool Project cost per child was not impossibly higher than what is available to Head Start programs today. However, the differences in how this money is spent are striking. Simply put, most of the Perry Preschool program dollars in the 1960s were spent on public school teacher salaries, whereas most Head Start dollars today are spent on community teacher salaries (about half of public school levels), family service workers at similar levels, and various program coordinators or specialists, such as education coordinators, special services coordinators, and so forth. These patterns constitute two sharply different models of how to spend money on preschool programs for young children living in poverty.

Development of the High/Scope Curriculum

High/Scope Perry Preschool Project staff developed a systematic approach to classroom and home visit activities based on the idea that both teachers and children should have major roles in defining and initiating children's learning activities. Originally called the Cognitively Oriented Curriculum to distinguish it from approaches that did not include a systematic emphasis on cognitive development (Weikart, Rogers, Adcock, & McClelland, 1971), the education model was later named High/Scope (Hohmann, Banet, & Weikart, 1979; Hohmann & Weikart, 1995, 2002). From the beginning, the High/Scope Perry Preschool Project staff explicitly sought to support the development of young children's cognitive and social skills through individualized teaching and learning. Staff continued to develop the educational model as the program operated from 1962 through 1967, building on insights from their classroom experience and their review of the studies of Jean Piaget and others (e.g., Brearly & Hitchfield, 1966; Flavell, 1965; Hunt, 1961; Piaget, 1960, 1968; Piaget & Inhelder, 1969; Piaget, Inhelder, & Szeminska, 1964; Smilansky, 1968).

During the 5 school years of the program, staff developed their theoretical understanding and articulation of this educational model based on children's intentional learning and became more systematic in its application. In the first year, the enthusiastic staff engaged in thoughtful experimentation, and their lesson plans were not yet guided by an explicit developmental theory or systematic objectives (Weikart et al., 1978). In the second year, the teaching and research staff attended six seminars on Piaget's theory and began to better articulate developmental goals and make classroom teaching practices more individualized and developmentally appropriate. In the third year, staff began to adapt Piaget's theory, develop a daily routine based on children's intentional learning, and focus systematically on the needs and interests of individual children in daily planning and evaluation. In the fourth year, the daily routine was formalized into child planning time, work time, recall time, cleanup, juice and small-group times, whole-group activity (indoor or outdoor), circle time, and dismissal. In the fifth year, staff consolidated an essentially Piagetian theory base and formulated a coherent, explicit model of early childhood education.

Throughout the program, curriculum development focused on evolving a conceptual framework with clearly articulated decision rules to shape educational practices and permit systematic, objective evaluation of teacher and child activities. The program's success with the first classes of children could not have been sustained in later classes without this systemization of the educational model.

Features of the High/Scope Educational Model

The High/Scope early childhood educational model, used in the Perry Preschool classroom and home visits, was and is an open framework of educational ideas and practices based on the natural development of young children. Drawing on the child development ideas of Jean Piaget, it emphasizes the idea that children are **intentional learners,** who learn best from activities that they, themselves, plan, carry out, and review afterwards. Adults introduce new ideas to children through adult-initiated small- and large-group activities. Adults observe, support, and extend the children's play as appropriate. Adults arrange interest areas in the learning environment; maintain a daily routine that permits children to plan, carry out, and review their own activities; and join unobtrusively in children's activities, asking appropriate questions that extend their plans and help them think about their activities. Adults add complex language to the discussion to expand children's vocabulary. Using key experiences derived from child development theory as a framework, adults encourage children to make choices, solve problems, and engage in activities that contribute to their intellectual, social, and physical development.

While key experiences in child development are used to monitor children's progress, adults do not provide children with prescriptively sequenced lessons that cover a defined subject matter. Instead, they listen closely to children's plans and then actively work with them to extend their activities to challenging levels as appropriate. Adults' questioning style is important, emphasizing questions that initiate conversations with children and drawing out observations and reflections expressed in children's own language. Adults rarely ask questions merely to test children's grasp of letters, numbers, or colors. Instead, they ask for self-generated descriptions or ideas: What happened? How did you make that? Can you show me? Can you help another child? The questioning style permits free conversation between adult and child and serves as a model for conversations among children. This reflective approach permits adults and children to interact as thinkers and doers rather than to assume the traditional school roles of initiating teacher and responding pupil. All are sharing and learning as they work, adults as well as children.

To create a setting in which children engage in intentional learning activities, a consistent **daily routine** is maintained that varies only when the children have fair warning that things will be different the next day. Field trips are not surprises, nor are special visits or events initiated in the classroom on the spur of the moment. This adherence to routine gives the child the control that helps develop a sense of responsibility and offers the enjoyment of being independent. The daily routine includes a **plan-do-review** sequence, as well as large- and small-group activities. The plan-do-review sequence is the central device that gives children opportunities to express intentions about their activities and reflect on their experience, while keeping the adult intimately involved in the process.

Using the High/Scope participatory education model, adults use a set of **key experiences in child development** to assess and plan children's progress. The idea of key experiences was a part of the High/Scope model from the beginning of the High/Scope Perry Preschool Project, although not named and articulated as such until a few years later. Key experiences are a way of helping the teacher support and extend the child's self-designed activities to include developmentally appropriate experiences. The key experiences are a way of thinking about education that frees the teacher from the resource books of themes and activities that characterize some early childhood programs or the scope-and-sequence charts and workbooks that dominate behavioral approaches. The key experiences are crucial to the development of children the world over, regardless of nation or culture; they are simple and pragmatic. Ten types of preschool key experiences have been identified: creative representation, language and literacy, initiative and social relations, movement, music, classification, seriation, number, space, and time. Each category includes various types of key experiences. For example, the category of initiative and social relations includes making and expressing choices, plans, and decisions; solving problems encountered in play; taking care of one's own needs; expressing feelings in words; participating in group routines; being sensitive to the feelings, interests, and needs of others; building relationships with children and adults; creating and experiencing collaborative play; and dealing with social conflict. The language and literacy category includes talking with others about personally meaningful experiences; describing objects, events, and relations; having fun with language, listening to stories and poems, and making up stories and rhymes; writing in various ways—drawing, scribbling, letterlike forms, invented spelling, conventional forms; reading in various ways—reading storybooks, signs, symbols, and one's own writing; and dictating stories.

High/Scope's early childhood educational model provides explicit theoretical justification for what are often implicit, experience-based intuitions about how to deal with children. The model grew out of the constructive give-and-take of teachers and researchers with strong convictions who were nonetheless open to new ideas and practices. The High/Scope model has continued to develop since the High/Scope Perry Preschool Project ended (Hohmann, Banet, Weikart, 1979; Hohmann & Weikart, 1995, 2002) and has been widely accepted and used.

Versions of the High/Scope curriculum manual have been translated from English into Spanish, Portuguese, Dutch and Flemish, Norwegian, Finnish, Chinese, Turkish, French, Arabic, and Thai. In the U.S., a national survey found that each High/Scope certified trainer, on average, prepared 25 teachers to implement the educational model (Epstein, 1993, 1999). As of 2003, 1,500 High/Scope certified trainers have reached an estimated 37,500 teachers serving 375,000 children per year. The survey further indicated that 75% of these programs serve children from low-income families (50% Head Start and 25% state-funded prekindergarten programs). Of the 4.5 million preschoolers in out-of-home care in the U.S. today, 1.6 million are from low-income families. Extrapolating from these numbers, 8% of all U.S. preschool children and 18% of U.S. preschoolers from low-income families attend High/Scope programs. High/Scope is a major national provider of inservice staff development programs, especially in settings serving high-need communities. Participants in High/Scope training can obtain credit towards their associate's, bachelor's, or master's degree. From 1983 to 2003, there were 70,000 registrations for High/Scope training courses. Since 1994, High/Scope has provided an intensive training program to nearly 4,000 teachers in the statewide Georgia prekindergarten program (Epstein & Neill, 1995–1996).

Data Collection in the Study

The High/Scope Perry Preschool study has accumulated an unusually rich and comprehensive data set on young people growing up in poverty, with variables representing their status from birth through childhood and adolescence to early adulthood and midlife. The many variables encompass demographic characteristics, test performance throughout childhood and adolescence, school success, crime, socioeconomic success, health, family, and personal development. Table 2.6 lists the study's instruments and principal variables. In the study phases at ages 19, 27, and 40, we checked information from records against information from study-participant interviews and vice versa.

Low Attrition

One of the study's special strengths is that attrition in the study sample has been very low. Across the 48 measures of 123 cases, a median 7 cases (5.7%) were missing; 32 measures, including the age-40 interview, had 12 or fewer cases missing (0%–10%); and 10 measures had 13 to 25 cases missing (11%–20%). Four measures had 26 to 37 cases missing (21%–30%); 2 of these were teacher ratings instruments with a measure comprising data collected annually from kindergarten through grade 3; 2 were achievement tests given at grades 5 and 8. Two measures had 45 cases missing (36.6%); both were tests given at the end of the first preschool year to the last three classes only. At the age 40 interview, of the 123 original study participants, 112 were interviewed, 4 living ones were not, and 7 were

Table 2.6

MEASURES AND PRINCIPAL VARIABLES

Measure	Age of Study Participants	Principal Variables
Initial parent interview	3[a]	Parents' schooling, employment; persons, rooms in household, siblings
Stanford-Binet Intelligence Scale (Terman & Merrill, 1960)	3–9[b]	Intellectual performance
Adapted Leiter International Performance Scale (Arthur, 1952)	3–9	Nonverbal intellectual performance
Illinois Test of Psycholinguistic Abilities (ITPA, experimental version, McCarthy & Kirk, 1961)	3, 5–9	Psycholinguistic abilities
Peabody Picture Vocabulary Test (PPVT, Dunn, 1965)	3–9	Vocabulary
Wechsler Intelligence Scale for Children (Wechsler, 1974)	14	Intellectual performance
California Achievement Test (CAT, Tiegs & Clark, 1963, 1970)	7–11, 14	Reading, language, mathematics, and total school achievement
Adult APL Survey (American College Testing Program, 1976)	19, 27	School abilities in everyday life
Kaufman Functional Academic Skills Test (KFAST, Kaufman & Kaufman, 1994).	40	Reading, arithmetic, total achievement
Pupil Behavior Inventory (PBI, Vinter, Sarri, Vorwaller, & Wiegerink, 1966)	6–9	Classroom conduct, school motivation
Ypsilanti Rating Scale (YRS, Weikart, et al., 1970)	6–9	School potential, social maturity
Age 15 interview (from Bachman, O'Malley, & Johnston, 1978)	15	Commitment to schooling, homework, school conduct, employment history, delinquent behavior, memberships, peer relations, activities, health, parent relations, general attitudes, life objectives
Parent interview at youth age 15	15	Parent on youth's schooling, parent-youth relationship, parent time use Age 19 interview (from Freeberg, 1974, 1976)
Age 19 interview (from Freeberg, 1974, 1976)	19	High school satisfaction, employment history, employment, income, savings, ownership, job satisfaction, plans, self-reported crime and delinquency, arrests, memberships, help-seeking, people problems, pregnancies, family relations; activities, health, self-esteem
Age 21 case study interview	21	Parental role in discipline and education, role models, attitudes toward money, goal orientation, church and religion, sense of responsibility

Table 2.6 (Cont.)

MEASURES AND PRINCIPAL VARIABLES

Measure	Age of Study Participants	Principal Variables
Age 27 interview	27	Schooling, postsecondary programs, employment history, income, car ownership, health, health services, reproductive history, rearing of oldest child, people problems, self-reported offenses, crimes and arrests, welfare, marital status, living arrangements, community activities, ease in everyday activities, personal influences, life frustrations and positive aspects, interviewer ratings
Age 40 interview	40	Schooling, marital status and spouse, health and health services, current employment, employment history, money, living arrangements, childrearing, oldest child you had a major role in raising, oldest child age 19 or older, oldest child age 18 or younger, next oldest child you had a major role in raising, next oldest child age 19 or older, next oldest child age 18 or younger, neighborhood, family relations, crime, cars, community activities, the future, functional academic skills, interviewer judgments of the respondent
School records	15, 19, 27	Years of schooling, special services; grades, suspensions, expulsions
Police and court records	19, 27, 40	Juvenile and adult arrests, convictions, sentences
Social services records	19, 27, 40	Welfare assistance, use of social services

Note. Copies of the Pupil Behavior Inventory, Ypsilanti Rating Scale, and the interview forms at ages 15, 19, 27, and 40 are available upon request from the High/Scope Educational Research Foundation.

[a] Age 3 for the second to the fifth classes; age 4 for the first class.

[b] A dash indicates annual assessments between the indicated ages.

deceased. Criminal justice and social services records were considered to have no missing cases because the names of all the study participants were included in these searches, and the lack of a record indicated no arrests or no social services, although it is possible of course that some information was recorded in agencies whose records were not searched. School records were found for all but 11 cases (8.9%). The low rates of missing data mean that attrition had little if any effect on either sample representativeness or group comparisons. On the handful of measures for which attrition was greater, such as the age 14 school achievement tests, analyses revealed no attrition effect on the analyses (Schweinhart & Weikart, 1980).

The study's low attrition is largely attributable to the persistence of the interviewer and project staff in finding study participants. The interviewer at ages 19, 27, and 40, Van Loggins, was a long-time, well-known African American resident of the Perry neighborhood in Ypsilanti. Because he was a coach at Ypsilanti High School when the study participants were attending high school, he knew many of them and had coached several of them. He found many of them by obtaining information from their families and friends. His tenacity was extraordinary. He endured a strip-search at a prison in order to obtain one interview and, during another, had to take cover to avoid gunshots being fired in the neighborhood. At a late-night neighborhood party, he discovered the sister of a man he was unable to locate and scheduled an interview through her. He caught up with another study participant by bumping into her sister while they were in line to buy tickets for a show. He carried blank interview forms with him and once made a U-turn to follow a study participant to a Laundromat and conduct an interview. In addition, the continued collaboration and good will of schools, courts and police, social services agencies, and the study participants themselves all contributed to successful data collection.

Another factor in the study's low attrition was the geographic stability of the study participants through age 40, which was slightly higher than is typical in the U.S. National estimates based on the University of Michigan's Panel Study of Income Dynamics (PSID; Duncan, 1992) indicate that 54% of the nation's children lived in the same county 20 years later, as compared to 61% of the Perry Preschool sample 37 years later; and 76% lived in the same state 20 years later, as compared to 82% of the Perry Preschool sample 37 years later.

Age 40 Data

This age 40 report presents findings that are based on data from an interview of study participants at ages 38–43, crime and prison records, and social services records.

Age 40 interview development

We developed the age 40 interview to find effects of the program on study participants at age 40. We built the interview on two foundations—previous findings of program effects in this study and the research literature on midlife, particularly for African Americans born in poverty. We identified program effects both in this study and in the High/Scope Preschool Curriculum Comparison study that followed it (Schweinhart & Weikart, 1997a, 1997b). In the latter study, we identified effects as the differences between outcomes of the High/Scope preschool program and outcomes of two other preschool program models—traditional nursery school and direct instruction. Then we duplicated on the age 40 interview those items for which group differences had previously been found.

Sources useful in the development of the age 40 interview included the Midlife Development Inventory (MacArthur Foundation Research Network on Successful Midlife Development, 1997), parent interviews used in the first Head Start Quality Research Consortium studies (1995–2000), health items used in the Harlem Longitudinal Study of Urban Black Youth (Brunswick & Messeri, 1985), social items developed and used by Freeberg (1974), and misconduct items from the Monitoring the Future Study (Bachman & Johnston, 1978). The academic performance test given at age 40 was the Kaufman Functional Academic Skills Test (KFAST; Kaufman & Kaufman, 1994).

The age 40 interview

The High/Scope Age 40 Follow-up Interview is a series of 286 items, an item being a question or series of related questions, that were collected by the interviewer in a face-to-face meeting with each study participant. The interview has 23 sections, as follows:

- Identifying information (16 items)
- Schooling (7 items)
- Marital status and spouse (2 items)
- Health and health services (28 items)
- Current employment (8 items)
- Employment history (4 items)
- Money (22 items)
- Living arrangements (10 items)
- Childrearing (5 items)
- Oldest child you had a major role in raising (10 items)
  - Oldest child age 19 or older (21 items)
  - Oldest child age 18 or younger (23 items)
- Next oldest child you had a major role in raising (10 items)
  - Next oldest child age 19 or older (21 items)
  - Next oldest child age 18 or younger (23 items)
- Neighborhood (9 items)
- Family relations (5 items)
- Social behavior (crime, 2 items)
- Cars (3 items)
- Community activities (8 items)
- The future (5 items)
- Functional academic skills (29 items on the KFAST)
- Interviewer judgments of the respondent (15 items)

The interviewer asked each respondent to sign forms granting permission for release of personal information from school, police, social services, welfare, employment, and medical records. He paid each respondent $100 for the interview.

Age 40 interview statistics

Of the 123 original Perry study participants, we

- Interviewed 112 with the age 40 interview.

- Found but could not interview 2 (1 had refused since childhood, the other was approached about 50 times but never explicitly refused).

- Could not find 2 (both had been interviewed at age 27).

- Found that 7 were deceased—2 in the program group in the 1990s, 5 in the no-program group (1 by cancer, 2 by murder, 2 by suspected murder).

The retention rates for the age 40 interview were 91% of the original study participants and 97% of the living study participants.

Of the 114 who were found, 62 lived in Ypsilanti, 8 lived in other areas of Washtenaw County, 14 lived in other areas of southeastern Michigan, and 10 were incarcerated in Michigan jails and prisons. The remaining 20 lived in 12 other states—4 in California; 3 in Alabama; 2 each in Massachusetts, Nevada (including 1 incarcerated there), and Texas; and 1 each in Arizona, Florida, Georgia, Kansas, Ohio, Pennsylvania, and Washington, DC.

The mean age of the 112 study participants interviewed was 40.8, with a standard deviation of 1.4. The program group did not differ noticeably from the no-program group in age at interview. The youngest study participant interviewed was 38.2, and the oldest was 44.0. Of the 112 study participants interviewed, 9 were interviewed at 38 (8.1%); 31 were interviewed at 39 (27.8%); 18 were interviewed at 40 (16.2%); 32 were interviewed at 41 (28.8%); 14 were interviewed at 42 (12.6%); and 8 were interviewed at 43 (7.2%). Reflecting the strategy of interviewing the younger classes at younger ages, the mean ages of classes at interview differed significantly from one another, with every class differing significantly from every other class. The mean class ages at interview (with standard deviations in parentheses) were as follows:

- First class: 42.5 (0.8)

- Second class: 41.6 (0.6)

- Third class: 40.9 (0.8)

- Fourth class: 39.9 (0.7)

- Fifth class: 39.3 (0.5)

Of the 112 study participants interviewed with the age 40 interview, the interviewer conversed with 61 of them (55%) in their own homes, 21 (19%) in his home, 6 (5%) in someone else's home, 13 (12%) in a county jail or state prison, 8 (7%) in a motel or hotel, 2 (2%) in some other business establishment, and 1 (1%) in an airport terminal. For the 83 age 40 interviews for which duration was recorded, the average interview lasted 2 hours, 33 minutes, with 23% of the interviews lasting less than 2 hours, 61% lasting 2–3 hours, and 16% lasting over 3 hours. Of 88 interviews with starting times recorded, 31% began before 3:00 pm, 31% began between 3:00 and 6:00 pm, and 39% began after 6:00 pm.

When questions related to each other were asked (for example, concerning employment, earnings, and income), study participants sometimes gave inadequate or inconsistent answers. One of the authors—without knowledge of whether the study participants were in the program group or the no-program group—reviewed each interview and filled in missing answers when it was possible to do so from other available information. For example, if a study participant reported having been in the same job for the past 3 years, but did not report the number of months unemployed during the past 24 months, then the response to the latter item was changed from "missing" to 0; or if a study participant reported having never been employed in the past 5 years, the missing report of the number of months unemployed was changed to 24. Despite these efforts, however, a few inconsistencies and gaps in the interviews remained.

For the age 40 study, we reviewed official records of crime, driving, county jail, state prison, social services, and unemployment of the study participants.

Crime records through age 41

In 2001, we collected data from crime records regarding study participants' felonies, misdemeanors, and civil infractions through age 27; we had previously collected data for juvenile crimes, felonies, and misdemeanors, but not civil infractions.

We collected data from the federal court in Detroit, Washtenaw County's 22nd Circuit Court, and five district courts, making use of the circuit court's computer database; from neighboring Jackson County's 4th Circuit and 12th District Courts; and from neighboring Wayne County's 3rd Circuit Court. Because of the expense and expected low return, we did not collect data from Wayne County's 23 district courts. Ypsilanti and Ann Arbor are the largest cities in Washtenaw County; Jackson is the largest city in Jackson County and is home to a state prison; Detroit is the largest city in Wayne County. We searched records for the names of all study participants, including maiden and married names, nicknames, aliases, and spelling variants; we used birthdates and occasionally addresses and Social Security numbers to confirm matches. We then linked names with criminal case numbers, and pulled the paper file for each case number. While the circuit courts retain felony records indefinitely, district courts keep misdemeanor records 7–10 years and civil infraction records, 3 years.

At the state level, we collected data on the Internet from the Michigan State Police Law Enforcement Information Network (LEIN), a computer database used by police that maintains a statewide record of felony and high misdemeanor convictions and related information. The database does not include arrests that did not result in conviction and is sometimes incomplete with respect to the subsequent charging and adjudication of arrests. We also collected data from Secretary of State driving records. If the LEIN identified a study participant conviction in Michigan outside of Washtenaw, Jackson, and Wayne counties, or in Wayne County district courts, we contacted the county where the conviction occurred for further information.

At the federal level, the federal court clerk for eastern Michigan in Ann Arbor searched the federal records for all 123 study participants and identified five case numbers. We confirmed three of them with the Detroit and Flint District Court Services and two with the Chicago Records Center. A similar search of federal records for western Michigan in Grand Rapids found none of the study participants.

Of the 29 study participants who had ever lived in states other than Michigan since 1990, 21 had lived in 1 other state, 5 had lived in 2 other states, and 3 had lived in 3 other states—a total of 38 other state residences. These residences were in 19 states: 8 in California; 5 in Texas; 3 each in Alabama and Massachusetts; 2 each in Arizona, Georgia, Kentucky, and Ohio; and 1 each in 11 other states—Alabama, Colorado, Florida, Kansas, Louisiana, Nevada, New Hampshire, Oklahoma, Pennsylvania, Tennessee, and Washington.

For crimes outside Michigan, when study participants reported living or having lived in another state since 1990, we contacted its state police agency requesting a criminal record search for those individuals. We conducted searches for specific individual crime records in 11 states—Alabama, Arizona (via the state website), California, Florida, Georgia, Kansas, Massachusetts, Ohio, Pennsylvania, Texas, and Washington (via the state department of law enforcement website). We used the *Rapsheets*.com website (2003) to search for specific individual crime records in 7 other states—Alabama, Colorado, Kentucky, New Hampshire, Oklahoma, Nevada, and Tennessee. Louisiana did not release information on criminal activity that we requested, nor was it available at the *Rapsheets.com* website. We also contacted the Federal Bureau of Investigation regarding access to its national database of individual criminal information, but learned that access is limited to the individuals themselves who must supply their fingerprints, so we decided not to pursue it.

It is not known whether the 2 study participants who were not found (2 of the 4 not interviewed were found in Michigan) committed crimes outside of Michigan.

Prison records

We used the Michigan Department of Corrections' Offender Tracking Information System (2004) to identify study participants with Michigan state prison records. Then we obtained permission from the Department to interview current state prisoners. Subsequently, at our request, the Michigan Department of Corrections ran a search for all 123 study participants and found 12, then for a fee sent detailed information on them. The Washtenaw County Jail also ran a search for all 123 study participants.

Unemployment records

The Unemployment Agency in the Michigan Department of Consumer and Industry Services ran a search for all 123 study participants. They informed us that their records were complete and accurate for the previous 7 years, but incomplete before that due to periodic record purges.

School records

In previous data collections, public school records regarding special education services (including nonusage) were found for 91% of the study participants. Data on high school graduation status were obtained for all the study participants—94% from public school records, 3% from adult high school records, and 3% from unconfirmed self reports on the age 27 interview. The Ypsilanti school district had the records of 63% of the study participants; other Washtenaw County school districts had the records of 24% of the study participants; and school districts outside Washtenaw County had the records of 8% of the study participants. Staff of adult high school programs in Ypsilanti, Willow Run, and Ann Arbor conducted records searches; 10 study participants were identified in the Ypsilanti program, while none were identified in the other programs.

The Michigan Department of Education and the Washtenaw Intermediate School District searched their GED records for the 56 study participants with no record of high school graduation, including 8 who claimed GED certification. GED certificates were found for 5 of them (2 in the program group and 3 in the no-program group). Nine other study participants took, but did not pass, the national GED test or took the preparatory course, but did not take the test; some of these nevertheless reported in their age 19 and age 27 interviews that the GED was their highest level of schooling, probably because they took GED coursework after dropping out of high school.

Requests and signed consent forms for records were sent to all post-secondary education programs identified by study participants in their age 27 interview—18 schools in 6 states. Officials in 11 schools responded, in which 31 study participants were enrolled; officials at 7 schools did not respond, at which 8 study participants reported that they were enrolled.

Social services records

Michigan's Family Independence Agency agreed to our request for information on receipt of various social services from 1991 to 2001. Data prior to 1996 had been warehoused and they could not access it; in addition, local records are purged after 3 years. They have had a central record keeping system since 1997. In January of 2002, we sent them each study participant's name (including aliases), birthdate, Social Security number, and signed information release form, which they used to search records for the following:

- *Family Independence Program/Aid to Families With Dependent Children*—time on assistance and benefit amounts by month from 1995

- *State Disability Assistance/General Assistance*—time on assistance and benefit amounts by month from 1995

- *Food Stamps*—time on assistance and benefit amounts by month since July 1997

- *Medicaid*—eligibility by month since July 1997

- *Child Day Care*—time on assistance and benefit amounts since July 1997

- *Children's Protective Services*—involvement in a case by type of involvement (perpetrator or adult caretaker of child victim) since January 1990

- *Prevention*—listed as active on a Prevention Services case since July 1997

We received an Excel data file with this information in June 2002. Because of this centralized data source, we did not collect data from local records as we had for the age 27 study. Nor did we pursue any out-of-state searches for social service information.

We also collected information on the receipt of unemployment benefits. We sent a list of participants, as described above, to the Coordinator of the Michigan Unemployment Agency. We requested and received in August 2001 a list of participants and amounts from 1990 to June 2001.

Methods of Analysis

The analytic techniques presented in this report are based on comparisons of the program group and the no-program group with statistical adjustments to compensate for the effects of seven background covariates, listed below. The study's experimental design and the initial similarity of groups inspire scientific confidence that the performance of the no-program group represents what the performance of the program group would have been if the program group had not attended the preschool program. The statistical adjustments for small remaining group background differences increase this scientific confidence.

Seven background variables were selected as covariates for the outcome analyses reported in this monograph. As shown in Table 2.7, five of them—participant's gender, Stanford-Binet IQ at study entry, mother's schooling, father's occupational status, and household rooms per person—had statistically significant relationships with one or more of the key outcome variables. Another variable—mother's employment—was included because it had a statistically significant relationship with preschool experience (but not key outcomes) that resulted from the random-assignment departure of assigning some children of employed mothers to the no-program group. Another variable—father at home—was included due to its policy relevance and nearly statistically significant relationship with monthly earnings at age 40. Four other potential covariates collected at study entry—age, family on welfare, average of parents' years of schooling, and persons in home—had weaker correlations with the key outcomes than the ones selected. Preschool-experience group differences in background variables were examined by the chi-square statistic for nominal variables and t-tests for continuous variables.

Except for tested performance, the distributions of most outcome variables were not normal but L-shaped, that is to say, positively skewed

Table 2.7

CORRELATIONS BETWEEN PRESCHOOL EXPERIENCE, COVARIATES, AND MAJOR OUTCOMES

Variable	Preschool Experience[a]	Gender[b]	Stanford-Binet IQ at Study Entry	Mother's Schooling	Mother's Employment	Father at Home	Father's Occupational Status[c]	Household Rooms per Person
Preschool experience[a]	—	.03	.08	.02	-.28*	.04	.16	.03
Stanford-Binet IQ after 1 preschool year	.50*	.06	.45*	.25*	-.08	.09	.11	.05
School achievement at 14	.34*	.12	.13	.32*	.01	.08	.34*	.02
Literacy at 19	.22*	-.06	.26*	.22*	.08	.00	.13	.04
Years retained in grade up to 19	-.06	-.09	-.08	-.22*	-.11	.01	-.16	-.13
Monthly earnings at age 27	.21*	-.10	.10	.22*	.04	.05	.06	.10
Monthly earnings at age 40	.16	.00	.20*	.20*	.13	-.14	.01	.10
Lifetime educational attainment	.18*	.03	.21*	.30*	.05	-.11	.05	.25*
Lifetime arrests	-.22*	-.38*	-.21*	-.09	-.03	-.02	-.24*	-.02

Note. All variables in the top row were collected at study entry. Correlations are Pearson above the middle line and Spearman Rho below the middle line. Variables below the middle line are ordinal with categories defined in Chapters 3 to 5. *N*s are 88 to 123.

[a] 0 = no-program group, 1 = program group

[b] 0 = male, 1 = female

[c] 0 = unemployed or unskilled, 1 = semiskilled or skilled

* *p* (two-tailed) < .05.

to the right. We truncated these distributions by dividing the variable into segments that were as equal in size as possible, presenting in the tables the percentages of the program group and no-program group falling into each segment. Group differences in outcome variables, statistically adjusted by the seven covariates, were examined by binary logistic regression analysis for dichotomous variables, such as employment status, ordinal regression analysis for ordinal variables, such as arrests and earnings truncated from highly skewed count data, and ordinary least-squares regression analysis for normally distributed interval variables, such as tested performance. When the preschool-experience-by-gender interaction term had a statistically significant association with the outcome variable, the same analyses were used to compare program males to no-program males and program females to no-program females.

Effect sizes were calculated for background variables and for normally distributed interval outcome variables by dividing the difference between preschool experience groups by the standard deviation of the no-program group (Fitz-Gibbon & Morris, 1987).

Odds ratios were calculated for dichotomous and interval outcome variables instead of effect sizes, due to the lack of meaningful standard deviations. The odds ratio compares the odds of the program group having a better score on the variable to the odds of the no-program group having a better score. An odds ratio greater than 1 means the program group has greater odds than the no-program group of having a better score. An odds ratio less than 1 means the program group has worse odds than the no-program group of having a better score.

Throughout this report, unless otherwise noted (as in Chapter 6), a group difference is identified as significant if it is statistically significant with a one-tailed probability of chance occurrence of less than .05, that is, less than 1 in 20. Significance levels of less than .01, that is, less than 1 in 100, are also identified. The decision to focus on one-tailed rather than two-tailed probability (as was done in previous reports) was based on the fact that at this point the study's hypotheses are clearly directional: the obvious hypothesis was that the program group would do better than the no-program group; and directional hypotheses call for one-tailed tests (see the discussion of this point by Locurto, 1991, and Schweinhart & Weikart, 1991). A one-tailed probability is half of the size of the corresponding two-tailed probability. We also decided to treat statistical tests as independent of each other. Another approach would have been to treat statistical tests as interdependent, thus calling for multivariate statistical testing or, alternatively, making Bonferroni corrections for statistical probability by multiplying probability levels by the number of tests conducted. This approach is better suited to theory testing than to this exploratory research. The question herein was not whether the preschool program had a specified set of effects, but rather what its effects were.

III Education

The program group significantly outperformed the no-program group on highest level of schooling completed. Specifically, a much larger percentage of program than no-program females graduated from high school. This difference was related to earlier differences in the rates of treatment for mental impairment and repetition in grade for program versus no-program females. Overall, the program group significantly outperformed the no-program group on various intellectual and language tests from their preschool years up to age 7; school achievement tests at ages 9, 10, and 14; and literacy tests at ages 19 and 27. Despite significantly more placements in programs for speech and language impairment (13% vs. 5%) and compensatory education (41% vs. 22%), the program group had significantly fewer placements in programs for mental impairment than the no-program group (15% vs. 35%). The program group had significantly better attitudes toward school than the no-program group at ages 15 and 19, and program-group parents had better attitudes toward their 15-year-old children's schooling than did no-program-group parents.

New education data obtained at age 40 primarily update schooling completed as indicated in Table 3.1. In addition, the analyses presented throughout this report differ from those presented in previous reports in that odds ratios are presented for ordinal variables rather than effect sizes, statistical tests correct for the effects of seven covariates—participants' gender, Stanford-Binet IQ at study entry, mother's schooling, mother's employment, father at home, father's occupation, and household rooms per person—and statistical tests are one-tailed rather than two-tailed. Apart from these revisions, this chapter summarizes what has been presented in previous monographs (e.g., Schweinhart et al., 1993).

Educational Attainment

The educational attainment numbers reported here are based on some recoding of such data up to age 27—high school graduation status (new information), college degrees (redefined as associate's or bachelor's degrees), college courses (some students who had not graduated from high school took courses at a community college that did not carry college credit); and grade of school dropout (new information).

As Table 3.1 and Figure 3.1 show, **the program group had significantly higher educational attainment than the no-program group.** By age 40, 77% of the program group but only 60% of the no-program group had graduated from high school in some way. By age 19, 67% of the program group but only 45% of the no-program group had graduated from high school, with most of those who dropped out doing so at grades 9 or 10 (Table 3.2). From ages 19 to 40, 10% more of the program group and 15% more of the no-program group graduated from high school in some way. While most graduated from regular high school in their teen years, 12% of the program group and 16% of the no-program group instead either

Table 3.1

SCHOOLING COMPLETED, BY AGE BY PRESCHOOL EXPERIENCE BY GENDER

Schooling Completed	By Age 40			By Age 27			Up to Age 19		
	Program Group	No-Program Group	Odds Ratio	Program Group	No-Program Group	Odds Ratio	Program Group	No-Program Group	Odds Ratio
Highest level of schooling attained									
Overall, *n*	56	63		58	64		58	65	
Associate or higher degree	9%	5%	2.25*	3%	2%	2.94**	0%	0%	2.36*
Graduated from high school in some way[a]	68%	55%		69%	51%		67%	45%	
Did not graduate from high school	23%	40%		28%	47%		33%	55%	
Males, *n*	31	39		33	39		33	39	
Associate or higher degree	7%	3%	.89	0%	0%	.84	0%	0%	.73
Graduated from high school in some way[a]	61%	66%		64%	64%		54%	56%	
Did not graduate from high school	32%	31%		36%	36%		46%	44%	
Females, *n*	25	24		25	25		25	26	
Associate or higher degree	12%	8%	5.08*	8%	4%	12.55**	0%	0%	28.22**
Graduated from high school in some way[a]	76%	38%		76%	32%		84%	27%	
Did not graduate from high school	12%	54%		16%	64%		16%	73%	
Type of high school graduation									
Overall, *n*	57	64		58	65		58	65	
Graduated from regular high school	65%	45%	2.10*	64%	45%	2.38*	64%	40%	2.47**
GED/adult high school	12%	16%		8%	9%		3%	5%	
Did not graduate from high school	23%	39%		28%	46%		33%	55%	

Table 3.1 (Cont.)

SCHOOLING COMPLETED, BY AGE BY PRESCHOOL EXPERIENCE BY GENDER

Schooling Completed	By Age 40			By Age 27			Up to Age 19		
	Program Group	No-Program Group	Odds Ratio	Program Group	No-Program Group	Odds Ratio	Program Group	No-Program Group	Odds Ratio
Males, n	*32*	*39*		*33*	*39*		*33*	*39*	
Graduated from regular high school	50%	54%	.78	49%	54%	.80	48%	51%	.78
GED/adult high school	19%	15%		15%	10%		6%	5%	
Did not graduate from high school	31%	31%		36%	36%		46%	44%	
Females, n	*25*	*25*		*25*	*26*		*25*	*26*	
Graduated from regular high school	84%	32%	19.57**	84%	31%	24.31**	84%	23%	32.69**
GED/adult high school	4%	16%		0%	8%		0%	4%	
Did not graduate from high school	12%	52%		16%	61%		16%	73%	
College education, n	*56*	*63*		*58*	*64*		*58*	*64*	
Associate or higher degree	9%	5%	1.36	3%	2%	1.67	0%	0%	1.45
College courses	37%	33%		33%	28%		19%	13%	
No college education	54%	62%		64%	70%		81%	87%	

Note. Statistical tests are one-tailed. Statistical tests and odds ratios (but not group percentages) are based on ordinal regression analysis, adjusted for the effects of participants' gender, Stanford-Binet IQ at study entry, mother's schooling, mother's employment, father at home, father's occupation status, and household rooms per person. High school status is based on school records supplemented by self reports. All college courses and degrees at age 40 and part of them at age 27 are based on self reports and consistency checks for names of college and course, time and duration, and across ages. Five participants who reported college courses but without high school graduation up to age 40 were coded as no college education for lack of evidence that courses taken were not aimed at high school certificate or vocational training.

[a] In some way = regular high school graduation, adult high school graduation, or GED certification.

* *p* (one-tailed) < .05; ** *p* (one-tailed) < .01.

Figure 3.1

HIGHEST LEVEL OF SCHOOLING ATTAINED BY AGE 40,
BY PRESCHOOL EXPERIENCE BY GENDER

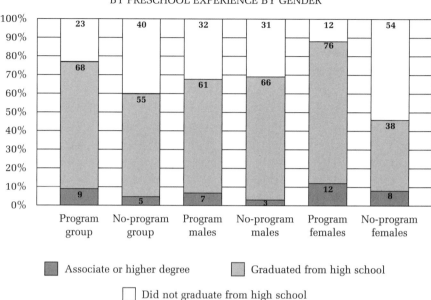

graduated from adult high school or passed the General Educational Development (GED) test by age 40. The odds of program-group members graduating from high school were 2 to 3 times as great as the odds of no-program group members graduating from high school. By age 40, 37% of the program group and 33% of the no-program group took college courses without attaining a degree, and 9% of the program group and 5% of the no-program group attained an associate's or bachelor's degree.

This group difference in educational attainment was due to females and not males. By age 40, 88% of the program females but only 46% of the no-program females had graduated from high school by some measure, a 42 percentage-point difference and nearly twice as many in the program as the no-program group. By age 19, 84% of the program females but only 27% of the no-program females had graduated from high school, a 57 percentage-point difference and over 3 times as many, with most of those dropping out doing so at grades 9 or 10 (Table 3.2). From ages 19 to 40, 4% more of the program females and 19% more of the no-program females either graduated from regular or adult high school or passed the GED test. Meanwhile, nearly identical percentages of program and no-program males had graduated from high school by some measure—68% versus 69% by age 40, 54% versus 56% by age 19—with increases of 14% versus 13% from ages 19 to 40. In short, the study's finding of a group difference in educational attainment is due to the difference in the regular high school graduation rates between program and no-program females, even though this difference was reduced by subsequent attainment of high school graduation by alternate routes. The odds ratio for female group differences varied from 5.08 to a remarkable 32.69, with the strongest odds ratio centered on their regular high school graduation by age 19.

The high school graduation rates of 64% of Perry study males, 88% of program-group females, and 46% of no-program-group females compare to U.S. rates for 40- to 44-year-olds in 2002 of about 85% for African American males and females and 89% for the whole population at that age (U.S. Census Bureau, 2003b). The generational improvement in high school graduation rates was substantial. A generation earlier, mostly in the South, 11% of the fathers of study participants had graduated from high school as compared to 64% of their sons; 21% of the mothers of study participants had graduated from high school, as compared to 35% of their daughters in the no-program group and 84% of their daughters in the program group.

Special Education

Table 3.2 presents the placements in all types of special school services identified on study participants' school records. Some of these placements were provided to students in regular classes while others were provided to students instead of regular classes. Assignment to special school services means, first, that the assigned student has been identified as someone who needs the service, and second, that the student's subsequent school experience was different from what it would have been if the student had not received the service.

As Table 3.2 and Figure 3.2 show, **a significantly smaller percentage of the program group than the no-program group received special education for mental impairment (15% vs. 35%),** with the group difference especially pronounced for those who received 6 or more years of such

Figure 3.2

PERCENT IN MENTAL IMPAIRMENT PROGRAMS AND RETAINED IN GRADE,
BY PRESCHOOL EXPERIENCE BY GENDER

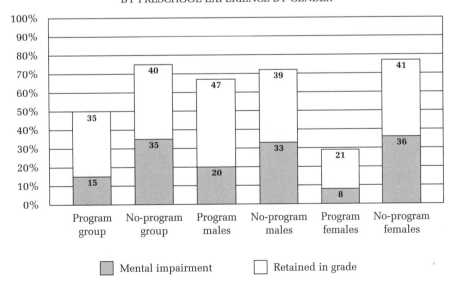

Table 3.2

GRADE AT DROPOUT, GRADE REPETITION, AND SPECIAL EDUCATION, BY PRESCHOOL EXPERIENCE BY GENDER

Variable	All			Males			Females		
	Program Group	No-Program Group	Odds Ratio	Program Males	No-Program Males	Odds Ratio	Program Females	No-Program Females	Odds Ratio
Grade at dropout, n	57	64		32	38		25	26	
No dropout	65%	44%	.36**	50%	55%	1.12	84%	27%	.04**
11–12	12%	16%		22%	16%		0%	15%	
9–10	23%	34%		28%	26%		16%	46%	
7–8	0%	6%		0%	3%		0%	12%	
Repeating a grade, n	54	58		30	36		24	22	
0 year	65%	60%	.93	53%	61%	1.97	79%	59%	.16*
1 year	18%	16%		24%	22%		13%	5%	
2–4 years	17%	24%		23%	17%		8%	36%	
Any special education, n	54	58		30	36		24	22	
0 year	35%	40%	.63	27%	42%	1.21	46%	36%	.26*
1–5 years	45%	24%		46%	25%		42%	23%	
6–18 years	20%	36%		27%	33%		12%	41%	
Mental impairment, n	54	58		30	36		24	22	
0 year	85%	65%	.23**	80%	67%	.36	92%	64%	.06**
1–5 years	6%	7%		10%	8%		0%	4%	
6–13 years	9%	28%		10%	25%		8%	32%	
Emotional impairment, n	54	58		30	36		24	22	
0 year	78%	79%	1.38	73%	75%	1.23	83%	86%	1.89
1 year	9%	12%		10%	17%		9%	5%	
2–9 years	13%	9%		17%	8%		8%	9%	

Table 3.2 (Cont.)

GRADE AT DROPOUT, GRADE REPETITION, AND SPECIAL EDUCATION, BY PRESCHOOL EXPERIENCE BY GENDER

Variable	All			Males			Females		
	Program Group	No-Program Group	Odds Ratio	Program Males	No-Program Males	Odds Ratio	Program Females	No-Program Females	Odds Ratio
Learning disability, *n*	*54*	*58*		*30*	*36*		*24*	*22*	
0 year	91%	90%	.82	83%	92%	2.51	100%	86%	--
1 year	2%	0%		4%	0%		0%	0%	
2–6 years	7%	10%		13%	8%		0%	14%	
Speech and language impairment , *n*	*54*	*58*		*30*	*36*		*24*	*22*	
0 year	87%	95%	3.74*	87%	92%	2.79	88%	100%	--
1 year	7%	3%		3%	5%		12%	0%	
2–5 years	6%	2%		10%	3%		0%	0%	
Compensatory education, *n*	*54*	*58*		*30*	*36*		*24*	*22*	
0 year	59%	78%	2.22*	57%	86%	4.98**	62%	64%	1.48
1 year	21%	12%		23%	8%		17%	18%	
2–8 years	20%	10%		20%	6%		21%	18%	
Disciplinary placement, *n*	*54*	*58*		*30*	*36*		*24*	*22*	
0 year	83%	79%	.69	80%	81%	.75	88%	77%	1.15
1 year	11%	11%		10%	8%		12%	14%	
2–4 years	6%	10%		10%	11%		0%	9%	

Note. Statistical tests are one-tailed. Statistical tests and odds ratios (but not group percentages) are based on ordinal regression analysis, adjusted for the effects of participants' gender, Stanford-Binet IQ at study entry, mother's schooling, mother's employment, father at home, father's occupation status, and household rooms per person.

* *p* (one-tailed) < .05; ** *p* (one-tailed) < .01.

service (9% vs. 28%). The odds of receiving treatment for mental impairment were only about one fourth as great for the program group as for the no-program group. On the other hand, **significantly larger percentages of the program group than the no-program group received special education for speech and language impairment (13% vs. 5%), and compensatory education (41% vs. 22%).** The meaning of the group difference in compensatory education indicated on school records is unclear because *all* of both groups were qualified for compensatory education by virtue of their family economic status. Groups did not differ significantly in their years placed in special education overall or for emotional impairment or learning disability; nor their years repeating a grade or receiving disciplinary placement. In comparison with the no-program group, the program group, on average, spent 1.7 fewer years in treatment for mental impairment, 0.6 more years in compensatory education, and 0.1 more of a year in speech and language programs—netting out 1 less year of receiving any of these special services. In all of the special services listed here, the program group averaged 1.2 fewer years than the no-program group (4.0 years vs. 5.2 years). This pattern of findings suggests that the preschool program improved the school performance or conduct of some study participants who would have received treatment for mental impairment enough so that they were placed instead more briefly in less serious and less expensive compensatory education programs.

Since the study participants were originally selected because they were at special risk of school failure, it is not surprising that they spent quite a few years receiving special school services. Despite the criticisms of intelligence tests, IQs continue to be a major determinant of treatment for mental impairment, and the American Association on Mental Deficiency identifies IQs between 70 and 85 with borderline mental impairment and IQs below 70 as constituting mental impairment (Grossman, 1973). In the Perry Preschool study, special education programs for mental impairment served 25% of the study participants; at age 3, 13% of the study participants had IQs below 70 and 72% had IQs between 70 and 85; at age 14, 16% had IQs below 70 and 56% had IQs between 70 and 85. Differences in school placements first appeared 5 years after the preschool program. At that time, by grade 4, it was reported that significantly fewer program-group children had been placed in special school programs or were repeating a grade (17% vs. 38%; Weikart et al., 1978).

Special Educational Treatment by Gender

Group-by-gender differences in special educational treatment were striking and account for some of the group-by-gender differences in high school graduation rates.

- **Program females differed significantly from no-program females in their rates of mental impairment treatment (8% vs. 36%), grade repetition (21% vs. 41%), and school dropout (12% vs. 54%), as**

Figures 3.1 and 3.2 show. It seems likely that, for females, preschool program participation, lack of mental impairment treatment, and lack of grade repetition served as protective factors against school dropout (see Barnes, 1991). All 17 of the program females *not* treated for mental impairment or repeating a grade graduated from high school, while only 2 of the 12 no-program females treated for mental impairment or repeating a grade did—100% versus 17%.

- Program males and no-program males, however, did not differ significantly in their rates of treatment for mental impairment (20% vs. 33%; Figure 3.2), grade repetition (47% vs. 39%), or school drop-out (32% vs. 31%). Despite the lack of a preschool program effect on mental impairment or grade repetition, just as with females, 26 of the 28 males (93%) not treated for mental impairment or repeating a grade graduated from high school, while only 15 of 34 males (44%) treated for mental impairment or repeating a grade did.

For females, the program/no-program differences were 26% for mental impairment treatment or grade repetition and 42% for high school graduation, so 62% of the program effect on female high school graduation could be mediated by treatment for mental impairment or grade repetition (26%/42%). For males, the program/no-program differences were 5% or less for mental impairment or grade repetition and high school graduation.

In thinking about how the preschool program might have affected males and females differently, teen pregnancy is an obvious choice for an explanation, since females become pregnant and males do not, and teen pregnancy is an obstacle to high school graduation. Indeed, in this study only 40% of the teen mothers graduated from high school as compared to 79% of the females who were not teen mothers—a difference of 39% ($p < .01$). However, even though at age 19 program females reported significantly fewer pregnancies than did no-program females (means of 0.6 vs. 1.2 pregnancies), they reported only slightly fewer births (means of 0.6 vs. 0.8 births), and 44% versus 54% reported being teen mothers. This 10% difference in teen motherhood is only one fourth the size of the 42% difference in high school graduation rates, so teen motherhood cannot account for much of the difference in female high school dropout rates.

The entire pattern of preschool-experience-by-gender findings on schooling variables suggests that the preschool program affected the school experience of females more than males. One interpretation of this pattern is that school staff paid scant attention to the preschool program's improvement of males' school ability, but did pay attention to the preschool program's improvement of females' school ability, and it was sustained and amplified by this attention, particularly the tracking of females according to their school ability—placing and keeping higher-ability females in the upper track of regular classes on grade while placing lower-ability females in the lower track of treatment for mental impairment and grade repetition. Subsequently, females in the upper track developed better school achievement and commitment to schooling than did the females in the lower track. When teen motherhood stood in the way of high school graduation for some females, most of those in the upper track, because of their stronger commitment to schooling, gradu-ated anyway, while most of those in the lower track did not. Gray et al. (1982), in their study of the Early Training Project, reported a similar pattern of findings for males and females.

Test Performance

The program group significantly outscored the no-program group on various intellectual and language tests up to age 7 and on various achievement tests from ages 7 to 27, reviewed chronologically below.

As shown in Table 3.3, **the program group significantly outscored the no-program group on the following intellectual and language tests up to age 7:**

- *Intellectual performance,* **annually from the end of their first pre-school year to age 7** (Stanford-Binet Intelligence Scale; Terman & Merrill, 1960)

- *Nonverbal intellectual performance,* **annually during their pre-school years** (Adaptation of the Leiter International Performance Scale; Arthur, 1952)

- *Vocabulary,* **annually from shortly after their first preschool year began until age 6** (Peabody Picture Vocabulary Test, PPVT; Dunn, 1965)

- *Language performance,* **at the end of their second preschool year** (Illinois Test of Psycholinguistic Abilities, ITPA, experimental ver-sion; McCarthy & Kirk, 1961)

The effect sizes associated with these significant group differences ranged from 0.34 to 1.16 standard deviations. Effect sizes exceeded 0.85 of a standard deviation on intellectual performance at the end of the first and second preschool years and on nonverbal intellectual perfor-mance, vocabulary, and language performance at the end of the second preschool year.

As shown in Table 3.4, **the program group significantly outscored the no-program group on various achievement tests from ages 7 to 27.** On the California Achievement Tests (Tiegs & Clark, 1963, 1971) given at ages 7, 8, 9, 10, 11, and 14, adjusting for the effects of the seven covari-ates, the program group significantly outscored the no-program group on the following:

- *Overall school achievement,* **at ages 9, 10, and 14**

- *Reading achievement,* **at ages 10 and 14**

- *Arithmetic achievement,* **at ages 9 and 14**

- *Language achievement,* **at ages 9 and 14**

Table 3.3

INTELLECTUAL AND LANGUAGE PERFORMANCE, BY PRESCHOOL EXPERIENCE

Variable	Age[a]	Program Group			No-Program Group			Effect Size
		n	Adjusted Mean	(SD)	n	Adjusted Mean	(SD)	
Intellectual Performance	P0	58	79.6	(5.9)	65	78.5	(6.9)	.16
(Stanford-Binet IQs)	P1	58	94.8	(11.5)	65	84.0	(10.0)	.88**
	P2	44	94.8	(13.0)	49	83.6	(10.2)	.87**
	6	56	90.6	(12.2)	64	86.9	(9.9)	.32*
	7	58	91.0	(11.7)	61	87.7	(10.2)	.30*
	8	55	87.8	(13.1)	62	87.1	(10.7)	.06
	9	56	87.0	(10.9)	61	87.4	(12.5)	−.03
	10	57	85.1	(11.3)	57	84.5	(11.2)	.05
(WISC Full IQ)	14	54	80.4	(11.2)	56	81.3	(10.9)	−.08
Nonverbal intellectual	P¼	58	69.0	(21.9)	64	59.6	(18.0)	.46**
Performance	P1	37	95.7	(15.7)	41	73.1	(20.6)	1.02**
(Leiter International	P2	44	89.9	(14.0)	49	77.9	(14.6)	.77**
Performance)	6	56	85.7	(11.7)	63	84.2	(13.1)	.12
	7	58	87.8	(11.9)	61	88.0	(11.3)	−.02
	8	54	87.7	(10.4)	62	88.6	(13.1)	−.07
	9	54	89.0	(10.0)	60	85.1	(12.3)	.34*
Vocabulary (PPVT)	P¼	58	66.4	(12.1)	60	62.7	(8.2)	.35*
	P1	37	74.7	(15.6)	41	63.4	(13.1)	.74**
	P2	44	81.1	(20.9)	49	62.8	(15.1)	.91**
	6	56	80.4	(15.7)	64	76.2	(14.2)	.28
	7	58	83.4	(12.9)	61	80.9	(12.5)	.19
	8	55	82.9	(14.7)	61	82.1	(10.3)	.06
	9	56	81.0	(13.6)	61	81.0	(14.3)	.00
Psycholinguistic abilities	P¼	55	2.85	(.78)	65	2.59	(.72)	.34*
	P2	44	4.78	(.70)	47	3.92	(.56)	1.16**
	6	55	5.18	(.69)	62	5.04	(.54)	.22
	7	54	6.06	(.80)	54	5.90	(.60)	.23
	8	48	6.74	(.94)	54	6.52	(.80)	.26
	9	54	7.42	(1.07)	56	7.24	(.92)	.18

Note. Statistical tests are based on regression analysis. All the means except Stanford-Binet IQ at study entry are adjusted for the effects of participants' gender, Stanford-Binet IQ at study entry, mother's schooling, mother's employment, father at home, father's occupation status, and household rooms per person.

[a] P0 = study entry at age 3 or 4; P¼ = within 3 months of study entry; P1 = end of first preschool year; P2 = end of second preschool year (excluded first class); 6–14 = age in years, at the end of grades kindergarten through eighth grade (except for children repeating a grade, from whom data were also collected).

*p (one-tailed) < .05; **p (one-tailed) < .01.

Table 3.4

SCHOOL ACHIEVEMENT AND GRADES, BY PRESCHOOL EXPERIENCE

Variable	Age	Program Group			No-Program Group			Effect Size
		n	Adjusted Mean	(SD)	n	Adjusted Mean	(SD)	
High school grade point average								
Overall		42	2.03	(.65)	44	1.73	(.74)	.42*
Male		24	1.82	(.63)	29	1.72	(.78)	.14
Female		18	2.35	(.54)	13	1.71	(.68)	.90**
Total school achievement	7	53	94.2	(39.9)	60	87.0	(37.7)	.18
	8	49	141.0	(48.0)	56	127.8	(45.7)	.28
	9	54	169.9	(69.8)	55	148.4	(76.5)	.29*
	10	49	225.7	(72.2)	46	199.0	(84.1)	.34*
	11	42	251.9	(70.2)	46	242.9	(71.1)	.13
	14	49	118.6	(41.6)	46	98.4	(35.5)	.49**
Reading achievement	7	53	38.6	(15.1)	60	36.3	(13.7)	.15
	8	49	55.7	(17.6)	56	51.4	(16.3)	.25
	9	54	47.8	(21.2)	55	42.8	(19.7)	.24
	10	49	61.0	(21.6)	46	51.9	(23.6)	.40*
	11	42	68.0	(19.8)	46	63.7	(19.9)	.21
	14	49	30.6	(12.1)	46	26.7	(9.9)	.34*
Arithmetic achievement	7	53	31.6	(18.0)	60	27.9	(17.8)	.20
	8	49	51.9	(18.9)	56	46.3	(21.4)	.27
	9	54	93.1	(40.2)	55	79.6	(45.7)	.31*
	10	49	124.5	(36.4)	46	112.1	(49.2)	.29
	11	42	137.7	(35.4)	46	136.2	(37.7)	.04
	14	49	30.5	(13.2)	46	26.1	(12.4)	.33*
Language achievement	7	53	24.1	(12.1)	60	23.2	(11.2)	.08
	8	49	33.2	(16.3)	56	30.3	(12.9)	.20
	9	54	30.5	(16.0)	55	25.3	(15.0)	.33*
	10	49	40.5	(18.5)	46	35.0	(15.9)	.31
	11	42	45.5	(18.5)	46	42.9	(17.6)	.15
	14	49	45.6	(16.0)	46	35.8	(12.6)	.63**

Note. Statistical tests are based on regression analysis. Means are adjusted for the effects of participants' gender, Stanford-Binet IQ at study entry, mother's schooling, mother's employment, father at home, father's occupation status, and household rooms per person.

*p (one-tailed) < .05; **p (one-tailed) < .01.

Despite significant differences in children's intellectual performance at age 7, no significant differences in achievement tests appeared at ages 7 or 8. Overall significant differences in achievement did appear at age 9 due to arithmetic and language and at age 10 due to reading, but not at age 11. Then at age 14, groups differed significantly on overall achievement and all the subtests, with an effect size of .49 for overall achievement and .63 for language, and about .33 for reading and arithmetic. Given the lack of significant intellectual test differences, the achievement test differences may be due to the fact that these group-administered tests demand task persistence while interactively administered intellectual tests do not. The unprecedentedly large achievement test differences found at age 14 also support this interpretation. It was the hardest of all the achievement tests: Although test-takers completed virtually all the items on earlier tests, on this test the program group failed to complete an average of 11% of the test items, while the no-program group failed to complete an average of 18% of them.

On average at age 14, the program group scored at the 13th percentile and the no-program group scored at the 6th percentile on total achievement, with similar gaps on the subtests (15th vs. 9th percentile on reading, 13th vs. 8th percentile on arithmetic, and 17th vs. 7th percentile on language). The reader should keep in mind that both groups were at risk of school failure and that the proper comparison is between groups rather than with the overall population, which is what percentiles do.

In addition to tests, on a 4.0 scale (A = 4, B = 3, C = 2, D = 1, F = 0), **the program group's high school grade point average (GPA) significantly exceeded the no-program group's average** (2.03 vs. 1.73). While program males had a slightly higher high school GPA than no-program males (1.82 vs. 1.72), **program females had a significantly and dramatically higher high school GPA than no-program females** (2.35 vs. 1.71), for an effect size of .90.

As shown in Table 3.5, on the Adult Performance Level Survey (American College Testing Program, 1976) given at ages 19 and 27, **the program group significantly outscored the no-program group as follows:**

- **Occupational knowledge and health information at ages 19 and 27**

- **Overall literacy, identifying facts and terms, reading, and writing at age 19**

- **Problem solving at age 27**

On the APL Survey, except for designated material to assess reading, the interviewer could read and repeat items if requested to do so by the respondent so that, for the study participants for whom reading was a problem, the test assessed abilities other than reading. At age 27, only 4 study participants, 2 in each group, declined to complete the APL Survey, for reasons that did not seem related to reading ability. At age 19, 12 study participants, 6 in each group, declined to complete the APL Survey—8 saying that they could not read, others possibly because of fatigue since the survey came after an interview lasting an hour to an hour and a half. According to the test's national norms defining scores of 0 to 23 as "below average," 39% of the program group, as compared to 62% of the no-program group, scored below average at age 19, and 47% of

Table 3.5

LITERACY BY AGE, BY PRESCHOOL EXPERIENCE

Variable	n	Program Group Adjusted Mean	(SD)	n	No-Program Group Adjusted Mean	(SD)	Effect Size
Age 40 K-FAST	36			40			
Total		99.7	(14.1)		100.2	(15.0)	−.03
Reading		103.4	(14.0)		101.4	(13.0)	.15
Arithmetic		98.1	(15.2)		101.0	(18.1)	−.17
Age 27 APL Survey	53			57			
Total (general literacy)		24.8	(6.4)		23.0	(6.4)	.28
Community resources		5.2	(1.6)		5.4	(1.6)	−.12
Occupational knowledge		5.2	(1.6)		4.5	(1.6)	.42*
Consumer economics		4.6	(1.7)		4.4	(1.7)	.09
Health information		5.4	(2.0)		4.4	(2.1)	.49**
Government and law		4.6	(1.6)		4.3	(1.4)	.20
Facts and terms		4.0	(1.4)		3.8	(1.6)	.12
Reading		5.1	(2.0)		4.9	(1.8)	.13
Writing		5.8	(1.5)		5.4	(1.4)	.25
Computation		3.8	(1.8)		3.8	(1.7)	.05
Problem solving		6.0	(1.3)		5.2	(1.8)	.48**
Age 19 APL Survey	52			57			
Total (general literacy)		24.3	(6.5)		22.0	(6.2)	.35*
Community resources		5.2	(1.6)		5.0	(1.6)	.13
Occupational knowledge		5.2	(1.7)		4.4	(1.7)	.47**
Consumer economics		4.6	(1.6)		4.4	(1.7)	.18
Health information		4.8	(1.9)		4.1	(1.9)	.33*
Government and law		4.4	(1.7)		4.1	(1.6)	.17
Facts and terms		3.7	(1.3)		3.3	(1.3)	.31*
Reading		5.7	(1.7)		4.9	(1.9)	.44*
Writing		5.4	(1.8)		4.9	(1.6)	.32*
Computation		4.2	(2.3)		3.8	(2.0)	.17
Problem solving		5.3	(1.7)		5.1	(1.8)	.05

Note. Statistical tests are based on regression analysis. Means are adjusted for the effects of participants' gender, Stanford-Binet IQ at study entry, mother's schooling, mother's employment, father at home, father's occupation status, and household rooms per person.

*p (one-tailed) < .05; **p (one-tailed) < .01.

the program group, as compared to 53% of the no-program group, scored below average at age 27.

Comparing the age 19 and age 27 APL Surveys, as shown in Table 3.5, the program group mean remained at virtually the same level in overall literacy, while the no-program group mean rose about one point to partially close the gap between the two groups. Perhaps the no-program group's educational and general life experiences from ages 19 to 27 helped them close the gap with the program group. In general, the mean scores were remarkably stable from age 19 to age 27. Both program-group and no-program-group means went up for health information, identifying facts and terms, writing, and problem solving; both went down for reading. The Pearson product-moment correlation between the age 19 and age 27 total scores was .501 (df = 108, p < .001), and the correlations between same sub-scales at age 19 and age 27 ranged from .361 to .491 (df = 108, p < .001).

At age 40, the Kaufman Functional Skills Test (K-FAST; Kaufman & Kaufman, 1994) was given to measure study participants' competence in reading and mathematics applied to realistic situations of daily life. As shown in Table 3.5, the program and no-program groups did not differ significantly on total reading or arithmetic. However, it appears that the lack of significant group differences on this test was due to the fact that the program group's better test performers refused to take the test, while the no-program group's better test performers did take the test. Only 76 of the 112 study participants interviewed at age 40 (68%) took the test. The Pearson correlation coefficient between the age 40 K-FAST scores and the age 27 APL Survey scores was .62 (p < .01). For those who took the age 40 test, program group and no-program group means on the age 27 test, adjusted for the effects of the seven covariates,[1] did not differ significantly (23.5 vs. 24.2, n = 71). However, **for those who did not take the age 40 test, the adjusted program group mean on the age 27 test was significantly and substantially greater than that of the no-program group (27.2 vs. 20.9, p < .01, n = 39).** This finding was echoed in other measures of academic performance and economic status. It explains the lack of a significant group difference on the age 40 test, but raises the question of why better test-takers in the program group refused to take the test while better test-takers in the no-program group did take the test. Perhaps the program group's high scorers were more likely than their no-program group's high scorers to refuse to take the test because it would challenge their self-image as successful people.

Test Performance Over the Years by Gender

No significant preschool experience by gender interaction effect was found for any of the test scores—Stanford-Binet, Leiter, PPVT, ITPA,

---

[1] Participants' gender, Stanford-Binet IQ at study entry, mother's schooling, mother's employment, father at home, father's occupation status, and household rooms per person

WISC, CAT total or subtests, APL Survey or subtests, or the K-FAST. This lack of significant interactions presents a strong argument that the preschool program did not affect the tested educational performance of females much more than the males, even though it did have more of an effect on females' school placement and highest year of schooling.

Regardless of their preschool experience, males significantly outscored females on several intellectual tests (not presented in a table)—vocabulary (on the PPVT) after 2 years of the preschool program and at ages 7, 8, and 9; psycholinguistic abilities (on the ITPA) at ages 8 and 9; and intellectual performance (on the WISC) at age 14. However, females significantly outscored males on several school achievement tests—the CAT total, reading, and language at age 8; the APL community resources subtest at age 19; and the APL government and law subtest at age 27. In other words, these males significantly surpassed these females in some of the abilities that they brought to school, but scored the same as or significantly worse than the females on the school achievement that they gained from their school experience.

Attitudes

Findings from ages 6 to 19 on the attitudes of study participants and their parents indicated the following **significant advantages for the program group over the no-program group:**

- **Higher value placed on schooling at age 15**

- **Better attitude at age 19 toward the last high school they had attended**

- **More who spent time on homework at age 15**

- **Fewer who reported that their parents talked with their teachers about their schoolwork at age 15**

- **More at age 15 who thought of going to college**

- **More parents who found their 15-year-old children willing to talk about school, who said their children had done as well in school as they would have liked, and who hoped their children would get college degrees**

- **Fewer parents who went to invited conferences with their children's teachers,** although about the same number got in touch with their children's teachers on their own

- **In addition, program females were absent from school fewer days per year in kindergarten through grade 6 than were no-program females.**

The program and no-program groups did not differ significantly in any of the attitudes towards school measured at age 27. At age 27, 90% of the study participants said that they planned to complete more schooling.

Table 3.6 presents indicators of teacher- and self-reported attitudes of study participants toward school from ages 6 through 19. When covariates were taken into account, kindergarten-through-third-grade teachers did not rate the program group significantly higher than the no-program group in school motivation or school potential. Without covariates, the program group was rated significantly higher in school motivation than the no-program group (Schweinhart et al., 1993). Although the program group did not differ significantly from the no-program group in days absent from elementary school, **program females were absent from elementary school significantly fewer days than the no-program females (19% vs. 53% absent over 15 days per year).**

At age 15, the program group placed significantly greater importance on high school than the no-program group (adjusted means of 24.1 vs. 22.7 on a 7-item scale with 4 points per item, developed by Bachman, O'Malley, & Johnston, 1978). **At age 19, the program group expressed a significantly better attitude toward their high school experience than did the no-program group** (adjusted means of 22.0 vs. 19.2 on a 16-item scale with 3 levels per item modeled after a job satisfaction scale developed by Freeberg, 1974).[2] **Significantly more of the program group than the no-program group reported that their schoolwork required preparation at home (68% vs. 40%),** with similar proportions reporting that they spent time each week on homework.

Study participants at age 15 were fairly accurate predictors of their future levels of schooling completed: 91% (49 of 54) of those who attended college had thought of doing so at age 15, while 60% (26 of 43) of those who did not attend college had not thought of doing so at age 15 ($r = .365$, $df = 96$, $p < .001$).

Table 3.7 presents indicators of parents' attitudes towards school when their children were age 15. As shown, **significantly more program-group parents than no-program-group parents**

- **Said that their teenaged child enjoyed talking about what they were doing in school (65% vs. 33%).**

- **Said that their teenaged child had done as well in school as they would have liked (51% vs. 28%).**

- **Hoped that their teenaged child would get a college degree (55% vs. 36%).**

This last finding contained a preschool-experience-by-gender interaction: While slightly more parents hoped for college degrees for program-group males than for no-program-group males, **significantly more parents hoped for college degrees for program-group females than for no-program-group females (63% vs. 33%).** These hopes, however devel-

---

[2] In addition to covariate adjustment, this finding differs from the one reported at age 19 (program-group mean = 21.3, no-program-group mean = 20.2, $p = .083$) because, this time, the direction of one item was reversed from positive to negative: "How often did you try to change something you didn't like about your school?" The previous interpretation focused on the positive aspect of trying to change the situation; the current interpretation focuses on the negative aspect of the school needing to be changed.

Table 3.6

TEACHER AND SELF ATTITUDES TOWARD SCHOOL THROUGH AGE 19,
BY PRESCHOOL EXPERIENCE

Continuous Variable	Age	Program Group		No-Program Group		Effect Size
		n	Adjusted Mean (SD)	n	Adjusted Mean (SD)	
Teacher-rated school motivation[a]	6–9	46	3.12 (.80)	49	2.93 (.74)	.24
Teacher-rated school potential[b]	6–9	50	4.04 (1.30)	55	3.73 (1.37)	.23
Value placed on schooling[c]	15	44	24.1 (3.23)	54	22.7 (3.56)	.39*
Attitude toward high school[d]	19	58	22.0 (7.63)	63	19.2 (8.78)	.33*

Ordinal Variable			%		%	Odds Ratio
Days absent per year, K–6	6–13	48		45		
1–7			33%		29%	.68
7.1–15			40%		31%	
Over 15			27%		40%	
Males		27		28		
1–7			30%		43%	1.66
7.1–15			37%		25%	
Over 15			33%		32%	
Females		21		17		
1–7			38%		6%	.04**
7.1–15			43%		41%	
Over 15			19%		53%	
School requires homework	15	44	68%	55	40%	2.97**
Days/week doing homework	15	44		55		
0			39%		62%	2.40*
1–2			29%		20%	
3–6			32%		18%	
Parents talk with teacher about my schoolwork	15	44	52%	53	79%	.27**
Thought of going to college	15	44	77%	53	60%	2.20*

Note. Statistical tests are based on regression analysis (for continuous variables) or ordinal regression analysis (for ordinal variables), adjusted for the effects of the seven covariates. A program-by-gender effect was found for days absent per year. Data sources are two scales on which teachers rated children: the Ypsilanti Rating Scale for school motivation and the Pupil Behavior Inventory for school potential; the age-15 and age-19 interviews for attitudes at these ages; and school records for days absent.

[a] Mean of 9 items scored 1 = very infrequently, 2 = infrequently, 3 = sometimes, 4 = frequently, 5 = very frequently (or the reverse) for at least 3 of 4 years from kindergarten to third grade, r_α over time = .829. Examples of items: Shows initiative, alert and interested in schoolwork, learning retained well, completes assignments, motivated toward academic performance.

[b] Mean of 3 items scored 1 = worst to 7 = best on at least 3 of 4 occasions, r_α over time = .839. Degree of imagination and creativity shown in handling materials and equipment, academic readiness, predicted future academic success.

[c] Sum of 7 items scored 1 = not at all, 2 = a little, 3 = pretty much, 4 = very much (or the reverse), r_α = .634. Examples of items: A real education comes from your own experience and not from things you learn in school; even if I could get a very good job at present I'd still choose to stay in school and get my education.

[d] Sum of 16 items scored 1 = worst response to 3 = best response, individually worded; r_α = .799. Examples of items: What are your feelings about the high school you went to? How much studying did you do? Did you feel that you were really part of the school, that you really belonged? How often did you try to change something you didn't like about your school?

*p (one-tailed) < .05, **p (one-tailed) < .01.

Table 3.7

PARENTS' ATTITUDES TOWARD THEIR CHILDREN'S SCHOOLING AT AGE 15,
BY PRESCHOOL EXPERIENCE

Variable	Program Group		No-Program Group		Odds Ratio
	n	%	n	%	
Is your child willing to talk about school?	48		54		
Enjoys it		65%		33%	**2.89****
Talks when asked		29%		56%	
Doesn't like to or refuses		6%		11%	
Has your child done as well as in school as you would have liked?	47	51%	53	28%	**2.78****
How much schooling would you hope your child would get?[a]	44		50		
College		55%		36%	**2.44***
Some college		29%		28%	
High school		16%		36%	
Over the years, have you gone to parent-teacher conferences when invited by a teacher?	48		54		
Always		42%		61%	**.25****
Most of the time		29%		22%	
Sometimes		10%		9%	
Once in a while		6%		8%	
Never		13%		0%	
How often have you gotten in touch with teacher on your own to talk about your child's progress?	47		53		
Often		19%		25%	.99
Occasionally		51%		47%	
Never		30%		28%	

Note. Statistical tests are based on ordinal regression analysis, adjusted for the effects of participants' gender, Stanford-Binet IQ at study entry, mother's schooling, mother's employment, father
at home, father's occupation status, and household rooms per person. Findings for "how much
schooling would you hope your child would get?" are not presented by gender in this table as by
Schweinhart et al. (1993) because no program by gender effect was found in ordinary regression
analysis. Data source is the parent interview at youth age 15.

[a] Numbers of cases are lower than for other items because the category "as far as he or she wants"
was treated as missing data in the analysis.

*p (one-tailed) < .05; **p (one-tailed) < .01.

oped, foreshadowed the preschool-experience-by-gender pattern for highest year of schooling completed. More generally, parents were fairly accurate predictors of whether their 15-year-old children would graduate from regular high school: 60% of parents (53 of 88) expecting their children to graduate from high school predicted accurately and 83% of parents (10 of 12) expecting their children to drop out of high school predicted accurately ($r = .266$, $df = 100$, $p < .01$).

Significantly *fewer* program-group parents than no-program-group parents said that they went to parent-teacher conferences when *invited* by their children's teachers (42% vs. 61%); however, groups did not differ significantly in how often they got in touch with teachers on their own. Corroborating this finding, only 52% of the program-group members, as compared to 79% of the no-program-group members, said their parents talked with their teachers about their schoolwork (Table 3.6, p. 68). Although this pattern of findings could be due to program-group parents wanting to be less involved in the schools, it seems more likely that it is due to their children having fewer problems with school work or discipline.

IV Economic Performance

The evidence indicates that significantly more of the program group than the no-program group were employed at age 27, especially females, and at age 40, especially males. The program group had significantly higher annual earnings than the no-program group at ages 27 and 40, and monthly earnings were higher at both ages. At ages 27 and 40, more of the program group than the no-program group owned their own homes rather than paying rent, receiving a subsidy, living with others, or being incarcerated. At age 40, program males paid significantly more per month for their dwelling than did no-program males. Significantly more of the program group than the no-program group had a car at ages 27 and 40, especially males. Indeed, at age 27, a significantly larger percentage of the program group than the no-program group had a second car, especially males. At age 40, significantly more of the program group than the no-program group had a savings account, especially males.

While the evidence of less use of social services by the program group than by the no-program group is strikingly consistent across various indicators of social services usage, the evidence of a significant group difference in use of social services is equivocal. By age 40, noticeably but not significantly less of the program group than the no-program group reported receiving social services at some time in their lives. At age 27, significantly less of the program group than the no-program group reported receiving social services at some time in the previous 10 years. Across the various categories of social services, the only significant differences, both with less of the program group than the no-program group, involved family counseling in the ages of 34 to 40 and General Assistance from ages 23 to 27.

With minor exceptions, the economic performance variables collected from and about study participants by interview at age 27 were collected again by interview at age 40 and are presented together here. A few variables were added at age 40 (e.g., life insurance, credit cards). The interviews also included questions on use of social services; in addition, we collected information from study participants' social services records at age 40 for the previous 7 years, that is, at ages 34 to 40. Although the interaction between preschool experience and gender was not significant for any of the economic performance variables, several of them exhibited significant group differences for males but not females; group differences by gender are presented for these variables.

Employment and Earnings

Table 4.1 and Figure 4.1 present employment rates by preschool experience at ages 27 and 40. **Significantly more of the program group than the no-program group were employed at age 27 (69% vs. 56%) and at age 40 (76% vs. 62%);** the odds of a program group member being employed were a little over twice as great as the odds of a no-program group member being employed, both at age 27 and at age 40. **This overall difference at**

Table 4.1

EMPLOYMENT AND EARNINGS, BY AGE BY PRESCHOOL EXPERIENCE

Variable	At Age 40			At Age 27		
	Program Group	No-Program Group	Odds Ratio	Program Group	No-Program Group	Odds Ratio
Currently employed,[a] **n**	54	58		55	61	
All	76%	62%	2.45*	69%	56%	2.29*
Males	70%	50%	3.58*	60%	56%	1.24
Females	83%	82%	.67	80%	55%	8.97*
Months unemployed in past 2 years, n	54	58		55	61	
0	57%	52%	.79	62%	44%	.45*
1–12	21%	14%		18%	22%	
13–24	22%	34%		20%	34%	
Previous year's earnings from work, n	54	58		54	59	
Median	$20,800	$15,300		$12,000	$10,000	
All Quartiles[b]						
Highest	26%	24%	2.01*	32%	20%	1.78*
Second highest	31%	19%		26%	24%	
Third highest	26%	24%		22%	27%	
Lowest	17%	33%		20%	29%	
Male Quartiles, n	30	36		29	37	
Highest	30%	28%	1.60	45%	24%	1.64
Second highest	33%	19%		14%	27%	
Third highest	20%	14%		24%	19%	
Lowest	17%	39%		17%	30%	
Female Quartiles, n	24	22		25	22	
Highest	21%	18%	1.65	16%	14%	1.50
Second highest	29%	18%		40%	18%	
Third highest	33%	41%		20%	41%	
Lowest	17%	23%		24%	27%	
Previous month's earnings from work, n	54	58		54	61	
Median	$1,856	$1,308		$1,020	$700	
All Quartiles[c]						
Highest	26%	24%	2.08*	35%	15%	2.52**
Second highest	33%	17%		24%	24%	
Third highest	24%	26%		17%	28%	
Lowest	17%	33%		24%	33%	

Table 4.1 (Cont.)

EMPLOYMENT AND EARNINGS, BY AGE BY PRESCHOOL EXPERIENCE

Variable	At Age 40			At Age 27		
	Program Group	No-Program Group	Odds Ratio	Program Group	No-Program Group	Odds Ratio
Male Quartiles, _n_	30	36		29	39	
Highest	30%	28%	2.14	45%	16%	2.01
Second highest	33%	14%		17%	33%	
Third highest	17%	19%		10%	23%	
Lowest	20%	39%		28%	28%	
Female Quartile, _n_	24	22		25	22	
Highest	21%	18%	1.61	24%	14%	1.96
Second highest	33%	23%		32%	9%	
Third highest	33%	36%		24%	36%	
Lowest	13%	23%		20%	41%	
Regularly receive money from family or friends,[d] _n_	54 4%	58 14%	.35	56 2%	61 16%	.06**

Note. Statistical tests and odds ratios (but not group percentages) are based on ordinal regression analysis, adjusted for the effects of participants' gender, Stanford-Binet IQ at study entry, mother's schooling, mother's employment, father at home, father's occupation status, and household rooms per person. No program-by-gender interaction effects were found for any of the variables.

[a] Participants' work during their prison service was defined as not employed.

[b] Ranges of the quartiles of annual earnings were $0–$2,250, $2,251–$17,280, $17,281–$31,525, and over $31,525 for age 40; and $0–$2,775, $2,776–$11,999, $12,000–$19,000, and over $19,000 for age 27.

[c] Ranges of the quartiles of monthly earnings were $0–$47, $48–$1,550, $1,551–$2,636, and over $2,636 for age 40; and $0, $1–$900, $901–$1,400, and over $1,400 for age 27.

[d] Those who answered "don't know" were coded as not regularly receiving money from family or friends.

*_p_ (one-tailed) < .05; **_p_ (one-tailed) < .01.

age 40 was due to the fact that 70% of the program males were employed as compared to only 50% of the no-program males, with no significant difference in the employment rates of program and no-program females (both at a little over 80%). However, the preschool-experience-by-gender situation at age 27 was the reverse of that at age 40: There was no significant difference in the employment rates of program and no-program males (both about 60%), but there was a significant difference between program and no-program females (80% vs. 55%). In this sample, except for no-program females at age 27, female employment rates were consistently higher than male employment rates.

At age 27, significantly less of the program group than the no-program group reported being unemployed in the past 24 months (38% vs. 55%), mainly because fewer of them were unemployed 13 to 24 months (20% vs. 34%). At age 40, the group difference in unemploy-

Figure 4.1

EMPLOYMENT RATES, BY PRESCHOOL EXPERIENCE BY AGE

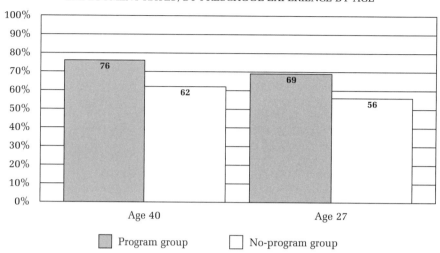

ment was not significant, but the percentage of groups unemployed 13 to 24 months (22% vs. 34%) was similar to what it had been at age 27.

Table 4.1 and Figure 4.2 present **a consistent picture of the program group having significantly greater earnings than the no-program group, annually and monthly, at ages 27 and 40:**

- **At age 40, median annual earnings for program and no-program groups were $20,800 versus $15,300—a $5,500 difference, 36% of the no-program group earnings.**

- **At age 27, median annual earnings for program and no-program groups were $12,000 versus $10,000—a $2,000 difference, 20% of the no-program group earnings.**

- **At age 40, median monthly earnings for program and no-program groups were $1,856 versus $1,308—a $548 difference, 42% of the no-program group earnings.** These figures times 12 months would be $22,272 versus $15,696—a $6,576 difference. As might be expected, the reported monthly earnings times 12 months were a little greater than the reported annual earnings, presumably because of irregularity in monthly earnings.

- **At age 27, median monthly earnings for program and no-program groups were $1,020 versus $700—a $320 difference, 46% of the no-program group earnings.** These figures times 12 months would be $12,240 versus $8,400—a $3,840 difference. The no-program group monthly earnings times 12 months were surprisingly lower than the no-program group annual earnings, by $1,600.

In Table 4.1, statistical tests presented for earnings are based on ordinal regression analysis of sample quartiles. Dividing the sample in half by earnings regardless of group, the program group had 57% of the sample

Figure 4.2

MEDIAN ANNUAL EARNINGS, BY PRESCHOOL EXPERIENCE BY AGE

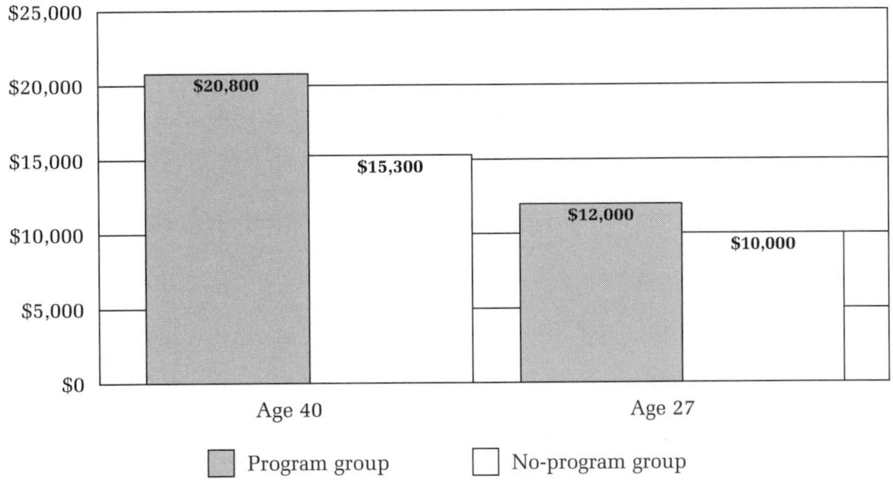

members with higher annual earnings at age 40, 58% of the sample with higher annual earnings at age 27, 59% of the sample with higher monthly earnings at age 40, and 59% of the sample with higher monthly earnings at age 27. The consistency of these measures is indicated by the fact that these percentages vary by only 2%. The odds of program group members having a higher level of earnings than no-program group members were 1.8 to 2.5 times as great as for the no-program group to have a higher level of earnings. However, when program males were compared to no-program males and when program females were compared to no-program females, their monthly and annual earnings at age 40 did not differ significantly.

Living Status

Table 4.2 presents group comparisons at ages 27 and 40 for dwelling, car ownership, and various financial amenities. Dwelling arrangements were ranked in terms of their indication of self-sufficiency, from home owner-ship with a mortgage, to rental, to public subsidy or living with others, to imprisonment. By this measure, **at ages 27 and 40, the program group had significantly more self-sufficient dwelling arrangements than the no-program group,** as shown in Figure 4.3. At age 40, 37% of the program group and 28% of the no-program group owned their own homes with a mortgage, and 85% of the program group and 68% of the no-program group either owned or rented their homes. At age 27, 27% of the program group and 5% of the no-program group owned their own homes with a mortgage, and 81% of the program group and 70% of the no-program group owned or rented their homes. The odds of the program group having more stable dwelling arrangements were 2.7 times greater at age

Table 4.2

LIVING STATUS, BY AGE BY PRESCHOOL EXPERIENCE

Variable	At Age 40			At Age 27		
	Program Group	No-Program Group	Odds Ratio	Program Group	No-Program Group	Odds Ratio
Dwelling arrangement, n	54	58		56	61	
Mortgage	37%	28%	1.87*	27%	5%	2.66**
Rent	48%	40%		54%	65%	
Public subsidy or live with others	9%	17%		12%	23%	
Incarcerated	6%	15%		7%	7%	
Dwelling payment[a]						
All						
(quartiles of the sample), n	51	51		50	57	
Highest	28%	20%	1.64	32%	14%	1.64
Second highest	29%	24%		22%	32%	
Third highest	23%	23%		24%	24%	
Lowest quartile	20%	33%		22%	30%	
Males						
(quartiles of the sample), n	28	32				
Highest	28%	12%	2.49*			
Second highest	32%	19%				
Third highest	11%	25%				
Lowest	29%	44%				
Females						
(quartiles of the sample), n	23	19				
Highest	26%	32%	1.42			
Second highest	26%	31%				
Third highest	39%	21%				
Lowest	9%	16%				
Had a car[b]						
All	82%	60%	3.36**	73%	59%	2.16*
Males	80%	50%	4.75**			
Females	83%	77%	1.40			
Had a second car[b]						
All	39%	36%	.99	30%	13%	3.91**
Males				36%	15%	7.21**
Females				24%	9%	2.88
Had a savings account[b]						
All	76%	50%	3.30**	57%	46%	1.64
Males	73%	36%	5.67**			
Females	79%	73%	.93			

Table 4.2 (Cont.)

LIVING STATUS, BY AGE BY PRESCHOOL EXPERIENCE

	At Age 40			At Age 27		
Variable	Program Group	No-Program Group	Odds Ratio	Program Group	No-Program Group	Odds Ratio
Had a checking account[b]	48%	43%	1.12	23%	25%	.89
Had life insurance[b]	67%	53%	1.48		NA	
Had credit card[b]	50%	41%	1.35		NA	

Note. Statistical tests and odds ratios (but not group percentages) are based on ordinal regression analysis, adjusted for the effects of participants' gender, Stanford-Binet IQ at study entry, mother's schooling, mother's employment, father at home, father's occupation status, and household rooms per person. No program-by-gender interaction effects were found for any of the variables, however, findings are presented by gender for the variables that had significant program effects for at least one gender.

[a] Ranges of the quartiles of dwelling cost are $0–$200, $201–$500, $501–$700, and over $700 for age 40; and $0–$99, $100–$250, $251–$400, and over $400 for age 27. Schweinhart et al. (1993) reported findings for dwelling payments that were based on the mistaken coding of study participants in prison at that time as paying a mortgage. For the dwelling cost, those in prison have now been assigned $0.

[b] Those who answered "don't know" were coded as not having the service, and all the sample size are 117 (56 for program, and 61 for no-program group) for age 27, and 112 (54 for program, and 58 for no-program group) for age 40. NA = Not available for age 27.

*p (one-tailed) < .05; **p (one-tailed) < .01.

Figure 4.3

DWELLING ARRANGEMENT, BY PRESCHOOL EXPERIENCE BY AGE

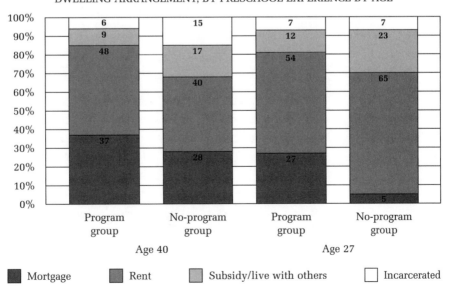

27 and 1.9 times greater at age 40 than the odds of the no-program group having more stable dwelling arrangements.

Although the program group consistently made greater dwelling payments than the no-program group, the amount of the program group's dwelling payment did not differ significantly from that of the no-program group, either at age 40 or at age 27. However, **at age 40, program males did pay significantly more for their dwellings than did no-program males.** Dividing the sample of males in half by dwelling payment, 60% of the program males made greater dwelling payments at age 40, as compared to 31% of the no-program males.

As illustrated in Figure 4.4, significantly more of the program group than the no-program group had a car at age 27 (73% vs. 59%) and at age 40 (82% vs. 60%), especially males (80% vs. 50%). Similarly, significantly more of the program group than the no-program group had second cars at age 27 (30% vs. 13%), especially males (36% vs. 15%). The odds ratios favored the program group's car ownership over the no-program group's by 2 to 4 times as much.

Significantly more of the program group than the no-program group had a savings account at age 40 (76% vs. 50%), especially males (73% vs. 36%). The odds ratios favored the program group's savings over the no-program group's by 3.3 times as much. The difference was in the same direction at age 27, but not to a statistically significant extent.

While groups did not differ significantly at age 40 in having checking accounts, life insurance, or a credit card, in all instances more of the program group than the no-program group had these amenities. About half of the program group had checking accounts and credit cards, while two thirds had life insurance.

Figure 4.4

CAR OWNERSHIP BY PRESCHOOL EXPERIENCE

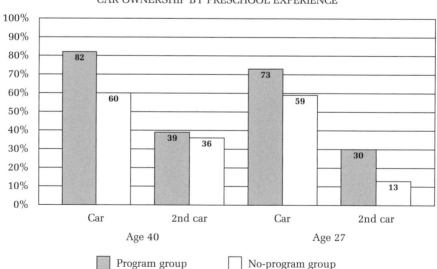

Social Services

Table 4.3 presents the major findings for social services. Age 40 findings are based on independent data from records and interviews, while age 27 findings combined data from records and interviews. From a lifetime perspective, the coverage of social services usage was spotty. State records, the most reliable data source, were collected at age 40 for the previous 7 years, from ages 34 to 40. Age 40 self-report was for the previous 15 years, from ages 26 to 40. Age 27 time spans were either the previous 10 years (ages 18 to 27) or the previous 5 years (ages 23 to 27); and of course self-report is often unreliable on details.

Only one lifetime indicator is presented—receiving any social services by age 40. It indicates whether a study participant received any type of service on any of four variables:

1. In the previous 10 years at age 27 (combining records and self-report)

2. Age 40 self-report of the past 15 years

3. State social service records from 1996 to 2002

4. Age 40 unemployment insurance records over an undetermined period of time

By this indicator, 71% of the program group and 86% of the no-program group had received any social services by age 40. This difference was nearly statistically significant at $p = .053$ (one-tailed). On one component of that measure, combining records and self-report, **significantly fewer of the program group than the no-program group received any social services in the previous 10 years at age 27 (59% vs. 80%).**

These two measures are the broadest and strongest evidence of less use of social services by the program group than by the no-program group. Beyond them, the evidence, although not statistically significant for single variables, is strikingly consistent across almost all the indicators of social services usage in Table 4.3. Only four of them reversed this pattern, and these only by 1% or 2%. Nonetheless, the evidence of significant group differences in the use of specific social services is equivocal. Regarding various types of social services, state records for ages 34 to 40 found that **significantly fewer of the program group than the no-program group received family counseling (13% vs. 24%),** but that groups did not differ significantly in months on assistance, cash, food, or medical assistance. Nor did they differ in the social services usage they reported at the interview or in the previous 15 years. **At age 27, in findings from both records and self-report, significantly fewer of the program group than the no-program group reported receiving General Assistance in the previous 5 years (10% vs. 23%),** but groups did not differ significantly in months on assistance in the previous 10 years; or in usage of AFDC, food stamps, General Assistance, or even the loosely described "money from the government" either at interview or in the previous 5 years.

Table 4.3

SOCIAL SERVICES RECEIVED, BY PRESCHOOL EXPERIENCE

Variable	Program Group	No-Program Group	Odds Ratio
Received any social services by age 40 (records &/or self report)	71%	86%	.41
Age 40			
Received any services in previous 7 years (records)	54%	56%	1.11
Months on assistance in the previous 7 years (records)			
0	46%	44%	1.09
1–48	25%	28%	
Over 48	29%	28%	
Type of assistance in previous 7 years (records)			
Cash	38%	39%	.96
Food	50%	54%	.99
Medical	40%	43%	.98
Family counseling	13%	24%	.33*
Years received service in previous 15 years (self-report)			
0 years	67%	61%	.81
1–2 years	18%	21%	
Over 2 years	15%	18%	
Received any social service at interview (self-report)	22%	22%	1.02
Type of assistance at interview			
TANF	0%	0%	
Food	7%	6%	
Child care	4%	4%	
General assistance	0%	2%	
Age 27			
Received any social services in previous 10 years (records &/or self report)	59%	80%	.32**
Months on assistance in the previous 10 years, *n*	53	60	
0	60%	53%	.59
1–30	23%	22%	
Over 30	17%	25%	
Type of assistance in previous 5 years			
AFDC	28%	26%	1.29
Food stamps	29%	31%	1.19
General assistance	10%	23%	.35*

Table 4.3 (Cont.)

SOCIAL SERVICES RECEIVED, BY PRESCHOOL EXPERIENCE

Variable	Program Group	No-Program Group	Odds Ratio
Type of assistance at interview, _n_	56	61	
AFDC	7%	16%	
Food stamps	11%	20%	
General assistance	2%	5%	
Money from the government	14%	31%	

Note. Statistical tests are based on ordinal regression analysis, adjusted for the effects of participants' gender, Stanford-Binet IQ at study entry, mother's schooling, mother's employment, father at home, father's occupation status, and household rooms per person. Unless otherwise noted, sample size at 40 and 27 is 123 (58 for program, 65 for no-program group); that for age 40 state record data is 102 (48 for program, 54 for no-program group); and that for age 40 self reported data varies between 108 and 110 (54 for program, 54–56 for no program group).

$^*p$ (one-tailed) $< .05$; $^{**}p$ (one-tailed) $< .01$.

V Crime

The study presents strong evidence of a lifetime effect of the High/Scope Perry Preschool Project in preventing total arrests and arrests for violent, property, and drug crimes and subsequent prison or jail sentences. Over their lifetimes by age 40, the program group had significantly fewer arrests than the no-program group and significantly fewer arrests for violent, property, and drug crimes. Significant group differences favoring the program group in various types of crime occurred at various times of life—crimes other than violent, property, or drug in adolescence; total arrests and drug crimes in early adulthood; and violent and property crimes in midlife. By age 40, compared to the no-program group, the program group had significantly fewer arrests for property and drug felonies and violent and property misdemeanors—significantly fewer arrests for property crimes by age 27 and significantly fewer arrests for violent felonies, drug felonies, and property misdemeanors from ages 28 to 40. By age 40, compared to the no-program group, the program group had engaged in significantly fewer of 3 of the 78 types of crimes cited at arrest—dangerous drugs, assault and/or battery, and larceny under $100. All 3 types of crimes had significant group differences by age 27; assault and/or battery also had a significant group difference at ages 28–40. The program group was sentenced to significantly fewer months in prison or jail by age 40, specifically from ages 28 to 40. Also from ages 28 to 40, the program group was sentenced to significantly fewer months in prison for felonies and had served significantly fewer months in prison.

This age 40 report adds findings from crime records data collected on study participants from ages 28 to 40, as described in Chapter 2. It integrates the data into lifetime patterns, organized as juvenile, adult up to 27, and adult from 28 to 40. It includes felonies, misdemeanors, and civil infractions; and violent, property, drug, and other types of crimes.

Arrests and General Types of Crimes

Table 5.1, Figure 5.1, and Figure 5.2 present findings for arrests and general types of crimes cited at arrest by age 40, further broken out by age. **Compared to the no-program group, the program group had significantly fewer arrests by age 40, specifically adult arrests by age 27,** but no fewer juvenile arrests or arrests from ages 28 to 40. The odds of lifetime arrests were half as great for the program group as the no-program group—a little less than the odds reduction for juvenile arrests (despite the lack of a significant difference for this variable) and adult arrests through age 27:

- 55% of the no-program group but only 36% of the program group were arrested 5 or more times in their lifetimes.

Table 5.1

ARRESTS AND CRIMES CITED AT ARREST, BY AGE BY PRESCHOOL EXPERIENCE

Crime Cited at Arrest	Lifetime by Age 40			Juvenile by Age 19			Adult By Age 27			Adult Ages 28-40		
	Program Group	No-Program Group	Odds Ratio	Program Group	No-Program Group	Odds Ratio	Program Group	No-Program Group	Odds Ratio	Program Group	No-Program Group	Odds Ratio
Arrests												
0	29%	17%	.54*	85%	75%	.47	52%	43%	.51*	45%	29%	.83
1–4	35%	28%		12%	20%		41%	28%		26%	34%	
5–10	22%	24%		3%	5%		2%	14%		19%	22%	
11 or more	14%	31%		0%	0%		5%	15%		10%	15%	
Violent												
0	67%	52%	.46*	95%	94%	.94	74%	71%	.80	86%	69%	.17**
1–2	23%	28%					21%	20%		14%	22%	
3 or more	10%	20%					5%	9%		0%	9%	
Property												
0	64%	42%	.41**	88%	81%	.60	72%	65%	.59	85%	68%	39*
1–2	26%	32%					23%	15%		8%	21%	
3 or more	10%	26%					5%	20%		7%	11%	
Drug												
0	86%	66%	.38*	100%	98%	—	91%	75%	.34*	90%	77%	.44
1–2	7%	23%					6%	22%		7%	18%	
3 or more	7%	11%					3%	3%		3%	5%	
Other												
0	40%	26%	.64	97%	89%	.22*	66%	54%	.79	48%	37%	.94
1–4	32%	34%		3%	11%		29%	38%		30%	37%	
5 or more	28%	40%					5%	8%		22%	26%	

Note. Adult arrests are for both felonies and misdemeanors. Statistical tests and odds ratios (but not group percentages) are based on ordinal regression analysis, adjusted for the effects of participants' gender, Stanford-Binet IQ at study entry, mother's schooling, mother's employment, father at home, father's occupation status, and household rooms per person. The odds ratio compares the odds of the program group having more crimes (using the ordinal categories) to the no-program group having more crimes.

* *p* (one-tailed) < .05; ** *p* (one-tailed) < .01; the odds ratio cannot be calculated because one group had 0 arrests.

Figure 5.1

PERCENT WITH 5 OR MORE ARRESTS BY AGE BY PRESCHOOL EXPERIENCE

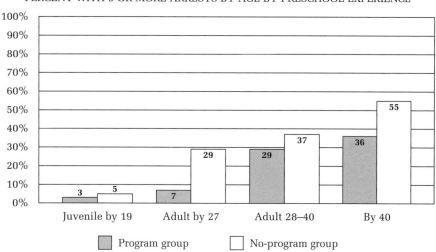

- 29% of the no-program group but only 7% of the program group were arrested 5 or more times as adults by age 27.[3]

Crimes are generally divided here into violent, property, drug, and other. *Violent crimes* involve violence against persons, such as kidnapping, intent to murder, hindering or obstructing the legal system, larceny (i.e., robbery), and assault and/or battery. *Property crimes* involve taking or damaging someone else's property, such as fraud, theft, arson, and breaking and entering. *Drug crimes* involve making or selling drugs illegally, such as sale, possession, or delivery of controlled substances and possession of drug paraphernalia. *Other crimes* include certain fraudulent activities, passing bad checks, a variety of driving offenses, disorderly conduct, criminal mischief, and weapons offenses.

Compared to the no-program group, the program group had significantly fewer lifetime arrests for violent, property, and drug crimes by age 40, but no fewer arrests for other crimes. The odds of violent, property, and drug crimes were about half as great for the program group as for the no-program group. Over their lifetimes by age 40,

- 48% of the no-program group but only 32% of the program group were arrested for one or more violent crimes.

- 58% of the no-program group but only 36% of the program group were arrested for one or more property crimes.

- 34% of the no-program group but only 14% of the program group were arrested for one or more drug crimes.

---

[3] The 29% represents arrest records and excludes an additional 6% who had self-reported arrests, which were included in the analysis reported by Schweinhart et al. (1993).

Figure 5.2

PERCENT ARRESTED AND CRIME TYPES BY AGE 40 BY PRESCHOOL EXPERIENCE

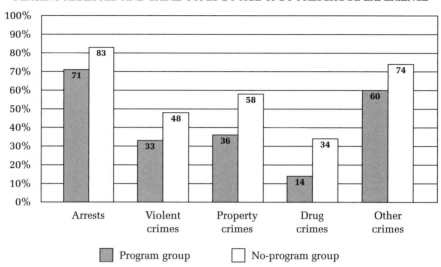

Crime patterns differed at different ages. Compared to the no-program group, the program group had significantly fewer arrests for other crimes as juveniles by age 19, but no fewer arrests for violent, property, or drug crimes. The odds of other crimes were 78% lower in the program group than in the no-program group. By age 19,

- 11% of the no-program group but only 3% of the program group were arrested for crimes other than violent, property, or drug as juveniles.

Compared to the no-program group, the program group had significantly fewer arrests for drug crimes as adults by age 27. The odds of drug crimes were 66% lower in the program group. By age 27,

- 25% of the no-program group but only 9% of the program group were arrested for drug crimes as adults.

Compared to the no-program group, the program group had significantly fewer arrests for violent and property crimes as adults from ages 28 to 40, but no fewer arrests for drug or other crimes. The odds of violent crimes were 83% lower in the program group than in the no-program group, and the odds of property crimes were 61% lower. From ages 28 to 40,

- 31% of the no-program group but only 14% of the program group were arrested for violent crimes.

- 32% of the no-program group but only 15% of the program group were arrested for property crimes.

Arrests and General Types of Crimes by Gender

Because, in general, males commit more crimes than females, we examined the crime outcome variables for group-by-gender interaction effects, that is, patterns in which a program effect was found for males but not females or females but not males. Although the regression analyses found no group-by-gender interaction effects for any of the crime or sentencing variables, Table 5.2 examines this question for arrests and general types of crime by age 40, using the less stringent standard of whether statistically significant group differences were also statistically significant for males, females, or both taken separately. Recall that overall program and no-program group differences for all four of these variables were statistically significant.

Table 5.2

ARRESTS AND CRIMES CITED AT ARREST BY AGE 40,
BY GENDER BY PRESCHOOL EXPERIENCE

Crime Cited at Arrest	Program Males	No-Program Males	Odds Ratio	Program Females	No-Program Females	Odds Ratio
Arrests						
0	18%	5%	.45*	44%	35%	.52
1–4	37%	26%		32%	31%	
5–10	21%	28%		24%	19%	
11 or more	24%	41%		0%	15%	
Violent crimes						
0	49%	38%	.47	92%	73%	.12*
1–2	33%	31%		8%	23%	
3 or more	18%	31%		0%	4%	
Property crimes						
0	52%	28%	.43*	80%	62%	.20*
1–2	30%	36%		20%	27%	
3 or more	18%	36%		0%	11%	
Drug crimes						
0	82%	51%	.34*	92*	89%	.78
1–2	6%	39%		8%	0%	
3 or more	12%	10%		0%	11%	

Note. Statistical tests and odds ratios (but not group percentages) are based on ordinal regression analysis, adjusted for the effects of participants' gender, Stanford-Binet IQ at study entry, mother's schooling, mother's employment, father at home, father's occupation status, and household rooms per person. The odds ratio compares the odds of the program group having more crimes (using the ordinal categories) to the no-program group having more crimes.

*p (one-tailed) < .05; **p (one-tailed) < .01.

Compared to no-program males, program males had significantly fewer arrests and significantly fewer arrests for property and drug crimes. Compared to no-program females, program females had significantly fewer arrests for violent and property crimes. Arrests for property crimes showed a significant difference among males and females separately. The biggest difference was for female arrests for violent crimes, 8% for program females versus 27% for no-program females. While the group difference in arrests for violent crimes by 40 was not significant for males, it was significant for males from 28 to 40, with 21% of program males with one such arrest versus 43% of no-program males with one or more such arrest (odds ratio = .14, $p < .01$).

Arrests and General Types of Felonies and Misdemeanors

Table 5.3 presents findings for adult felony arrests and general types of felonies cited at arrest and adult misdemeanor arrests and general types of misdemeanors cited at arrest. Felonies are more serious crimes and misdemeanors are less serious crimes. A person may be charged with one or more felonies in a felony arrest, but is charged with only one misdemeanor in a misdemeanor arrest. **Compared to the no-program group, the program group had significantly fewer arrests for property and drug felonies by age 40,** but no fewer felony arrests or arrests for violent or other felonies. The odds of being arrested for property felonies were 59% less and for drug felonies, 81% less in the program group than in the no-program group. Over their lifetimes by age 40,

- 32% of the no-program group but only 19% of the program group were arrested for a property felony.

- 28% of the no-program group but only 7% of the program group were arrested for a drug felony.

Compared to the no-program group, the program group had significantly fewer arrests for property felonies by age 27, but no fewer arrests for violent, drug, or other crimes. The odds of being arrested for property felonies were 58% lower in the program group than in the no-program group. By age 27,

- 26% of the no-program group but only 14% of the program group were arrested for a property felony.

Compared to the no-program group, the program group had significantly fewer arrests for violent and drug felonies from ages 28 to 40, but no fewer total felony arrests or property or other crimes. The program group's odds were 89% less than the no-program group's for violent felonies and 76% less for drug felonies. From ages 28 to 40,

- 12% of the no-program group but only 2% of the program group were arrested for a violent felony.

Table 5.3

ADULT FELONIES AND MISDEMEANORS CITED AT ARREST,
BY AGE BY PRESCHOOL EXPERIENCE

Crime Cited at Arrest		By Age 40			By Age 27			Ages 28–40		
		Program Group	No-Program Group	Odds Ratio	Program Group	No-Program Group	Odds Ratio	Program Group	No-Program Group	Odds Ratio
Felonies										
Arrests	0	69%	52%	.54	72%	65%	.78	83%	69%	.54
	1–2	17%	25%		18%	17%		12%	25%	
	3 or more	14%	23%		10%	18%		5%	6%	
Violent	0	79%	77%	.99	79%	81%	1.46	98%	88%	.11*
	1	12%	6%		14%	8%		2%	4%	
	2 or more	9%	17%		7%	11%		0%	8%	
Property	0	81%	68%	.41*	86%	74%	.42*	90%	86%	.68
	1	10%	12%		9%	9%		3%	6%	
	2 or more	9%	20%		5%	17%		7%	8%	
Drug	0	93%	72%	.19**	93%	83%	.33	97%	85%	.24*
	1	2%	16%		4%	9%		0%	11%	
	2 or more	5%	12%		3%	8%		3%	4%	
Other	0	83%	79%	.94	93%	86%	.50	88%	89%	1.57
	1	10%	15%		5%	9%		9%	11%	
	2 or more	7%	6%		2%	5%		3%	0%	
Misdemeanors										
Arrests	0	35%	26%	.68	57%	46%	.52	47%	37%	.80
	1–4	31%	25%		36%	31%		24%	29%	
	5–9	22%	21%		5%	17%		24%	15%	
	10 or more	12%	28%		2%	6%		5%	19%	
Violent	0	81%	63%	.28**	95%	83%	.19**	86%	74%	.42
	1	14%	19%		5%	6%		9%	18%	
	2 or more	5%	18%		0%	11%		5%	8%	
Property	0	76%	59%	.50*	83%	73%	.62	90%	72%	.31*
	1	15%	15%		12%	12%		5%	14%	
	2 or more	9%	26%		5%	15%		5%	14%	
Drug	0	90%	80%	.50	96%	89%	.34	92%	84%	.49
	1	5%	8%		2%	6%		5%	11%	
	2 or more	5%	12%		2%	5%		3%	5%	
Other	0	41%	29%	.78	67%	60%	.78	48%	40%	.95
	1–4	31%	37%		28%	32%		31%	34%	
	5 or more	28%	34%		5%	8%		21%	26%	

Note. Statistical tests and odds ratios (but not group percentages) are based on ordinal regression analysis, adjusted for the effects of participants' gender, Stanford-Binet IQ at study entry, mother's schooling, mother's employment, father at home, father's occupation status, and household rooms per person. The odds ratio compares the odds of the program group having more crimes (using the ordinal categories) to the no-program group having more crimes.

*p (one-tailed) < .05; **p (one-tailed) < .01.

- 15% of the no-program group but only 3% of the program group were arrested for a drug felony.

Compared to the no-program group, the program group had significantly fewer arrests for violent and property misdemeanors over their lifetimes by age 40, but no fewer total misdemeanor arrests, drug arrests, or arrests for other misdemeanors. The program group's odds were lower than the no-program group's odds by 72% for violent misdemeanors and by 50% for property misdemeanors. By age 40,

- 37% of the no-program group but only 19% of the program group were arrested for a violent misdemeanor.

- 41% of the no-program group but only 24% of the program group were arrested for a property misdemeanor.

Compared to the no-program group, the program group had significantly fewer arrests for violent misdemeanors by age 27. The program group's odds were lower than the no-program group's odds by 81%. By age 27,

- 17% of the no-program group but only 5% of the program group were arrested for a violent misdemeanor.

Compared to the no-program group, the program group had significantly fewer arrests for property misdemeanors from ages 28 to 40, but no fewer total misdemeanor arrests or arrests for violent, drug, or other misdemeanors. Compared to the no-program group's odds, the program group's odds of being arrested for this reason were 69% less. From ages 28 to 40,

- 28% of the no-program group but only 10% of the program group were arrested for a property misdemeanor.

Specific Types of Crimes

Table 5.4 presents the percentages of the program group and the no-program group that were arrested for each specific type of felony and misdemeanor—13 types of violent crimes, 28 types of property crimes, 5 types of drug crimes, and 32 types of driving and other crimes. Most of these specific types of crimes were committed by under 10% for the no-program group by age 40; 18 specific types of crimes were committed by 10% or more of the no-program group by age 40. Of these 18, 8 were committed by 20% or more of the no-program group by age 40, half of them driving misdemeanors (driving with an suspended license, without a license, under the influence of liquor, or with a improper license plate); the others were larceny under $100, dangerous drugs, interfering with police, and assault and/or battery (see Table 7.4, p. 140).

Table 5.4

ADULT INDIVIDUAL CRIMES CITED AT ARREST, BY AGE BY PRESCHOOL EXPERIENCE

Crime Cited at Arrest	By Age 40		By Age 27		Ages 28-40	
	Program Group	No-Program Group	Program Group	No-Program Group	Program Group	No-Program Group
Violent crimes						
Felonies						
Assault with a dangerous weapon	3%	11%	3%	11%	0%	0%
Aggravated assault	5%	11%	5%	8%	0%	5%
Armed robbery	7%	11%	7%	8%	0%	5%
Murder	2%	5%	2%	2%	0%	3%
Criminal sexual conduct	7%	9%	7%	5%	0%	5%
Assault with intent of body harm	2%	3%	2%	3%	0%	0%
Kidnapping	2%	2%	0%	2%	2%	0%
Fleeing and eluding with violence	0%	0%	0%	0%	0%	0%
Aggravated child abuse	0%	0%	0%	0%	0%	0%
Assault with intent to murder	3%	2%	3%	0%	0%	2%
Failure to stop at scene of injury	2%	0%	2%	0%	0%	0%
Misdemeanors						
Assault and/or battery	19%	37% *	5%	17% **	14%	26% *
Child abuse or negligence	2%	0%	0%	0%	2%	0%
Property crimes						
Felonies						
Larceny over $100	5%	15%	2%	12% +	5%	6%
Larceny in a building	2%	8%	0%	6%	2%	3%
Larceny from a person	0%	3%	0%	3%	0%	0%
Vehicle theft	0%	3%	0%	3%	0%	0%
Breaking and entering felony	14%	17%	10%	12%	5%	8%

Table 5.4 (Cont.)

ADULT INDIVIDUAL CRIMES CITED AT ARREST, BY AGE BY PRESCHOOL EXPERIENCE

Crime Cited at Arrest	By Age 40		By Age 27		Ages 28-40	
	Program Group	No-Program Group	Program Group	No-Program Group	Program Group	No-Program Group
Retail fraud over $25,000	0%	2%	0%	0%	0%	2%
Receive and/or conceal stolen property	5%	5%	5%	5%	0%	2%
Forgery	3%	2%	2%	2%	3%	2%
Fraudulent use of credit card over $300	0%	0%	0%	0%	0%	0%
Unlawful driving away	0%	0%	0%	0%	0%	0%
Arson	0%	0%	0%	0%	0%	0%
Malicious destruction of property	0%	0%	0%	0%	0%	0%
Trespassing	0%	0%	0%	0%	0%	0%
Theft of rental property	0%	0%	0%	0%	0%	0%
Embezzlement	0%	0%	0%	0%	0%	0%
Welfare fraud	2%	0%	0%	0%	2%	0%
Misdemeanors						
Larceny under $100	9%	22% *	9%	20%	2% *	6%
Retail fraud under $25,000	5%	11%	0%	0%	5%	11%
Shoplifting under $100	0%	5%	0%	5%	0%	0%
Malicious destruction of property	7%	12%	2%	3%	5%	9%
Breaking and entering misdemeanor	2%	6%	0%	0%	2%	6%
Larceny from a building	2%	5%	2%	5%	0%	0%
Trespassing	2%	5%	2%	3%	0%	2%
Scheme to defraud	3%	5%	3%	5%	0%	0%
Receive or conceal stolen property	2%	2%	2%	2%	0%	0%
Food stamp or welfare fraud	0%	0%	0%	0%	0%	0%
Fraudulent use of credit card	0%	0%	0%	0%	0%	0%
Embezzlement	0%	0%	0%	0%	0%	0%

Table 5.4 (Cont.)

ADULT INDIVIDUAL CRIMES CITED AT ARREST, BY AGE BY PRESCHOOL EXPERIENCE

Crime Cited at Arrest	By Age 40		By Age 27		Ages 28-40	
	Program Group	No-Program Group	Program Group	No-Program Group	Program Group	No-Program Group
Drug crimes						
Felonies						
Dangerous drugs	3%	20% **	3%	14% **	0%	9%
Drug sale, possession, or trafficking	5%	12%	3%	6%	3%	6%
Misdemeanors						
Possession marijuana under 20 grams	3%	11%	0%	6%	3%	5%
Possession drug paraphernalia	5%	9%	3%	6%	2%	8%
Controlled substance use	3%	6%	0%	0%	3%	6%
Other crimes						
Felonies						
Miscellaneous other felonies	5%	9%	0%	5%	5%	6%
Escape	2%	5%	2%	5%	0%	2%
Tampering with witness	0%	2%	0%	0%	0%	2%
Fraudulent activities	2%	3%	0%	3%	2%	0%
Habitual offender	2%	3%	0%	2%	2%	2%
Obstructing police	2%	0%	0%	0%	2%	0%
Carrying a concealed weapon	7%	5%	7%	5%	0%	0%
Fraudulent uttering and publishing	3%	0%	0%	0%	3%	0%
Misdemeanors						
Interfering with police	10%	23%	5%	9%	5%	15%
Driving without license	26%	37%	2%	2%	26%	35%
Driving with suspended license	29%	39%	16%	22%	28%	26%
Disorderly conduct or disturbing peace	7%	17% +	5%	11%	2%	9%

Table 5.4 (Cont.)

ADULT INDIVIDUAL CRIMES CITED AT ARREST, BY AGE BY PRESCHOOL EXPERIENCE

Crime Cited at Arrest	By Age 40		By Age 27		Ages 28-40	
	Program Group	No-Program Group	Program Group	No-Program Group	Program Group	No-Program Group
Driving under influence of liquor	12%	20%	5%	9%	9%	15%
Other driving misdemeanors	3%	9%	0%	0%	3%	9%
Public nuisance	3%	6%	2%	3%	2%	5%
Probation violation	2%	5%	2%	5%	0%	0%
Frequenting illegal places	3%	5%	3%	3%	0%	2%
Invasion of privacy	0%	2%	0%	2%	0%	0%
Weapon	7%	9%	3%	5%	3%	5%
Miscellaneous other misdemeanors	10%	12%	9%	5%	3%	8%
Accosting and soliciting	2%	2%	2%	0%	0%	2%
Failure to stop at accident	2%	2%	0%	2%	2%	0%
Gambling	0%	0%	0%	0%	0%	0%
Failure to appear under bond	0%	0%	0%	0%	0%	0%
Eluding a law enforcement officer	3%	2%	0%	2%	3%	0%
Building code violation	0%	0%	0%	0%	0%	0%
Driving without insurance	0%	0%	0%	0%	0%	0%
Driving without child safety seat	0%	0%	0%	0%	0%	0%
Reckless driving	3%	2%	0%	0%	3%	2%
Indecent exposure	2%	0%	0%	0%	2%	0%
Criminal mischief	2%	0%	0%	0%	2%	0%
Improper license plate	35%	29%	0%	0%	35%	29%

Note. Statistical tests (but not group percentages) are based on ordinal regression analysis, adjusted for the effects of participants' gender, Stanford-Binet IQ at study entry, mother's schooling, mother's employment, father at home, father's occupation status, and household rooms per person.

+ *p* (one-tailed) < .10; *p* (one-tailed) < .05; **p* (one-tailed) < .01.

We examined the data for group differences using one-tailed tests and probability levels up to .10 to maximize the sensitivity of significance tests to these differences—not to identify and confirm specific program effects, but to learn more about what specific types of crimes constituted the broader program effects. Despite the liberal standards, only four group differences were found for specific types of crimes by age 40—assault and/or battery, larceny under $100, dangerous drugs, and disorderly conduct or disturbing the peace. These findings were reflected in findings by age 27 (assault and/or battery, larceny over $100, and larceny under $100) and at ages 28–40 (assault and/or battery). Comparing these findings to those presented in Tables 5.1 and 5.2, the significant group differences in specific types of crimes were important to the significant group differences in general types of crimes: assault and/or battery in violent misdemeanors and crimes; larceny under $100 in property misdemeanors and crimes; and dangerous drugs in drug felonies and crimes.

To facilitate consideration of the nature of the group differences in crime, within general type of felonies and misdemeanors, Table 5.4 presents specific types of crimes—from those with the largest differences favoring the program group, through those with no differences between the groups, to those with the largest differences favoring the no-program group. Figure 5.3 presents the specific types of crimes with the largest group differences. Of the 78 specific types of crimes by age 40 listed, a smaller percentage of the program group than the no-program group were arrested for 43 types (55% of the total), by a mean difference of 5.4%; the same percentages of the two groups were arrested for 22 types (28% of the total, 17 types with 0%, 4 with 2%, and 1 with 5%); and a larger percentage of the program group than the no-program group were arrested for 12 types (15% of the total, by a mean difference of 2.1%).

Figure 5.3

PERCENT ARRESTED FOR SELECTED CRIMES BY AGE 40
BY PRESCHOOL EXPERIENCE

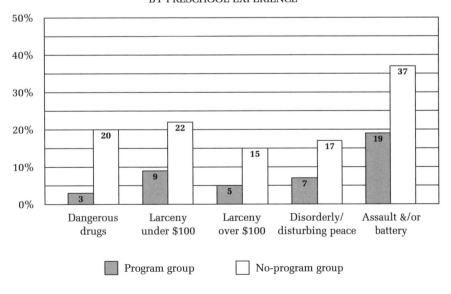

Criminal Sentences

Table 5.5 and Figure 5.4 present group comparisons on adult criminal sentences, by age 40 and broken out up to age 27 and at ages 28 to 40.[4] **Program group members were sentenced to significantly fewer months in prison or jail by age 40 than were no-program group members.** The odds of the program group spending time in prison or jail were 52% less than they were for the no-program group. Over their lifetimes,

- 52% of the no-program group but only 28% of the program group were sentenced to any time in prison or jail.

The program group had less sentencing than the no-program group on every measure of sentencing, but not to a statistically significant extent for any other single measure—undropped misdemeanor cases, convicted felony crimes, sentenced to prison for felonies, months sentenced to probation, or months served in prison.

This table also presents group comparisons on criminal sentences through age 27, and from age 28 to age 40. Compared to the no-program group, the program group had no significant differences in sentencing by age 27. **Compared to the no-program group, the program group had**

Figure 5.4

PERCENT SENTENCED TO PRISON OR JAIL BY AGE BY PRESCHOOL EXPERIENCE

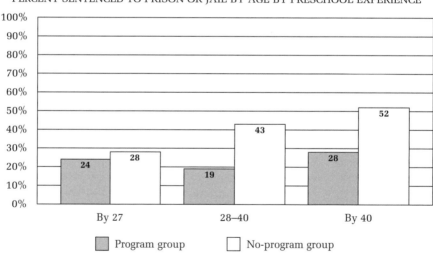

[4] Findings for sentences through age 27 differ slightly from those reported by Schweinhart et al. (1993). One variable reported at age 27, "Served time on probation or parole," is not reported here because the variable is now based on *state* prison records, in which only 3 study participants had any history of probation, and parole history was kept only for those persons currently on parole. (Probation is a sentence instead of prison; parole occurs after a prison sentence.) Thus, we could neither confirm findings for parole through age 27, nor determine it in subsequent years.

Table 5.5

ADULT CRIMINAL SENTENCES, BY AGE BY PRESCHOOL EXPERIENCE

Variable	By Age 40			By Age 27			Ages 28–40		
	Program Group	No-Program Group	Odds Ratio	Program Group	No-Program Group	Odds Ratio	Program Group	No-Program Group	Odds Ratio
Misdemeanor cases not dropped									
0	38%	29%	.61	57%	46%	.52	54%	42%	.83
1–4	34%	25%		36%	31%		24%	31%	
5–9	19%	25%		5%	17%		19%	18%	
10 or more	9%	21%		2%	6%		3%	9%	
Convicted felony crimes									
0	74%	65%	.70	79%	75%	.98	83%	74%	.57
1–2	14%	17%		14%	14%		15%	17%	
3 or more	12%	18%		7%	11%		2%	9%	
Sentenced to prison for felonies	19%	31%	.54	19%	20%	1.20	7%	25%	.22**
Months sentenced to prison or jail									
0	72%	48%	.48*	76%	72%	1.13	81%	57%	.41*
1–24	16%	29%		12%	17%		14%	29%	
25 or more	12%	23%		12%	11%		5%	14%	
Months sentenced to probation									
0	74%	63%	.64	88%	81%	.73	81%	74%	.69
1–24	16%	19%		5%	11%		14%	18%	
25 or more	10%	18%		7%	8%		5%	8%	
Months served in prison									
0	86%	78%	.62	86%	84%	.92	91%	79%	.37*
1–100	7%	8%		12%	8%		2%	12%	
101 or more	7%	14%		2%	8%		7%	9%	

Note. Statistical tests and odds ratios (but not group percentages) are based on ordinal regression analysis, adjusted for the effects of participants' gender, Stanford-Binet IQ at study entry, mother's schooling, mother's employment, father at home, father's occupation status, and household rooms per person. The odds ratio compares the odds of the program group having more crimes (using the ordinal categories) to the no-program group having more crimes.

*p (one-tailed) < .05; **p (one-tailed) < .01.

Table 5.6

SELF- AND TEACHER-REPORTED MISCONDUCT OVER TIME, BY PRESCHOOL EXPERIENCE

Variable	Program Group		No-Program Group		Effect Odds Ratio
	n	%	n	%	
Self-reported arrests					
Age 40					
All	54	30%	56	46%	.47
Males	30	33%	35	60%	.27*
Females	24	25%	21	24%	1.17
Age 27					
All	56	25%	61	38%	.46*
Males	31	36%	39	46%	.59
Females	25	12%	22	23%	.43
Age 19					
All	52	31%	57	51%	.36**
Males	31	39%	37	57%	.39*
Females	21	19%	20	40%	.24*
Self-reported misconduct[a]					
Age 40	53		57		
0		72%		67%	1.01
1–3		17%		21%	
6–38		11%		12%	
Age 27	55		61		
0–2		45%		36%	.67
3–6		33%		31%	
7–35		22%		33%	
Age 19	58		63		
0–5		40%		32%	.85
6–11		34%		36%	
12–70		26%		32%	
Age 15	44		55		.42*
0–2		57%		35%	
3–8		20%		38%	
9–35		23%		27%	

significantly fewer members sentenced to prison for felonies from ages 28 to 40, was sentenced to significantly fewer months in prison or jail, and served significantly fewer months in prison, but there were no significant group differences in undropped misdemeanor cases, convicted felony crimes, or months sentenced to probation. Compared to the odds for the no-program group, the odds of the program group being sentenced to prison for felonies were 78% less, of being sentenced to prison or jail were 59% less, and of serving months in prison were 63% less. From ages 28 to 40,

- 25% of the no-program group but only 7% of the program group were sentenced to prison for felonies.

- 43% of the no-program group but only 19% of the program group were sentenced to prison or jail.

- 21% of the no-program group but only 9% of the program group served time in prison.

Table 5.6 (Cont.)

SELF- AND TEACHER-REPORTED MISCONDUCT OVER TIME, BY PRESCHOOL EXPERIENCE

Variable	Program Group		No-Program Group		Effect Size
	n	Mean *(SD)*	n	Mean *(SD)*	
Teacher ratings					
Personal misconduct, ages 6–9[b]	45	0.84 (0.49)	49	1.02 (0.51)	0.36[*]
School misconduct, ages 6–9[c]	46	1.36 (0.65)	49	1.61 (0.60)	0.40[*]

Note. Statistical tests on odds ratios are based on ordinal regression analyses adjusted for the seven covariates; effect size of teacher ratings is based on ordinary least-squares regression analysis.

[a] Developed by Martin Gold of the University of Michigan's Institute for Social Research, the scales at ages 15, 19, 27, and 40 had 13-16 items, with alpha coefficients ranging from .774 to .863. The items were scored by number of times ranging from 0 (not at all) to 5 (5 or more). The age-19 items, for example, were as follows: Have you ever: hurt someone badly enough to need bandages or a doctor, used a knife or a gun or some other thing like a club to get something from a person, set fire to someone's property on purpose, hit an instructor or supervisor, gotten into a serious fight at school or work, taken part in a fight where a group of your friends were been against another group, taken a car that didn't belong to someone in your family without permission of the owner, gone into some house or building when you weren't supposed to be there, taken something not belonging to you worth under $50, taken something not belonging to you worth over $50, taken something from store without paying for it, damaged school property on purpose, damaged property at work on purpose?

[b] 6 teacher ratings scored 1 = very infrequently, 2 = infrequently, 3 = sometimes, 4 = frequently, 5 = very frequently; $r_\alpha = .754$; absences or truancies, inappropriate personal appearance, lying or cheating, steals, swears or uses obscene words, poor personal hygiene.

[c] 12 teacher ratings scored 1 = very infrequently, 2 = infrequently, 3 = sometimes, 4 = frequently, 5 = very frequently; $r_\alpha = .762$. Examples: Blames others for trouble, is resistant to teacher, attempts to manipulate adults, influences others toward troublemaking.

[*]p (one-tailed) < .05; [**]p (one-tailed) < .01.

Although significant group differences in arrests and crimes cited at arrest appeared consistently throughout study participants' lifetimes, the significant group differences in sentencing appeared only at ages 28 to 40. It would seem that the preschool program's effect on sentencing was catching up with its effects on criminal activity.

Self-Reported Misconduct

Table 5.6 presents self- and teacher-reported misconduct over time, by preschool experience. It complements this presentation of findings based on official criminal records. No one source of information on antisocial behavior is without challenges to its validity. Some see arrests as indicating more about the behavior of police toward certain racial and ethnic groups than about the behavior of those arrested. In its simple form, this argument is tangential to the validity of the findings reported here because all study participants were African American. To apply, the argument would have to maintain that the program group engaged in behavior less likely to prejudice police than did the no-program group. Criminal behavior itself is the parsimonious explanation. On the other hand, it is obvious that many people commit crimes for which they are not arrested, and self-report is the reasonable way to count such crimes—if, and it is a big if, those committing such crimes report them accurately to the interviewer. However, social desirability encourages respondents to undercount crimes, and memory becomes less precise as the number of crimes exceeds 2 or 3. In addition, the best self-reported indicator of crime is self-reported number of arrests; asking respondents to characterize actions for which they were not arrested as criminal or not requires them to make judgments for which they are neither legally competent nor particularly disposed to make.

In fact, program group members reported significantly fewer arrests than no-program group members at age 19 (31% vs. 51%) and at age 27 (25% vs. 38%), with a similar trend at age 40 (30% vs. 46%). The difference was statistically significant for males and females at age 19 and for males at age 40. Comparing these figures to the arrest figures in Table 5.1, it can be seen that individuals under-reported whether they were ever arrested, so that the self-reported arrest group percentages at ages 27 and 40 were two thirds of the recorded arrest group percentages. However, surprisingly, at age 19 the self-reported arrest group percentages were double the recorded arrest group percentages, probably because the wording at age 19 was, "Have you ever gotten into trouble with the police because of something you did," rather than being restricted to being "picked up or arrested," as it was at ages 27 and 40. In addition, the juvenile arrest records were not nearly as complete as the adult arrest records.

Program group members reported significantly fewer acts of misconduct than no-program group members at age 15 (43% vs. 65% reporting three or more such acts), but not significantly fewer at ages 19, 27, or 40.

Teacher-Rated Misconduct

According to the ratings of kindergarten through third grade teachers, the program group engaged in personal and school misconduct significantly less frequently than the no-program group at ages 6 through 9. Personal misconduct (called personal behavior in earlier monographs) had 6 items—absences or truancies, inappropriate personal appearance, lying or cheating, steals, swears or uses obscene words, and poor personal hygiene. School misconduct had 12 items, such as blames others for trouble, is resistant to teacher, attempts to manipulate adults, and influences others toward troublemaking. All the items on both scales were scored very infrequently, infrequently, sometimes, frequently, or very frequently.

Crime Patterns

Several questions can be raised about the evidence presented in this chapter—whether it truly leads to the conclusion that the High/Scope Perry Preschool Project prevented crime and what such a conclusion really means. At first glance, data in Tables 5.1 and 5.2 show that the evidence is strong, but not totally consistent with this conclusion. For arrests and crimes by age 40, favorable significant group differences were not found for felonies or misdemeanors as such. However, such an emphasis on statistical significance misses the broader pattern: **Every single odds ratio of arrests, crimes, or sentences by age 40 favored the program group over the no-program group.** The same was true of all but three of the odds ratios of arrests, crimes, and sentences by age 27 and from ages 28 to 40. In these three instances (other crimes from ages 28 to 40, sentenced to prison for felonies by age 27, and months sentenced to prison or jail by age 27), the unadjusted percentages were lower for the program group than for the no-program group. The chances of this overall pattern occurring in the absence of a crime prevention effect are negligible.

With respect to the meaning of this conclusion, data presented in Table 5.1 suggest that the preschool program's crime prevention effect centered on violent, property, and drug crimes, rather than driving or other crimes. It suggests a consistent effect on drug crimes and an effect on violent and property crimes that was stronger in midlife (ages 28–40) than in early adulthood (by age 27). This intensification of crime reduction effect is all the more striking because of the program effect reducing sentencing to prison or jail from 43% to 19% from ages 28 to 40. Table 5.3 indicates that the program effect was strongest for assault and/or battery, larceny under $100, dangerous drugs, and disorderly conduct or disturbing the peace. These types of crimes appear to indicate a lack of impulse control. Use of dangerous drugs also indicates a grave disregard for long-term consequences. With its daily routine of children planning, doing, and reviewing their activities, the preschool program focused on strengthening their abilities to make decisions and plan their lives intelligently. Many violent, property, and drug crimes result from bad decision-making, disregard for consequences, and a lack of impulse control. It would seem that the preschool program helped children avoid these negative traits to a greater extent than they would have otherwise.

For this explanation to apply, impulse control must be a behavioral trait that can be influenced by preschool experience and then remain stable until the onset of opportunities for criminal activity. The preschool curriculum-based explanation above focuses on variables that are proximal to the antisocial behavior that sometimes becomes crime, the type of variables often featured in crime theorizing (e.g., Snyder, Reid, & Patterson, 2003). As such, it could apply both in the preschool setting and in the families of origin, contexts that have sometimes been cast as alternative explanatory paths (Barnett, Young, & Schweinhart, 1998). Family and preschool setting may instead be seen as mutually reinforcing pathways for the behavioral complex in which people's social and antisocial behaviors are embedded. Then the question is not whether one of them is responsible for the development of antisocial behavior, but rather how much each of them contributes. Parents' involvement in home visits and subsequent childrearing places family as a potential mediator of the program effects. The involvement of some of the study participants in the preschool program makes it a potential fountainhead for recurrent cycles of success and motivation for success.

The structural-equation model presented in a later chapter tracks preschool program effects through educational variables—postpreschool program intellectual performance, commitment to schooling, school achievement, and educational attainment—to arrests by age 40 and earnings at age 40. This model neither confirms nor denies the causal speculation presented above. Rather, it suggests that such causal paths would probably operate in the context of study participants' schooling, just as the presented model does. The many variables in this study, selected to cover all aspects of study participants' development, were not limited to the explanatory variables suggested by our post hoc speculation.

Why were the violent and property crime prevention effects stronger at ages 28–40 than up through age 27? One explanation is that the no-program group committed more violent and property crimes over a longer period of their lives than did the program group. Another way to interpret this finding is to say that the program group stopped committing these crimes earlier in their lives. The impulse control hypothesis readily enlarges to the lifespan perspective: Over their lifetimes, the program group members were more purposeful in avoiding these crimes than were the no-program group.

VI Family, Relationships, and Health

Jeanne Montie

High/Scope Educational
Research Foundation

The High/Scope Perry Preschool study provides evidence of statistically significant findings related to family, relationships, and health. Consider that program group members have been married significantly more times than no-program group members. In particular, 71% of the program males and 54% of the no-program males have married, and 29% of program males and 8% of no-program males have married 2 or 3 times. Program males were less likely to have children they did not raise: 43% of program males had children they did not raise, compared to 70% of no-program males. Program group members were significantly more likely to say they have a positive relationship with their families than were those in the no-program group (100% vs. 91%) and more likely to say their families thought they were doing well (71% vs. 56%). Program group members were significantly more likely to believe their neighborhoods were dangerous after dark (31% vs. 14%), especially females (46% vs. 18%). Although there were few group differences related to the prevalence of health problems, significantly fewer people in the program than the no-program group had health problems that stopped them from working for at least 1 week (43% vs. 55%). Moreover, program males were significantly less likely than no-program males to abuse prescription drugs (17% vs. 43%), marijuana (48% vs. 71%), or heroin (0% vs. 9%).

Previous chapters have presented findings related to study participants' education, economic performance, and criminal records. It is logical to assume that those who received the program would have a more positive outcome in regard to these areas of their lives, and it is clear that more education, higher earnings, and less crime are positive outcomes. Each is an area in which a directional hypothesis (one-tailed statistical significance test) based on the original treatment makes sense: The program group members are assumed to have a better life because of the preschool program they experienced. This chapter presents findings in domains that do not lend themselves as readily to directional hypotheses: marriage, family and household composition, and health status. For this reason, all of the tables in this chapter except one (family relationships) present findings using two-tailed statistical significance tests, which do not assume a directional hypothesis as does a one-tailed test.

The chapter also presents findings related to the participants' children. Looking at the possibility of preschool program effects on the next generation is an unprecedented move for a study of program effects. Most such studies are limited to a look at immediate effects or, occasionally, effects 1 or 2 years later. This examination of potential next-generation effects is justified by the fact that this study has already identified so many powerful and lasting program effects that next-generation effects seem plausible.

Marital Status

When interviewed at age 40, the study participants were questioned in detail about their current marital status and their marital history. Table 6.1

Table 6.1

MARITAL STATUS, BY AGE BY PRESCHOOL EXPERIENCE

Variable	At Age 40			At Age 27		
	Program Group	No-Program Group	Odds Ratio	Program Group	No-Program Group	Odds Ratio
Years in marriage						
Total sample, *n*	56	63		58	64	
Over 10 years	32%	19%	1.79	2%	0%	1.49
6–10 years	23%	19%		20%	11%	
Up to 5 years	13%	13%		19%	22%	
Never married	32%	49%		59%	67%	
For those ever married	38	32				
Mean years	10.34	9.06		5.48	4.05	
Number of marriages						
Overall, *n*	56	63		58	64	
0	32%	49%	2.38*	59%	67%	1.42
1	48%	45%		39%	33%	
2–3	20%	6%		2%	0%	
Male, *n*	31	39				
0	29%	46%	2.81*	—	—	
1	42%	46%				
2–3	29%	8%				
Female, *n*	25	24				
0	36%	54%	1.86	—	—	
1	56%	42%				
2–3	8%	4%				
Marital status						
Overall, *n*	54	58		58	62	
Married, cohabiting	37%	24%	1.76	32%	20%	1.50
Unmarried, cohabiting	11%	12%		18%	18%	
Single, not cohabiting	52%	64%		50%	62%	
Male, *n*	30	36		33	39	
Married, cohabiting	43%	25%	2.31	26%	26%	.98
Unmarried, cohabiting	17%	8%		26%	20%	
Single, not cohabiting	40%	67%		48%	54%	
Female, *n*	24	22		25	23	
Married, cohabiting	29%	23%	1.07	40%	9%	2.45
Unmarried, cohabiting	4%	18%		8%	14%	
Single, not cohabiting	67%	59%		52%	77%	

Note. Statistical tests and odds ratios (but not group percentages) are based on ordinal regression analysis, adjusted for the effects of participants' gender, Stanford-Binet IQ at study entry, mother's schooling, mother's employment, father at home, father's occupation status, and household rooms per person. The odds ratio compares the odds of the program group having a higher level of each variable (using the ordinal categories) to the odds of the no-program group having a higher level. Data were checked for consistency across two ages and updated based on the principle of most-recent-memory.

"—" means no significant preschool experience effect was found.

*p (two-tailed) < .05; **p (two-tailed) < .01.

presents findings related to marital status at ages 40 and 27 and the number of years spent in marriage. The total number of years spent in a marital relationship was calculated from information that the study participants gave about the starting and ending date of each marriage. Over their lifetimes, the program group members spent nearly significantly more years in marital relationships than those in the no-program group (10.34 vs. 9.06 years, two-tailed p = .10). As shown in the table, by age 40, 55% of the program group members had been in marital relationships 6 or more years, compared to 38% of the no-program group. Compared to 49% of the no-program group, 32% of those in the program group have never been married.

Related to the number of years spent in marital relationships is the fact that **the program group members have been married significantly more times than those in the no-program group (20% vs. 6% married two or three times), especially males (29% vs. 8% married two or three times).** By age 40, the program group members were 2.4 times more likely to have been married one or more times than no-program group members, and program males were 2.8 times more likely to have been married one or more times than no-program males. There was no significant difference in total number of marriages between program and no-program females at age 40, nor was there any difference between the two groups or by gender in number of marriages or number of years married at age 27.

The percent married at age 40 was noticeably but not significantly greater for the program group than the no-program group (37% vs. 24%), the same pattern as at age 27 (32% vs. 20%). By gender, noticeably but not significantly more program males than no-program males were married at age 40 (43% vs. 25%), but not at age 27 (26% vs. 26%). In contrast, noticeably but not significantly more program females than no-program females were married at age 27 (40% vs. 9%[5]), but the difference was much smaller at age 40 (29% vs. 23%). About 12% of the members of each group were unmarried but cohabiting with a partner at age 40, compared to 18% of each group at age 27.

Parental Status

In the 1960s, many of the High/Scope Perry Preschool Project participants were raised in single-parent homes (47%) and extended family arrangements. It was not uncommon, then, in poor African American families, for grandparents and other relatives to assume childrearing responsibilities if biological parents were unable or unwilling, and this practice continues 40 years later. For this reason, when the study participants were interviewed at age 40, every effort was made to capture all possible family configurations and childrearing arrangements. To gather accurate

---

[5] This age-27 finding, reported as significant by Schweinhart et al. (1993), did not reach statistical significance when reanalyzed with covariates controlled (Stanford-Binet IQ at entry, mother's schooling, mother's employment, father at home, father's occupation status, and household rooms per person).

and comprehensive information about the number of children born and raised, study participants were questioned carefully about their biological children, as well as any other children they had raised. Females were asked about the number of pregnancies, abortions, miscarriages, and births they had experienced, and the number of children they had a major role in raising for at least 4 years, and whether the child was their biological offspring or not. Males were asked about the number of biological children they had and how many children they had a major role in raising.

Program and no-program group members did not differ significantly in the number of children they had (including both biological and stepchildren). At age 40, the mean number of children for members of the program group was 2.58 (range 0–8), compared to 1.92 for the no-program group (range 0–12). Table 6.2 presents findings related to childbirth and child raising at ages 27 and 40; four fifths of the members of each group had 1 or more children by age 40. The groups did not differ significantly in the number of children who were born out of wedlock; 86% of the members of each group who had children had 1 or more of them born out of wedlock by age 40. This information was not asked directly in the interview, but was calculated by comparing children's birthdates to the years that their parents reported being married. Similar results were found at age 27, although each group had fewer children at that time. At age 27, 60% of the program group members and 69% of the no-program group members had children; of those who had children, 86% of the program group and 82% of those in the no-program group had at least one of them out of wedlock.

The age at birth of the first child was calculated for both male and female study participants using data collected at ages 19, 27, and 40. Results for the groups were similar: Median age at first birth for the program group members was 20; for no-program group members, 21. As Table 6.2 shows, 43% of program group members and 48% of no-program group members had their first child by age 19.

At age 40, but not at age 27, study participants were asked, "How many children have you had a major role in raising for at least four years, whether the child was biological or not?" Overall, groups did not differ significantly: 29% of the program group members, compared to 43% of those in the no-program group, did not have a major role in raising one or more of their children. However, there was a significant effect by gender. As shown in Figure 6.1, **significantly fewer program males than no-program males had children they did not raise (43% vs. 70%).** Not surprisingly, females were more likely to have raised all their children—over 85% in both groups.

In addition to questions about biological and stepchildren, which were asked of all study participants, female study participants were asked about the number of pregnancies, voluntary abortions, and miscarriages they had experienced in their lives. The groups did not differ significantly on any of these three variables either at age 27 or age 40; however, sample sizes were small—about 25 in each group. By age 27, 76% of the program females had been pregnant at least once, compared to 96% of the no-program females. These numbers increased only slightly by age 40, when 84% of the program females and 96% of the no-program females had experienced at least one pregnancy. In contrast, group differences in the number of voluntary abortions by age 40 were large; only 16% of program females had had 1 or more abortions compared to 46% of the no-program females. The

Table 6.2

CHILDBIRTH AND RAISING, BY AGE AND PRESCHOOL EXPERIENCE

Variable	At Age 40			At Age 27		
	Program Group	No-Program Group	Odds Ratio	Program Group	No-Program Group	Odds Ratio
Number of children,[a] _n_	_56_	_63_		_58_	_64_	
0	20%	19%	1.08	40%	31%	.64
1–2	34%	37%		45%	44%	
3–4	30%	33%		10%	20%	
5 or over	16%	11%		5%	5%	
Children born out of wedlock,[b] _n_	_43_	_49_		_35_	_44_	
0	14%	14%	.96	14%	18%	.71
1	23%	31%		43%	34%	
2	37%	20%		34%	23%	
3 or over	26%	35%		9%	25%	
Age at first birth, _n_	_44_	_50_				
13–16	7%	10%	1.34			
17–19	36%	38%				
20–24	27%	32%				
25 or older	30%	20%				
Children raised by others,[c] _n_				NA	NA	
Overall, _n_	_45_	_51_				
0	71%	57%	.52			
1–2	20%	21%				
3 or over	9%	22%				
Males, _n_	_23_	_30_				
0	57%	30%	.29*			
1–2	26%	37%				
3 or over	17%	33%				
Females, _n_	_22_	_21_				
0	86%	95%	3.45			
1–2	14%	0%				
3 or over	0%	5%				
Pregnancies, _n_	_25_	_23_		_25_	_24_	
0	16%	4%	1.42	24%	4%	.59
1–2	12%	35%		44%	54%	
3–4	40%	22%		20%	29%	
5 or over	32%	39%		12%	13%	

Table 6.2 (Cont.)

CHILDBIRTH AND RAISING, BY AGE AND PRESCHOOL EXPERIENCE

Variable	At Age 40			At Age 27		
	Program Group	No-Program Group	Odds Ratio	Program Group	No-Program Group	Odds Ratio
Abortions, *n*	*25*	*22*		*25*	*23*	
0	84%	54%	.67	96%	78%	.40
1	8%	23%		4%	22%	
2-3	8%	23%		0%	0%	
Miscarriages, *n*	*25*	*22*		*25*	*23*	
0	68%	55%	1.12	88%	74%	.86
1	20%	36%		8%	26%	
2–3	12%	9%		4%	0%	

Note. Statistical tests and odds ratios (but not group percentages) are based on ordinal regression analysis, adjusted for the effects of participants' gender, Stanford-Binet IQ at study entry, mother's schooling, mother's employment, father at home, father's occupation status, and household rooms per person. The odds ratio compares the odds of the program group having higher numbers (using the ordinal categories) to the odds of the no-program group having higher numbers.

[a] All children are biological except for 4 participants with nonbiological children at age 40. Includes children of deceased participants and children not raised by participants.

[b] Only for those having biological children.

[c] For those with any children.

NA = not collected at age 27 interview. Data were checked for consistency across ages and updated based on the principle that the most recent memory is the most likely to be accurate.

[*]*p* (two-tailed) < .05; [**]*p* (two-tailed) < .01.

Figure 6.1

CHILDREARING AND HEALTH FINDINGS AT AGE 40 BY PRESCHOOL EXPERIENCE

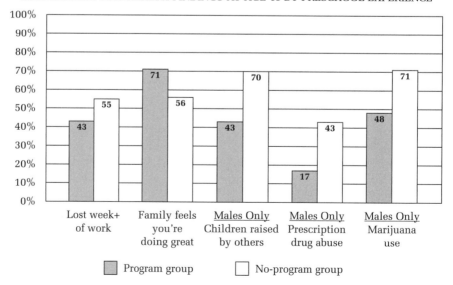

lack of statistical significance for this finding is surprising and is due to the effects of several covariates in the logistic regression analysis. Higher Stanford-Binet IQs at study entry, father's presence at home, mother's employment, and father's occupation in skilled work were all related to fewer abortions in both groups ($p < .05$). By age 27, the percentage of program group members compared to no-program group members who had had an abortion was also smaller, 4% versus 22%, and the only significant covariate was father's occupation in skilled work. The percentages of study participants who had miscarriages was more similar in each group, 12% versus 26% at age 27 and 32% versus 45% at age 40.

Children's Outcomes

By midlife, the study participants were nearing the end of their childbearing years; in fact, many had children already in their 20s. There is a natural interest in their childrearing experiences and curiosity about their children's outcomes; however, in this study, findings related to their offspring do not lend themselves to meaningful between-group comparisons, for two important reasons. First, the no-program group has a higher percentage than the program group of children not raised by their study-participant parents; second, the children's ages range widely, making it necessary to divide them into age groups, with resulting small numbers per group. These issues are elaborated below.

As Table 6.2 illustrates, not all study participants have children of their own, and among those who do, some have not raised their own children. During the age 40 interview, the study participants were questioned only about children they have had a major role in raising for at least 4 years. Each study participant who had raised 1 or more children answered a series of questions about their oldest child and next oldest child, if they had more than 1 child. The questions related to their children's school performance, any behavior problems, employment, health, receipt of social services, and marital and childbearing status. Thus, the child outcomes data involve only the study participants who have raised their own children and only the first 2 children born to, and raised by, study participants.

To assess whether the subgroups of study participants who had raised their own children were representative of their whole group, a series of statistical tests were performed on the three major age 40 outcome variables. First, study participants who had children ($n = 96$) were compared to those who did not have children ($n = 23$) on lifetime arrests, education, and annual income. Then, using those who had children as the sample base, a comparison was made on the same variables between study participants who did not raise their own children ($n = 28$) and those who did ($n = 68$). Table 6.3 presents the results. There were no significant differences on major age 40 outcome variables between those who *had* children and those who did not. However, among those who had children, there were significant differences between those who *raised* their children and those who did not, on two of the three age 40 outcomes tested. Those who did not raise their own children had more lifetime arrests ($p < .001$) and

Table 6.3

MAJOR AGE 40 OUTCOMES FOR THE TOTAL SAMPLE BY CHILDREARING STATUS

Age 40 Outcome	Did Not Have Children	Had Children	Odds Ratio	Did Not Raise Their Children	Raised Children	Odds Ratio
n^a	23	96		28	68	
Lifetime arrests						
0	22%	22%	1.16	4%	29%	0.11**
1–4	35%	31%		18%	37%	
5–10	26%	23%		21%	24%	
>10	17%	24%		57%	10%	
Educational attainment						
No high school graduation	39%	30%	1.32	46%	23%	3.13**
High school graduate	52%	64%		54%	68%	
Associate degree or higher	9%	6%		0%	9%	
Annual income						
$0–2,250	38%	22%	1.44	30%	19%	1.39
$2,251–17,280	19%	26%		22%	28%	
$17,281-31,525	14%	28%		26%	28%	
>$31,525	29%	24%		22%	25%	

Note. Statistical tests and odds ratios (but not group percentages) are based on ordinal regression analysis, adjusted for the effects of participants' gender, Stanford-Binet IQ at study entry, mother's schooling, mother's employment, father at home, father's occupation status, and household rooms per person. The odds ratio compares the odds of those who had or raised children having a higher level of a particular variable (using the ordinal categories) to those who did not have or raise children.

[a] Sample includes the 7 participants who were deceased at age 40.

*p (two-tailed) < .05; **p (two-tailed) < .01.

lower educational attainment ($p < .01$). Thus, the study participants who raised their own children did not represent the entire sample; as a group they were better off in terms of educational attainment and less criminal behavior. Further analysis found that the percentage of first and second born children not raised by their study participant parent was significantly higher in the no-program group than the program group (33% vs. 18%, chi square = 5.39, $p < .05$). For these reasons, statistical comparisons of children's outcomes based on their parents' group status do not constitute a fair test of preschool program effects.

Program group members had 129 biological children (ranging from 6 months to 25 years old), and the no-program group had 134 children (ranging from 1 to 27 years old). Table 6.4 presents the major outcomes for the 2 oldest children combined, for the program and no-program groups. To provide the most complete picture of the sample of study participants' children, the table also includes the number of oldest and next oldest

Table 6.4

TWO OLDEST CHILDREN ACHIEVING SELECTED OUTCOMES, BY STUDY PARTICIPANT'S PRESCHOOL EXPERIENCE

Variable	Children of Program Group	Children of No-Program Group
Age Under 19		
School performance, *n*	*48*	*40*
Did not repeat grade	67%	60%
Repeated a grade	13%	5%
Not raised by the study participant	20%	35%
Age Over 18		
School performance, *n*	*27*	*38*
Regular high school graduation	41%	37%
GED or equivalent	7%	8%
Dropped out	37%	18%
Not raised by the study participant	15%	37%
Marital status, *n*	*29*	*40*
Married	0%	8%
Cohabiting with partner	3%	10%
Single, not cohabiting	83%	47%
Not raised by the study participant	14%	35%
Childbearing status, *n*	*29*	*40*
Have biological children	41%	38%
Pregnant with first child	0%	5%
No children	45%	22%
Not raised by the study participant	14%	35%
Ever been arrested, *n*	*29*	*40*
No	55%	45%
Yes	31%	20%
Not raised by the study participant	14%	35%
Employed, *n*	*29*	*39*
Yes	59%	38%
No	27%	26%
Not raised by the study participant	14%	36%
Received welfare, *n*	*29*	*39*
No	55%	44%
Yes	31%	20%
Not raised by the study participant	14%	36%

Note. $N = 69$ for the reported children over 18 and 95 for under 19. Missing cases = 0 for marital status, childrearing, and arrests; 1 for employment and welfare; and 4 for school performance over age 18. For school performance under age 19, data for 7 cases were not available because the children were younger than 6 years old.

*p (one-tailed) < .05; **p (one-tailed) < .01.

children *not raised* by their study-participant parent for each variable. Because the age range of the children varied widely, they were divided into those under 19 and those over 18 for reporting these outcomes.

Findings for school performance are reported using high school graduation for those over 18 and repeating a grade for those under 19. Less than half of those over 18 in both groups had graduated from high school. Some context for these findings can be gained by comparing the results to similar findings for the study participants themselves. By age 19, 67% of the program group and 45% of the no-program group had graduated from regular high school. Among the children of study participants less than 18 years of age, 67% of program group members' children and 60% of no-program group members' children did not repeat a grade. Among study participants themselves, 65% of program group members and 60% of no-program group members did not repeat a grade.

More program group members' children than no-program group members' children over 18 were single (83% vs. 47%). Many of the study participants' children had children of their own—41% of the program group members' children compared to 38% of the no-program group members' children. A generation earlier, at age 27, 64% of the program group members and 69% of those in the no-program group had had children. Fifty-nine percent of the program group members' children who were over 18 were employed, compared to 38% of the no program group members' children.

Compared to 20% of the no-program group members' children, 31% of the program group members' children had been arrested. Similar percentages of each group had received welfare (31% of the program group's children, 20% of the no-program group's children). A generation earlier, at age 27, 57% of the program group and 69% of the no-program group had been arrested at least once, and 59% of the program group and 80% of the no-program group had received welfare. Although the findings across generations are not directly comparable because of age differences in the samples and changes in welfare regulations, it is encouraging to note that percentages of welfare receipt and arrests are lower in this small sample of the study participants' children when compared to age 27 findings for the study participants themselves.

For every variable presented in the table, the percentage of children not raised by their study-participant parents is higher in the no-program group than in the program group. We do not know how those children fared, but since their parents had poorer outcomes on education and criminal behavior, it seems likely that their children were at greater risk.

Household Members and Neighborhood

To obtain basic information about household configuration, study participants were asked how many adults and children under 18 years old were living in their households at ages 27 and 40. Table 6.5 shows that groups did not differ significantly on these variables at either age. At age 40, in both groups, there was a median of 2 adults and 1 child per household. At age 27, the median number of adults in the household was also 2 for both

Table 6.5

HOUSEHOLD MEMBERS AND NEIGHBORHOOD BY PRESCHOOL EXPERIENCE

Variable	At Age 40			At Age 27		
	Program Group	No-Program Group	Odds Ratio	Program Group	No-Program Group	Odds Ratio
Adults in household, _n_	_50_	_48_		_50_	_53_	
Median	2	2		2	2	
1	20%	25%	0.85	24%	23%	0.70
2	58%	44%		52%	41%	
3–5	20%	31%		22%	28%	
6–14	2%			2%	8%	
Children under age 18 in household, _n_	_50_	_48_		_50_	_53_	
Median	1	1		1	2	
0	34%	40%	1.11	34%	26%	0.81
1	22%	21%		24%	23%	
2–3	36%	31%		32%	32%	
4–9	8%	8%		10%	19%	
Neighborhood safe to walk around after dark[a]						
Overall, _n_	_52_	_48_				
Completely safe	15%	29%	2.17			
Fairly safe	54%	56%				
Somewhat dangerous	27%	9%				
Extremely dangerous	4%	6%				
Females, _n_	_24_	_22_				
Completely safe	0%	32%	6.13**			
Fairly safe	54%	50%				
Somewhat dangerous	46%	9%				
Extremely dangerous	0%	9%				
Own a handgun, _n_	_50_	_49_				
Yes	8%	14%	0.76			

Note. Statistical tests and odds ratios (but not group percentages) are based on ordinal regression analysis, adjusted for the effects of participants' gender, Stanford-Binet IQ at study entry, mother's schooling, mother's employment, father at home, father's occupation status, and household rooms per person. The odds ratio compares the odds of the program group having a higher level of each variable (using the ordinal categories) to the odds of the no-program group having higher levels.

[a] There was a significant group by gender effect, with significant preschool experience differences for females, but not males.

*_p_ (two-tailed) < .05; **_p_ (two-tailed) < .01.

groups; however, the median number of children was 2 for no-program group households compared to only 1 in program group households. At age 27, 34% of the program group members and 26% of the no-program group members had no children living in their households.

At age 40, study participants were asked whether their neighborhood was safe to walk around in after dark. **Significantly more of the program group than the no-program group (31% vs. 14%) reported that they felt their neighborhood was somewhat or extremely dangerous; this finding was due to females (46% vs. 18%), not males.** This finding is difficult to interpret, given that the program females were better off in general than the no-program females. Further analysis shows that 73% (11) of the 15 females who said their neighborhood was dangerous lived in Ypsilanti. Perhaps program females had closer ties to their hometown and preferred to live there regardless of perceived danger. Nevertheless, 66% (21) of the 32 females who lived in Ypsilanti said they lived in a safe neighborhood, so most of the females in the study considered Ypsilanti safe. Only a small number of those in each group said they owned a handgun (8% of the program group vs. 14% of the no-program group).

Family and Social Relationships

In both the age 27 and the age 19 findings reported by Schweinhart et al. (1993), the two groups did not differ in their estimates of how well they were getting along with their families or in their estimates of how their families felt they were doing. However, at age 40, there were significant group differences favoring the program group on both of these variables. Table 6.6 presents the results of the age 40 analysis. **The program group members were 2.4 times more likely to say they had a positive relationship with their families than those in the no-program group (100% vs. 91%). When asked their opinion of how their family felt about how they were doing, program group members were twice as likely to say their families thought they were doing great (71% vs. 56%).** Groups did not differ significantly in participants' estimations of whether they were turning out as their families expected.

Study participants were asked about their relationships with other people in their lives. Specifically, the interviewer asked if any of the following types of people were "giving you a hard time": spouse or partner, roommate, family members, co-workers, supervisors at work, teachers, police, courts, social workers, lawyers, collection agencies, doctors, neighbors, people at church, friends, and others. As Table 6.6 shows, when grouping the categories into family, co-workers, authority figures, and others, groups did not differ significantly in their responses. Similarly, at ages 27 and 19, there were no significant group differences in response to this question. Overall, at age 40, about 30% of study participants in both groups had difficulty getting along with authority figures compared to other types of people. There was a significant group by gender effect for authority figures. Fewer program than no-program males (20% vs. 41%) said they were having difficulty getting along with author-

Table 6.6

FAMILY AND SOCIAL RELATIONS AT AGE 40

Variable	Program Group	No-Program Group	Odds Ratio
Family relations			
How well getting along with family, n	*52*	*55*	
Very Well	75%	64%	2.40*
Fair	25%	27%	
Not too good	0%	9%	
How family feels about how you're doing, n	*52*	*55*	
Doing great	71%	56%	2.11*
Getting by	29%	35%	
Not doing anything worth much	0%	9%	
Turning out as family expected, n	*52*	*55*	
Better than expected	48%	35%	1.60
As expected	39%	42%	
Not as well as expected	13%	24%	
Other social relations			
People giving you a hard time, n	*54*	*56*	
Family			
0	76%	77%	0.87
1	20%	18%	
2 or more	4%	5%	
Co-workers			
0	83%	86%	1.31
1	11%	12%	
2 or more	6%	2%	
Authority figures[a]			
0	69%	68%	0.86
1	26%	18%	
2	5%	14%	
Others			
0	91%	91%	0.97
1	5%	9%	
2 or more	4%	0%	

Note. Statistical tests and odds ratios (but not group percentages) are based on ordinal regression analysis, adjusted for the effects of participants' gender, Stanford-Binet IQ at study entry, mother's schooling, mother's employment, father at home, father's occupation status, and household rooms per person. The odds ratio compares the odds of the program group having a higher level of each variable (using the ordinal categories) to the odds of the no-program group having higher levels.

[a] There was a significant group by gender effect for authority figures.

*p (one-tailed) < .05; **p (one-tailed) < .01.

ity figures, while more program than no-program females (46% vs. 18%) had the same difficulty. However, neither of the group differences within gender reached statistical significance.

Community Involvement

Study participants were questioned about their community involvement at ages 27 and 40. Groups did not differ significantly on any measured aspect of community involvement at either age. Table 6.7 presents the responses for the program and no-program group members at age 40 and the whole sample at age 27. Study participants tended to be more involved at age 40 than at age 27. At both ages, most study participants considered religion to be very important and had registered to vote. At age 40, 52% of the program group members and 46% of those in the no-program group said they had voted in the last presidential election. These figures are comparable to the 51% national average of the voting age population who voted in the 2000 presidential election and higher than the 42% national average of African Americans who voted in the 1998 national election (Federal Election Commission, 1998, 2000). In local elections, 35% of the program group and 25% of the no-program group had voted. The voting percentages were somewhat lower at age 27: 39% of the sample voted in the previous presidential election and 19% voted in the last state or local election. Approximately one third of the sample participated in volunteer work at both ages.

Table 6.7

COMMUNITY INVOLVEMENT

Variable	At Age 40			At Age 27
	Program Group	No-Program Group	Odds Ratio	Combined Groups
Considered religion very important	83%	75%	1.59	60%
Registered to vote	74%	63%	1.82	62%
Voted in last presidential election	52%	46%	1.54	39%
Voted in last state or local election	35%	25%	1.85	19%
Attended school board or city council meeting	30%	27%	1.21	13%
Participated in volunteer work	32%	36%	0.94	29%

Note. *N*s vary between 116 and 110, depending on the age and the particular question. There were no statistically significant differences between the program and no-program groups at age 40 on any variable. Statistical tests and odds ratios (but not group percentages) were based on ordinal regression analysis, adjusted for the effects of participants' gender, Stanford-Binet IQ at study entry, mother's schooling, mother's employment, father at home, father's occupation status, and household rooms per person. The odds ratio compares the odds of the program group having a higher level of each variable (using the ordinal categories) to the odds of the no-program group having higher levels.

Health

Information about study participants' health and use of health services was gathered by interview at age 40. They were first asked to rate their general health and to describe any recent illnesses and hospitalizations. They were also asked about their use of routine health services, such as yearly physical and dental exams. Table 6.8 presents these findings. Groups did not differ significantly in their ratings of their general health. About 60% of the study participants in both groups said they were in very good or excellent health. In addition, groups did not differ significantly in hospitalizations and surgeries during the past year; 18% to 20% of the participants reported undergoing hospitalizations or surgeries. **At age 27, significantly more of the program group than the no-program group reported being hospitalized in the past 12 months (30% vs. 15%),** but this significant difference did not reappear at age 40. Groups did differ significantly in the number who reported that their health stopped them from working for at least 1 week during the past 15 years. As shown in Figure 6.1 (p. 112), **significantly fewer program group members than no-program group members missed work during that time (43% vs. 55%).**

Most of the study participants (87%) reported having at least one routine visit to a physician in the previous 12 months. This percentage has increased slightly since age 27, when 77% of the study participants reported having annual health exams. Noticeably but not significantly more of the program group than the no-program group had one or more routine dental and eye exams at age 40 (two-tailed $p = .056$ for dental exams and .074 for eye exams), perhaps due to a greater awareness of the benefits of preventive health care. The two groups did not differ significantly in the number of visits made to urgent care centers or emergency rooms; 20% of the sample made one or more visits to these facilities.

Health care access was not a problem for the majority of the study participants. More than 80% of the sample had one particular place they went to for medical care. Most people in the sample (77%), reported that they had health insurance coverage, which was most often paid through their own or their spouse's employer. However, 45% of the sample said that there were times in the past 15 years when they were without health insurance, usually because they were unemployed at the time. Eighteen percent of the sample said there was at least one time in the past 12 months that they needed a doctor but did not go because of the cost.

Study participants were questioned about several chronic health problems that are prevalent in the U.S. or African American population in midlife. Specifically, they were asked if a doctor had ever told them they had high blood pressure, diabetes, asthma, or arthritis. As shown in Table 6.9, the groups did not differ significantly in the prevalence of these chronic diseases, although slightly more of the program group than the no-program group said they had been told they had high blood pressure (35% vs. 25%).

Table 6.8

GENERAL HEALTH

| | At Age 40 | | | At Age 27 | | |
Variable	Program Group	No-Program Group	Odds Ratio	Program Group	No-Program Group	Odds Ratio
General health, n	*54*	*58*		*56*	*61*	
Excellent	19%	21%	.79			
Very good	42%	38%			.	
Good	20%	20%				
Fair or poor	19%	21%				
Hospitalized in previous 12 months	20%	18%	1.30	30%	15%	2.76*
Health stopped respondent from working for 1 or more weeks in past 15 years	43%	55%	0.41*			
Number of routine visits in previous 12 months, n	*54*	*57*		*55*	*60*	
Physician						
0	17%	11%	0.72	25%	22%	0.97
1	48%	51%		75%	78%	
2 or more	35%	38%		—	—	
Dentist						
0	24%	37%	2.07			
1	35%	35%				
2 or more	41%	28%				
Eye doctor						
0	50%	63%	2.11			
1	43%	33%				
2 or more	7%	4%				
Number of visits to urgent care or emergency in previous 12 months						
0	78%	79%	1.33			
1	17%	19%				
2 or more	5%	2%				
Number of visits for scheduled treatment or surgery in previous year						
0	78%	86%	1.48			
1	18%	10%				
2 or more	4%	4%				

Note. Statistical tests and odds ratios (but not group percentages) are based on ordinal regression analysis, adjusted for the effects of participants' gender, Stanford-Binet IQ at study entry, mother's schooling, mother's employment, father at home, father's occupation status, and household rooms per person. The odds ratio compares the odds of the program group having a higher level of each variable (using the ordinal categories) to the odds of the no-program group having higher levels.

*p (two-tailed) < .05; **p (two-tailed) < .01.

Table 6.9

CHRONIC HEALTH PROBLEMS

	At Age 40			
Variable	Program Group	No-Program Group	Odds Ratio	Population Prevalence
Disease,[a] n	*54*	*56*		
High blood pressure	35%	25%	2.32	11%
Diabetes	8%	4%	2.25	4%
Asthma	13%	11%	1.68	11%
Arthritis	19%	13%	1.48	9%[b]
Body Mass Index				
Overall, n	*48*	*55*		
Under 25	27%	31%	1.25	
25–29 overweight	46%	42%		
Over 29 obese	27%	27%		
Males, n	*30*	*35*		60.7%[c] (BMI >24)
Under25	20%	29%	1.28	
25–29 overweight	47%	40%		
Over 29 obese	33%	31%		
Females, n	*18*	*20*		77.3%[c] (BMI >24)
Under 25	39%	35%	0.91	
25–29 overweight	44%	45%		
Over 29 obese	17%	20%		
Tobacco use, n	*53*	*58*		
Smoke or use other forms of tobacco	42%	55%	0.52	22.4%[d]

Note. Statistical tests and odds ratios (but not group percentages) are based on ordinal regression analysis, adjusted for the effects of participants' gender, Stanford-Binet IQ at study entry, mother's schooling, mother's employment, father at home, father's occupation status, and household rooms per person. The odds ratio compares the odds of the program group having a higher level of each variable (using the ordinal categories) to the odds of the no-program group having higher levels.

[a] Prevalence statistics cited for African Americans age 18–44 years from National Center for Health Statistics (Lucas, Schiller, & Benson, 2004).

[b] Prevalence cited is for "arthritic symptoms."

[c] Prevalence statistics cited for BMI 25 or over for African Americans 20–74 years old (1999–2000 National Health and Nutrition Examination Survey).

[d] Prevalence statistics cited for African-Americans aged 18 or over (Centers for Disease Control and Prevention Morbidity and Mortality Weekly Report, May 28, 2004).

*p (two-tailed) < .05; **p (two-tailed) < .01.

The last column in Table 6.9 shows prevalence statistics for these diseases among African Americans in the general population (Lucas, Schiller, & Benson, 2004). It is striking to note that for each of the four chronic diseases, the prevalence was higher for study participants in both groups than for the general population. This is likely due, in part, to the fact that the incidence of each of these diseases increases with age, and the population prevalence statistics cited include adults between 18 and 44 years while the study sample is at the upper end of this range. It is also true that the prevalence of these diseases tends to be higher in populations defined as "near poor" (persons having incomes 1 to 2 times the poverty threshold), a characteristic that describes many of the study participants.

Obesity has recently been recognized as a leading U.S. health problem. Studies show that nearly two thirds of U.S. adults are overweight or obese (National Institute of Diabetes & Digestive & Kidney Diseases, 2003). To gather information about obesity in this study, study participants were asked to state their height and weight, from which their body mass index (BMI) was calculated.[6] According to guidelines from the National Institutes of Health, a BMI of 18.5 to 24.9 is normal, 25.0 to 29.9 is overweight, and 30.0 or greater indicates obesity. As Table 6.9 indicates, 71% of the study participants fell in the categories of overweight or obese, more than the national average. Although gender was not statistically significant in the analysis, results are reported in the table separately for males and females and compared to national averages for African American men and women. Seventy-five percent of the males in the study had BMIs in the range of overweight or obese, more than the national average of 61% for African-American men aged 20–74 years. The percentage for study females, 63%, was lower than the national average of 77% for African American women. Since the obesity data were gathered by self-report, it is likely that overweight and obesity are underreported in the study sample; indeed, 17% of the study females declined to state their weight.

The final item in the chronic health problems table is the prevalence of tobacco use. Study participants were asked if they "now smoke cigarettes or use other forms of tobacco." The percentage of the program group members who answered yes (42%) was somewhat lower than that in the no-program group (55%). Interestingly, these percentages are about twice as high as the 22.4% of African Americans aged 18 years or older who say they smoke cigarettes (Husten, Jackson, & Lee, 2004). A minor qualification is that the questions asked in the two studies differed slightly; this study asked about tobacco use, while the national study cited asked specifically about cigarette smoking. Researchers have documented that the prevalence of smoking is higher in those living below the poverty level and those with "less than some college education." Both of these factors may play a role in this study.

---

[6] Body mass index was calculated by the following formula: (weight in pounds/height in inches²) × 703.

Drug and Alcohol Use

Study participants answered a series of questions about their use of alcohol, illegal substances, and prescription drugs (e.g., sedatives, amphetamines, painkillers, and antidepressants) not prescribed by a doctor. Although there is no way to directly test the veracity of their responses, in only two cases did the interviewer note that he thought the respondent was not being completely truthful.

Table 6.10 presents the findings related to alcohol use. Groups did not differ significantly in the average number of drinks they had on the days they consumed alcoholic beverages in the past month. Slightly more than half of each group did not consume alcohol at all in the prior month; 25% of the program group members and 12% of the no-program group members said they had 3 or more drinks on the days they consumed alcohol. When questioned about heavy drinking—"How many times in the past month did you have 5 or more drinks on an occasion?"—a nearly significant group difference was found (two-tailed $p = .058$). Program group members were more likely than those in the no-program group to have consumed 5 or more drinks on one or more occasions (25% vs. 12%). Of drinkers, 50% of the program group and 27% of the no-program group consumed 5 or more drinks on one or more occasions. These percentages can be compared to the national average of 32% of current drinkers who had 5 or more drinks on at least 1 day in the past year (National Center for Health Statistics, 2004a). Study participants were also asked how many times during the past month they had driven a car when they had probably had too much to drink; about 14% of the members of each group said that they had done so on at least one occasion.

The use of illegal drugs, especially cocaine and crack, was a significant societal problem in the years that the study participants were growing up and becoming young adults, the 1970s and 1980s. Drug abuse has been a particular problem in communities affected by limited employment opportunities, poverty, illiteracy, or low education levels (Anthony & Helzer, in press), communities like those in metropolitan southeastern Michigan where most of the study participants were living. The age 40 interview included detailed questions about study participants' use of illegal drugs and prescriptions in the past 15 years on their own, defined as "without a doctor's prescription, in larger amounts than prescribed, or for a longer period than prescribed." Table 6.11 presents the findings related to drug abuse grouped by soft drugs (e.g., marijuana and prescription drugs such as sedatives, tranquilizers, and pain killers) and hard drugs (e.g., cocaine, LSD, and heroin).

Survey data from the general U.S. population indicate that 33% have ever used marijuana and only 2% to 5%, depending on the type of drug, have ever used stimulants, sedatives, tranquilizers, and analgesics for nonmedical purposes (National Institute on Drug Abuse, 2003). Thus, abuse of soft drugs, especially prescription drugs, among the study participants, especially no-program males, was much higher than survey estimates for the general population. Two factors probably contribute to this difference:

Table 6.10

ALCOHOL USE AT AGE 40

Variable	Program Group	No-Program Group	Odds Ratio
Number of drinks per day, *n*	*53*	*57*	
0	51%	54%	1.34
1–2	21%	34%	
3–5	17%	7%	
6 or more	8%	5%	
Number of occasions in past month had 5 or more drinks, *n*	*52*	*57*	
0	75%	88%	2.77
1–2	10%	5%	
3 or more	15%	7%	
Number of occasions driving when had too much to drink, *n*	*52*	*57*	
0	87%	88%	1.26
1	4%	3%	
2 or more	9%	9%	

Note. Statistical tests and odds ratios (but not group percentages) are based on ordinal regression analysis, adjusted for the effects of participants' gender, Stanford-Binet IQ at study entry, mother's schooling, mother's employment, father at home, father's occupation status, and household rooms per person. The odds ratio compares the odds of the program group having a higher level of each variable (using the ordinal categories) to the odds of the no-program group having higher levels.

*p (two-tailed) < .05; **p (two-tailed) < .01.

1. The ever-used survey data were not broken down by age or race.

2. The sample for the survey data did not include incarcerated or homeless individuals, subgroups that were likely to have a higher prevalence of drug use.

In addition, the Perry Preschool study sample surely included a higher percentage of study participants living in disadvantaged neighborhoods than the population-based sample.

Age 40 study data about the use of hard drugs revealed no significant differences between the percentages of program and no-program participants using cocaine and cocaine-related drugs (23% vs. 29%) or LSD (4% vs. 7%). Again, the program group members were slightly less likely to have used these drugs. None of the program group members said they used heroin in the past 15 years, while 9% of the no-program group members said they had used heroin. (An odds-ratio could not be computed because of zero occurrences in the program group.) The use of hard drugs was noticeably but not significantly more prevalent for males than females in both groups: About 35% of males in both groups reported

Table 6.11

USE OF ILLEGAL DRUGS IN THE PAST 15 YEARS AT AGE 40

Variable	Program Group	No-Program Group	Odds Ratio
Soft Drugs			
Overall, *n*	*53*	*57*	
Sedatives, sleeping pills, tranquilizers	23%	32%	.66
Marijuana, hashish	45%	54%	.60
Males, *n*	*29*	*35*	
Sedatives, sleeping pills, tranquilizers	17%	43%	0.28*
Marijuana, hashish	48%	71%	0.15**
Females, *n*	*24*	*22*	
Sedatives, sleeping pills, tranquilizers	29%	14%	2.14
Marijuana, hashish	42%	27%	2.27
Hard Drugs			
Cocaine, crack, free base, *n*	*53*	*56*	
	23%	29%	0.64
LSD or other hallucinogens, *n*	*53*	*57*	
	4%	7%	0.27
Heroin, *n*	*53*	*57*	
	0%	9%	—[a]
Drug or alcohol treatment (for those who ever used)			
Overall, *n*	*38*	*49*	
Negative effects of drugs or alcohol on life	40%	49%	0.91
Ever been treated for drug or alcohol abuse	32%	38%	0.99
Males, *n*	*22*	*33*	
Negative effects of drugs or alcohol on life	59%	46%	2.77
Ever been treated for drug or alcohol abuse	50%	38%	3.25
Females, *n*	*16*	*16*	
Negative effects of drugs or alcohol on life	13%	56%	0.16
Ever been treated for drug or alcohol abuse	6%	38%	0.11

Note. Statistical tests and odds ratios (but not group percentages) are based on ordinal regression analysis, adjusted for the effects of participants' gender, Stanford-Binet IQ at study entry, mother's schooling, mother's employment, father at home, father's occupation status, and household rooms per person. The odds ratio compares the odds of the program group having a higher level of each variable (using the ordinal categories) to the odds of the no-program group having higher levels. Results are presented for males and females when a significant group by gender effect was found.

[a] An odds ratio could not be calculated for heroin use because there were no occurrences in the program group.

*p (two-tailed) < .05; **p (two-tailed) < .01.

using hard drugs compared to 4% of the program females and 23% of the no-program females.

National survey estimates show the following percentages of the general population that have ever used various hard drugs: cocaine—10.6%, crack—2.0%, LSD—9.9%, and heroin—1.1% (National Center for Health Statistics, 2004b). The age 40 study sample reports a much higher prevalence of cocaine-related drug use; however, the data for the general population report statistics for cocaine and crack separately and are subject to the same measurement differences cited above for soft drug use. Nevertheless, crack cocaine constituted a powerful, negative intervention into the lives of many in the study sample.

Table 6.11 also presents findings regarding study participants' perceptions about the negative effects of their use of drugs or alcohol on their lives and whether they had ever been treated for drug or alcohol abuse. Of those who used drugs or alcohol, 45% of the sample said they had suffered negative effects on their lives from substance abuse. Approximately one third of the sample who used drugs or alcohol had been treated for substance abuse. Although there were significant preschool by gender effects for both of these variables, no significant group differences appeared when males and females were examined separately. Program males were the most likely to say they had suffered negative effects from drug or alcohol abuse (59%) and were the most likely to have been treated (50%), while program females were the least likely to say they suffered negative effects (13%) and to have been treated (6%).

Overall, the findings related to drug and alcohol use show much higher rates of use by both groups than the general population. The program group had a significantly higher prevalence of heavy drinking, which is negative but legal behavior, while the no-program group had significantly higher use of illegal soft drugs.

VII Lifetime Cost-Benefit Analysis

W. Steven Barnett

National Institute for Early Education Research
Rutgers, The State University of New Jersey

Clive R. Belfield

Teachers College, Columbia University

Milagros Nores

Teachers College, Columbia University

*In constant 2000 dollars discounted at 3%, the estimated economic return
to society for the High/Scope Perry Preschool Project was $258,888 per
participant on an investment of $15,166 per participant—$17.07 per dollar
invested. Of that return, $195,621, $12.90 per dollar invested, went to the
general public and $63,267 went to each participant. Of the public return,
88% came from crime savings, and 1% to 7% came from either education savings, increased taxes due to higher earnings, or welfare savings.
Remarkably, 93% of the public return was due to males because of the
program's large reduction of male crime, and only 7% was due to females.*

This chapter reports a cost-benefit analysis of the High/Scope Perry
Preschool Project using new data on the careers and livelihoods of the
program group and no-program group up to age 40. A full cost-benefit
analysis of the High/Scope Perry Preschool Project was conducted by
Barnett (1996), using data on individuals up to age 27 (for analysis up to
age 19, see Barnett, 1985a). Barnett (1996) found that the program yielded
a high positive return both for society and for participants, describing it
as a "social program from which everybody wins." (Similarly positive
results have been obtained from economic evaluations of other preschool
programs: see Massé & Barnett, 2002; Reynolds et al., 2001; and Conyers,
Reynolds, & Ou, 2003). This chapter reassesses the long-term benefits
that arise from participation in the program and rederives the net present
value of providing the program. It serves as both an affirmation and an
extension of the earlier analysis up to age 27. The results presented here
are based on a full cost-benefit analysis available as a separate monograph
(Barnett et al., in press).

This new analysis draws on updated information about the study
participants up to age 40, i.e., over a sizeable proportion of their productive working lives. Prior studies had to project forward the likely
behaviors and outcomes after age 27; unavoidably, these cost-benefit
analyses relied on plausible predictions, rather than actualities. It is
therefore important to reaffirm the above conclusions (and see how the
predictions compared to actuality). Using more complete, high-quality,
and detailed data, it is possible to see whether the prior predictions
were overly conservative or overly optimistic. Furthermore, a lifetime
approach allows for a fuller consideration of the path-dependency of
circumstances and behaviors to determine if there are sufficiently strong
educational influences on future life opportunities. Growing attention is
being paid to how early cognitive development presages later life behaviors, opportunities, and experiences (Shore, 1997; Shonkoff & Phillips,
2000). Thus, when preschool programs dissuade participants from later
juvenile delinquency, for example, they may also dissuade them from a
life of crime (see Farrington, 2003). Such an effect would have important
economic consequences.

This cost-benefit analysis uses the same framework for comparing costs and benefits for participants and society applied by Barnett
(1996). This analytical technique is well developed, although only
infrequently applied to educational interventions (see Levin & McEwan,
2002a, 2002b). Simply, the costs of a program should be compared to its

benefits, expressed in money terms. Those programs with high positive net benefits are preferred over those with low or negative net benefits. Because benefits accrue to the individual and to society, separate cost-benefit analyses are necessary for each. Also, because the benefits occur much later than the costs are incurred, these benefits need to be discounted (valued at a lower rate).[7]

The efficacy of cost-benefit analysis depends fundamentally on two key aspects. First, accurate information on the costs of the program is necessary. For the purposes of this analysis, these costs have already been established: Barnett (1996) reports highly detailed and itemized costs of the High/Scope Perry Preschool Project, and these data are reapplied below. Second, all program benefits (or at least the most salient) must be measurable in money terms. This is the main challenge addressed below: Using individual-level data on program and no-program groups and national datasets, the advantages from program participation are calculated in dollar amounts for up to age 40 and projected forward for ages up to 65. As described in earlier chapters, these advantages are primarily gains in earnings, reductions in crime, and changes in welfare receipt, accounting for differences in schooling and adult education costs. After applying a discount rate, these pecuniary benefits are compared against the costs of the program to derive the net present value of the program. For exposition, all money values are expressed in 2000 dollars.

The cost-benefit analysis is set out below in five sections. In the next section, the earnings profiles are derived using self-reported data. Next, criminal behaviors taken from state records are related to the costs of crimes; estimates are generated of the overall costs to victims and the criminal justice system attributable to each individual. In the following section, welfare receipt and payments are calculated, based on self-reported and official information sources. Throughout these sections, undiscounted values are reported, with separate analyses for males and females by program status. In the next section, the costs of the program are reported, along with the impact of child care on the program, the savings to the school system, and the additional costs and savings in adult education. All the items from these sections are then incorporated into a cost-benefit analysis presented in the next section. Net present value figures are calculated, both for the overall program and by gender. This section also includes a sensitivity analysis to test whether the results are robust to the assumptions made in the calculations. The final section summarizes the results and draws policy conclusions; it also considers whether the results would be upheld if the program were implemented under current economic conditions and whether the program can be generalized to other groups in society.

---

[7] Discounting is necessary because $100 received immediately is worth more than $100 received a decade later. (This equation is separate from whether there is inflation or not.) For example, the immediate $100 could be invested, and after 10 years it would be worth more. Discounting also reflects the uncertainty of money now versus money later. Thus, a discount rate must be applied to all money streams, with streams discounted more the further away they are from the initial investment time (Levin & McEwan, 2002a).

Earnings Profiles

Constructing Lifetime Earnings Profiles

One important benefit of the High/Scope Perry Preschool Project is that it enhances labor market opportunities—through enhanced skills and/or through educational attainment. As indicated in Chapter 4, labor market participation and earnings advantages convey benefits to the individual and to society in the form of higher tax contributions. Using new data from interviews at age 40, it is possible to calculate lifetime economic differences between the program group and the no-program group.

The earnings profile is derived separately for three age periods: up to age 27, from ages 28 to 40, and beyond age 40. For the period up to age 27, annual earnings are constructed from a linear trend beginning with declared earnings at ages 16–19 up to declared earnings at age 27. For the period for ages 28 to 40, the earnings profile was created by working backwards from the self-reported earnings for age 40, as well as from self-reported earnings from previous jobs. Data for these years are also used to extrapolate forward for earnings over the age-profile 41–65.

A range of information was used to construct the earnings profiles for individuals, with separate analysis for males and females. The age 40 survey provides information for the current job(s) on annual and monthly earnings, hours of work, and the start date; for the last three jobs, there is similar information. It also provides information on last year's earnings. These are the main sources of data for constructing the career earnings profiles. However, many study participants do not have stable careers, but change jobs frequently and have multiple part-time jobs. Therefore, interpolating and extrapolating from these earnings data must be done cautiously. Although individuals may more accurately report monthly earnings, translating these figures into annual amounts would over-estimate earnings for individuals with intermittent labor market participation. Annual earnings, on the other hand, are corrected for months unemployed, but may be reported less precisely. In addition, information is used on spells of unemployment and incarceration. Notably, labor market participation rates do vary across the program and no-program groups and by gender (see Chapter 4). At age 40, program males were more likely to be employed (70% vs. 50%), less likely to be incarcerated (9% vs. 26%), and had more months of unemployment over the preceding 2 years (9.6 months vs. 7.6 months). This information on participation is also factored into the creation of earnings profiles.

Finally, all earnings are adjusted for employment-related fringe benefits (Office of Compensation and Working Conditions [OCWC], 2002). All types of benefits are included, such as leave, Social Security, and insurances; these represent 27.3% of total compensation, adding 37.6% to earnings.

Estimated Lifetime Earnings Profiles

The earnings profile is derived separately for three age periods: up to age 27, ages 28 to 40, and beyond age 40.

For the period up to age 27, annual earnings are constructed from a linear trend beginning with declared earnings at ages 16–19 up to declared earnings at age 27. For the period from ages 28 to 40, the earnings profile was created by working backwards from the self-reported earnings for age 40, as well as from self-reported earnings from previous jobs. At any given time period when earnings data are not reported and individuals are either on welfare, in prison, or unemployed, earnings are assumed to be zero. This approach uses more information than a simple linear trend, by tracking the job history of each individual between the two interviewed ages. For years with no information, linear trends are applied to fill the gaps. Finally, for the age period beyond 40, it is necessary to project earnings. Information was obtained on African Americans' average annual earnings by education level and gender from the March 2002 Current Population Survey (CPS; Bureau of Labor Statistics, 2002). Average earnings in the CPS are weighted in accordance with educational attainment for program and no-program males and females. Also, survival rates by gender are incorporated (National Center for Health Statistics, 1998) to adjust these projected earnings for mortality.

Earnings profiles by age period, gender, and program status are reported in the top panel of Table 7.1. For each age period, program males and females have considerably higher earnings than their no-program counterparts. Over their lifetimes, program males have earned $1.39 million, which is $143,230 (11.5%) more than no-program males (also see Figure 7.2, p. 154). Similarly, program females have earned, on average, $1.08 million, which exceeds the earnings of no-program females by $169,751 (18.6%). This represents a sizeable enhancement in economic well-being of the program group members.

Tax Contributions

Part of the benefits attached to lifetime earnings accrue to the general public in the form of tax revenues. Higher earnings translate into higher absolute amounts of income tax payments (and sales tax payments); with tax progressivity, higher earnings may also lead to proportionately higher income tax payments. (For individuals with incomes below poverty thresholds, there are net government disbursements through welfare support; these are considered below.)

Accordingly, tax incidence was estimated across gender and age profiles for program and no-program individuals on the basis of earnings. The marginal income tax rate applied for all years across the age-profiles was 15%, which was the U.S. marginal income tax rate for a married couple with taxable income in the corresponding years. In addition, Federal Insurance Contributions payable both by the employer and employee are included (OCWC, 2002). Thus, taxes are 31% of net earnings (excluding fringe benefits).

Table 7.1

LIFETIME FULL EARNINGS AND TAX CONTRIBUTIONS PER PERSON

	Program Group		No Program Group	
Source	Males	Females	Males	Females
Earnings profile				
Up to age 27	$206,235	$141,301	$184,759	$90,607
Ages 28–40	380,805	312,158	293,434	248,381
Ages 41–65	804,268	626,808	769,885	571,528
Total lifetime	*$1,391,307*	*$1,080,267*	*$1,248,077*	*$910,516*
Program differentials	+143,230	+169,751		
Tax contributions				
Up to age 27	$46,462	$31,833	$41,623	$20,412
Ages 28–40	85,790	70,325	66,106	55,957
Ages 41–65	179,402	139,483	173,778	128,080
Total lifetime	*$311,653*	*$241,640*	*$281,507*	*$204,449*
Program differentials	+30,146	+37,191		
N	*33*	*25*	*39*	*26*

Tax contributions across age-periods, gender, and program status are reported in the bottom panel of Table 7.1. Differences across contributions reflect the greater earnings of the program group. Over their lifetimes, these differences translate into a greater tax payment of $30,146 for program males and $37,191 for program females.

Impacts on Crime

Criminal Activity

Broadly, crime rates are lower for the High/Scope Perry Preschool Project program group than the no-program group; these behavioral differences are reported in full in Chapter 5. Here, a cost estimate is placed on these behavioral differences. Reductions in crime will produce savings in three domains: (1) victims' costs; (2) criminal justice costs for policing, arrest, and sentencing; and (3) incarceration and probation costs (see Anderson, 1999). These costs vary according to the type of crime (e.g., murder, burglary) and the seriousness of the crime (felony or misdemeanor). Multiplying the incidence of each crime by its unit cost yields the total economic burden of crime.

However, unit crime costs and criminal activities are rarely available together in the same format (e.g., the cost per burglary and the number of burglaries). To harmonize costs and activities, it is necessary to collapse the categories of crime.[8] These crime types are as follows: *felonies* of violent assault, rape, drugs, property, vehicle theft, and other; and *misdemeanors* of assault/battery, child abuse, drugs, driving, and other. Using the incidences reported in Chapter 5, each arrest was reclassified into one of these categories.[9] Predictions for criminal activity beyond age 40 are based on national data on arrest rate frequencies by age. Prior criminal activity is weighted according to these national frequencies.[10]

Table 7.2 reports the lifetime incidences across these categories. They show considerably lower rates of criminal activity for the program group, especially the males. (Even though these incidences—at a highly disaggregated level—are often not statistically significant, they may be economically meaningful.) For males, in only 2 out of 11 categories does total crime in the program group exceed that of the no-program group (felony other, and misdemeanor child abuse). For females, the results are much more equivocal, in part because the females have committed far less crime regardless of program status. In addition, Table 7.2 shows the numbers of months of probation and incarceration for each group. Correspondingly, these are higher for those not in the program.

It is important to note that there are far more crimes than arrests. Using arrest data alone would therefore greatly understate the actual incidence of crime: In 2002, for example, 5.34 million violent crimes were reported by victims, but there were only 0.62 million arrests (Bureau of Justice Statistics [BJS], 2002b; Federal Bureau of Investigation [FBI], 2002). Therefore, each arrest is assumed to represent only a fraction of total crimes committed by an individual, so arrest incidences must be adjusted accordingly to estimate numbers of crimes. BJS and FBI data on the numbers of crimes reported by victims and the numbers of arrests are used to estimate these factor increases. The final column of Table 7.2 shows the relationships between arrests and crimes. The ranges vary between 3 and 14 crimes per arrest. In the economic analysis, all the crimes are taken into account by using these estimates.

---

[8] Ideally, the categorization should be as fine as possible, down to each crime. However, categorization is driven by the availability of data for each crime type on incidences, victim costs, and criminal justice system costs.

[9] One important assumption relates to the treatment of differences in murder rates. Whereas the program group reported a murder incidence of 2%, the incidence for the no-program group was 5%. However, murder causes such high victim costs that it may dominate the evaluation and drive the results immediately toward the group with the lower murder rate. (This introduces considerable volatility when, as is the case here, there are few murders within the dataset.) Barnett (1996) subsumes murder under assault, which is the most clearly associated crime. More accurate data on victim costs are now available, indicating that fatal crimes are associated with victim costs of approximately $3 million, which is over 100 times the victim cost from assault. Nevertheless, Barnett's approach is used here to include murders under the category felony—violent assault.

[10] The new data up to age 40 should include information on the majority of all criminal activity over a lifetime. Most crime is committed during adolescence and the 20s (Brame & Paquerio, 2003). Using arrest rates by age, criminal activity up to age 40 represents 73% to 92% of total lifetime criminal activity, with proportions varying by crime type (Federal Bureau of Investigations, 2002). Age-specific arrest rates for each of the crime types for males and females are taken from the 2002 Uniform Crime Reports (Tables, 39 and 40; *www.fbi.gov/uer/02cius.htm*).

Table 7.2

ARREST INCIDENCES AND CRIME RANGE PER ARREST BY TYPE OF CRIME PER PERSON

Arrests by Type of Crime	Program Group		No Program Group		Crime Range per Arrest
	Males	Females	Males	Females	
Felony—Violent assault	0.780	0.150	0.825	0.048	5–8.61
Felony—Rape	0.187	0.000	0.411	0.000	3.21–4
Felony—Drugs	0.758	0.249	0.825	0.085	10.87–14
Felony—Property	0.610	0.231	2.152	0.338	6.64–12
Felony—Vehicle theft	0.000	0.000	0.141	0.000	6.64–10
Felony—Other	0.851	0.192	0.622	0.046	10.87–12
Misdemeanor—Assault/battery	0.462	0.050	1.368	0.635	3.55–14
Misdemeanor—Child abuse	0.041	0.000	0.000	0.000	10.87–14
Misdemeanor—Drugs	0.231	0.149	0.521	0.239	10.87–14
Misdemeanor—Driving	2.848	1.942	4.429	1.772	10.87–14
Misdemeanor—Other	1.770	0.498	2.996	1.389	10.87–14
Months sentenced to probation	15.768	4.531	22.243	4.909	—
Months served in prison	31.681	9.251	53.311	4.311	—
N	33	25	39	26	

Unit Costs of Crime

Each crime generates costs both to the victim and to the criminal justice system. These two costs are treated separately in this analysis.

The tangible and intangible costs of crime to victims are numerous. Victims face direct expenses for medical treatments and to replace property and assets (even with insurance claims). Victims' productivity at work and home is reduced, and they experience reduced quality of life from pain, fear, and suffering. These costs vary according to the type of crime; and many may be difficult to estimate with precision. Often, data are unavailable in an appropriate form, and cost estimation requires extrapolations and value judgments regarding the full intangible consequences of being a victim of crime.[11]

Victim cost figures across crime types are reported in the first column of Table 7.3. Only the costs applicable to the age 28 to 40 period are shown (the full analysis includes separate costs for each of the three age periods). These are derived from Miller, Cohen, and Wiersema (1996,

---

[11] The intangible losses of pain, suffering, and death are estimated from amounts people generally spend on avoiding these eventualities, e.g., the amount paid for safer cars or the wage premiums for more dangerous jobs (see Mrozek & Taylor, 2002). For nonfatal injuries, awards by juries are typically used to estimate the losses in terms of pain and suffering.

Table 7.3

UNIT VICTIM COSTS AND CRIMINAL JUSTICE SYSTEM COSTS PER TYPE
OF CRIME PER PERSON (2000 DOLLARS)

Arrests by Type of Crime	Victim Cost	Criminal Justice System Cost
Felony—Violent assault	$26,860	$19,319
Felony—Rape	97,368	57,299
Felony—Drugs	2,238	8,393
Felony—Property	8,953	18,452
Felony—Vehicle theft	41,409	8,393
Felony—Other	8,953	8,393
Misdemeanor—Assault/battery	10,520	4,360
Misdemeanor—Child abuse	30,218	8,393
Misdemeanor—Drugs	2,238	4,360
Misdemeanor—Driving	3,022	4,360
Misdemeanor—Other	1,567	4,360
Month of probation	0	141
Month of incarceration	0	2,282

Notes: Unit costs are reported for age 40. Victim costs, CJS costs, probation costs, and incarceration costs for juvenile to age 27 are taken from Barnett (1996). Victim costs for ages 28 to 40 are taken from Miller et al. (1996). CJS costs for ages 28 to 40 are averages of estimates from Cohen (1998) and the low estimates of Cohen et al. (2004). Probation costs per month and incarceration costs per month are taken from BJS databases (BJS, 2001, 2002a). Victim costs, CJS costs, probation costs and incarceration costs for ages 40–65 are extrapolated, based on the trend growth rate in criminal justice costs, 1960s–1990s.

Table 2) and incorporate costs relating to lost productivity, medical care/ambulance, mental health care, police/fire services, social/victim services, property loss/damage, and quality of life. These figures show four economically important crimes from the victims' perspectives: violent assault, rape, vehicle theft, and child abuse. Victim costs for vehicle theft are high because these crimes are often associated with auto accidents where there is a relatively high injury or fatality rate. Victim costs for child abuse are high because of the lifetime reductions in quality of life (labeled intangible victim costs by Miller et al., 1996). These victim costs per crime are multiplied by the crime rates listed in Table 7.2.

High criminal justice system costs are also incurred. In 2001, direct expenditures on the U.S. criminal justice system for arrests, trials, and sentencing were $110 billion; 34.2% of this expenditure was on the judicial system (not including incarceration) and 65.8% was on policing (BJS, 2001).

The second column of Table 7.3 reports the criminal justice system (CJS) costs per crime type (again, only for the age period 28 to 40). These estimates are adapted from Cohen (1998) and Cohen, Rust, Steen, and Tidd (2004). The figures show that violent assault and rape felonies impose high costs on the criminal justice system; as with the victim costs, these are the most economically important crimes. However, there are considerable CJS costs from other crimes, particularly felonies; for these crimes, the CJS costs exceed the victim costs. However, not all CJS costs should be weighted according to the crime:arrest ratios in Table 7.2. Specifically, policing costs are incurred per crime, but sentencing and trial costs are only incurred per arrest, not when a crime is committed. Thus, policing costs are assumed to be proportional to the numbers of crimes committed, with policing costs being 65.8% of total CJS costs (the national ratio). Similarly, sentencing and trial costs are assumed proportional to the number of arrests made, with these costs being 34.2% of total CJS costs.

A final cost item is incurred for those individuals on probation or incarcerated. Unit costs for probation and incarceration per month are reported in the bottom rows of Table 7.3. These produce cost-per-inmate-month estimates of probation at $141 and of incarceration at $2,282.[12]

Lifetime Costs of Crime

Using the information on impacts and on unit costs, lifetime costs from criminal activity can be calculated.

Table 7.4 shows the lifetime costs by age period, gender, and program status. Both victim costs and CJS costs are included in these figures. The disparities by program status are striking. Males in the program group impose an economic burden of $1,075,359 each. As shown in Figure 7.2, p. 154, although substantial, this figure is substantially less (at 59%) than the burden of $1,808,253 each that the no-program males impose (for similar estimates for at-risk youth, see Cohen, 1998). In contrast, females impose much lower burdens ($291,020 vs. $315,005); these are broadly similar across program status, but again show a gain to the general public from program participation (the program female crime costs are 92% of those not in the program). The program results in (undiscounted) savings of $732,894 per male participant and $23,985 per female participant. This is a substantial gain for society from the Perry Preschool Project.

It is noteworthy that these estimates of crime benefits differ significantly from those produced by Barnett (1996) at an earlier time. To some extent, this reflects the addition of new data. However, even the estimates through age 27 differ considerably between the two analyses. While the current estimates through age 27 are somewhat larger on average, the most striking difference is that estimated benefits for males are considerably larger, while those for females are much smaller. This tilts the bulk of estimated public benefits much more toward males than in

---

[12] The probation figure is calculated as total direct expenditures for state noninstitutional correctional activities in 1999 divided by the number of adults on probation under state jurisdiction (BJS, 2002, Tables 1.8 and 6.1). The incarceration figure is calculated from total direct expenditures for state institutional correctional activities in 1999 divided by the number of persons in state prisons in 1999 (BJS, 2002, Tables 1.8 and 6.12).

Table 7.4

LIFETIME COSTS OF CRIME PER PERSON

Time Span	Program Group		No Program Group	
	Males	Females	Males	Females
Up to age 27	$334,844	$107,795	$640,430	$123,402
Ages 28–40	484,623	117,598	773,265	125,577
Ages 4–65	255,892	65,627	394,558	66,026
Total lifetime	$1,075,359	$291,020	$1,808,253	$315,005
Program differentials	−732,894	−23,985		

Barnett's (1996) earlier analysis. The differences in outcomes between these two analyses is indicative of the extent to which changes in the categorization of crimes, the estimated costs attributed to specific crimes, and other decisions in the analysis can influence the outcome. This may be particularly true when looking at estimates for males and females separately, given the reduction in sample size. It also suggests caution in drawing conclusions about subgroups in the study of which males and females are the most obvious example—for this reason, and because the confidence intervals around estimates for subgroups are larger than for the sample as a whole.

Impacts on Welfare Receipt

Amounts of Welfare Receipt

Welfare payment effects are the third main component of the cost-benefit analysis. In general, welfare reliance is somewhat lower for the program group than the no-program group (see Chapter 4). Lower reliance on welfare mainly arises because of higher earnings and greater economic independence; yet, higher incarceration rates render more of the no-program group ineligible for welfare payments; and welfare reliance differs by gender, particularly when females are primary caregivers for children. However, the consequences from differences in welfare receipt across the program and no-program groups depend on whose perspective is adopted. The welfare payment, itself, is a transfer of income from taxpayers to welfare recipients. Thus, decreased payment represent a gain for society but a loss for the individual (see Wolfe, 2002). In addition, there are costs for administering welfare payments, and decreases in these represent gains for all members of society.

The impact across genders on welfare payments is estimated for the three age profiles: up to age 27, from ages 28 to 40, and extrapolated to ages 41 to 65. Welfare payments are calculated as the numbers of months on welfare times the monthly welfare receipt.

Table 7.5

LIFETIME WELFARE RECEIPT AND PAYMENTS PER PERSON

Source	Program Group		No Program Group	
	Males	Females	Males	Females
Months of welfare receipt				
Up to age 27	5.673	26.748	6.000	39.015
Ages 28–40	4.249	59.384	27.550	24.337
Ages 41–65	12.403	107.665	41.938	79.190
Total lifetime	*22.325*	*193.797*	*75.488*	*142.542*
Money amounts in welfare				
Up to age 27	$2,945	$32,246	$8,737	$36,070
Ages 28–40	739	15,652	5,724	6,763
Ages 41–65	2,158	28,377	8,713	22,006
Total lifetime	*$5,842*	*$76,275*	*$23,174*	*$64,839*
Program differentials	−17,331	11,438		
Societal cost				
Total lifetime	*$8,063*	*$105,261*	*$31,979*	*$89,477*
Program differentials	−23,916	15,784		
N	*33*	*25*	*39*	*26*

Notes: Welfare up to age 27 includes welfare receipt over 10 years (AFDC, Medicaid, GA, and Food Stamps). Welfare for ages 28–40 includes cash assistance, food assistance, medical assistance, family counseling, and other welfare. Societal cost adjusts for the error rate and administrative costs.

The top panel of Table 7.5 shows the monthly incidence of welfare claims across the three age-periods. For the period up to age 27, updated self-report records are used, although state records are also available (see Barnett, 1996).[13] Males report similar and relatively low levels of assistance, relying on welfare for approximately 6 months over the period. In contrast, females report considerable reliance on welfare systems: 27 months for the program females versus 39 months for the no-program females. For ages 28 to 40, newly obtained state records are used for tracking five different types of welfare programs. These estimates take into account reforms to the welfare system (reflected in the 1996 Personal Responsibility and Work Opportunity Reconciliation Act). Strong differences are apparent across genders and program status. Program females reported the greatest reliance on welfare, at an average of 59 months; this

---

[13] For the ages up to 27, self-report data are available on months of receipt of Social Security, Aid to Families with Dependent Children (AFDC), Medicaid to families/mothers, and General Assistance (GA). AFDC was primarily directed at single mothers, and Medicaid was usually tied with eligibility to other benefits. The General Assistance program was run by the State of Michigan.

is mainly food and medical assistance, as well as family counseling. In comparison, the no-program females report 24 months of welfare receipt. For program males, welfare reliance is relatively low at 4 months; but no-program males report very high levels of medical assistance, drawing on welfare support for 28 months over the age period. (These figures are months on any of the designated welfare programs: An individual on two welfare programs for 1 full year would therefore be counted as having 24 months of welfare receipt in total.) Finally, an age-weighted ratio is used to estimate welfare assistance for the age period 41 to 65, based on previous years' experience.

Welfare Payments

From months of incidence and estimates of per-month welfare benefits, total amounts of funding can be derived.

Estimated lifetime welfare payments are given in the bottom panel of Table 7.5. For the age period to 27, males in the program obtained welfare transfers of $2,945 on average; this compares favorably with no-program males who obtained $8,737 on average. However, these numbers are considerably smaller than the receipts to the females: $32,246 for the program females on average and $36,070 for the no-program females on average. For the ages 28 to 40, direct statements of financial assistance in cash and Food Stamps are available. Financial amounts for the three remaining welfare services are calculated from state records and eligibility rules obtained from the state government website (Michigan Government, 2004, *www.michigan.gov*). For this age period, program males report low welfare support compared to that allocated to the no-program males (averages of $739 vs. $5,724). For females, the program effect is in the opposite direction: Females in the program draw on $15,652 in welfare payments on average, compared to $6,763 for the no-program females on average. Finally, welfare receipt for the third age-profile is the product of total monthly welfare claims and per-month amounts of support. Per-month amounts are assumed to be the weighted average of the amounts for the prior age profiles. (There is very little growth in welfare payments in real terms.) These show welfare payments for program males averaging $2,158, compared to $8,713 for no-program males. For females, the payments average $28,377 and $22,006, respectively.

Across their entire lifetimes, members of the program group have received slightly less welfare. But this average obscures gender differences. Program males are estimated to have lower welfare receipts over their lifetimes by $17,331 per person; but program females are estimated to have more, by $11,438 per person.

For the social returns to the program, these welfare amounts are interpreted differently. Although welfare payments are a willing transfer between recipients and taxpayers, the net impact on taxpayers does not equal the absolute amount of transfers. The costs of administering the program, including the error rate in targeting the program, should be counted. The costs of administering all welfare disbursements are reported as 29.7% of total disbursements, and the error rate is 6.4%

(Family Independence Agency, 2003, *www.michigan.gov/fia*). Thus, the taxpayer cost of an additional welfare payment is 38% more than the amount the individual claimant receives. As shown in the bottom panel of Table 7.5, taxpayers save $23,916 per program male, but spend an additional $15,784 per program female. At the same time, the cost to society as a whole (taxpayers and recipients) is only the additional 38% administrative costs.

Program Costs and Additional Impacts

Costs of the Program

The costs of the program are taken directly from Barnett (1996). These costs have been described in full in earlier research. Information to derive these costs was taken from school district budgets and the program administration; both operating costs (instructional staff, administrative and support staff, overhead, supplies, and developmental screening) and capital costs (for classrooms and facilities) are included. However, these costs only refer to the expenditures on the program, which were funded by the taxpayer; they do not include expenditures by the program group members or their families. In undiscounted 2000 dollars, the cost of the program per participant was $15,827. (A discount rate must be applied to the program costs, because the program was extended over multiple years.) This cost is used in the cost-benefit analysis below.

Child Care and Educational Attainment Impacts of the Program

Additional program impacts that can be directly measured are child care and educational attainment. Child care over the period of the program unambiguously represents savings to parents, in free time and lower personal expenses. No new data are pertinent for these items, so earlier estimates from Barnett (1996) are used. Educational attainment counts both in the benefit and cost column: Where students progress more efficiently through the education system, there are savings; but, where the program promotes further educational attainment, costs are increased. The former effect is important: Both lower grade retention and less frequent placement in special education classes are associated with program participation (Barnett, 1996). These program costs are included in the cost-benefit analysis also.

Program participation is associated with higher educational attainment up to age 27 (see Chapter 3); this results in an increased financial burden on the taxpayer, as well as educational costs to the individual (see Barnett, 1996, pp. 35–38). In part because of higher on-time high school graduation rates, the program group had a lower rate of participation

Table 7.6

STATE AND INDIVIDUAL COSTS OF EDUCATIONAL ATTAINMENT AT
AGES 28 TO 40 PER PERSON

Educational Attainment at Ages 28 to 40	Program Group		No Program Group	
	Males	Females	Males	Females
State costs:	$2,814	$3,195	$2,455	$1,570
Program differentials	359	1,625		
Individual costs	*671*	*1,089*	*755*	*235*
Program differentials	*−84*	*855*		
N	*33*	*25*	*39*	*26*

Notes. Educational attainment costs for ages up to 27 are taken from Barnett (1996). No educational attainment costs are assumed for the age profile after 40.

in adult schooling up to age 27. The cost savings are not large, $338 for males and $968 for females. As regards higher education, program males reported fewer semester credits than did no-program males—the result is a saving of $916 per participant. For females, participation in the program is associated with considerably increased college progression, increasing the program costs by $1,933. These items are also carried over into the cost-benefit analysis.

As shown in Chapter 3, individuals continued to accumulate education credentials during the age profile 28 to 40. These extra credentials are costed using national data.[14] The extra educational attainment costs for the age period 28 to 40 are summarized in Table 7.6. (No additional educational attainment beyond age 40 is factored into this analysis, and GED recipients are regarded equivalent to high school graduates.) On average, the state incurred costs on educational attainment for those new high school graduates and for higher education attainment beyond high school. These amount to $2,814 per program male, compared to $2,455 per no-program male. For the program females, the amount is $3,195, compared to $1,570 for no-program females. For individuals, the expenses incurred were $671 per program male, compared with $755 per no-program male; and for the program females, expenditures were $1,089, considerably above the $235 expended by those not in the program.

[14] These data are from the *Digest of Education Statistics* (NCES, 2002b). For high school diplomas, the cost is assumed equivalent to the cost of 6 months of high school: in 2000, this was $3,827 (NCES, 2002b, Table 166). For associate and college degrees, the per full-time-equivalent median student expenditures in 1999–2000 were $8,924 at 2-year colleges and $13,517 at 4-year colleges; offsetting this are average tuition and fees payable by the students, which were $1,721 and $3,314, respectively (NCES, 2002b, Tables 312, 314, 334). For the Master's degrees, student expenditures are assumed to equal those at 4-year colleges, with the individual student contribution in tuition and fees at $8,429 (NCES, 2002b, Table 315). Each individual with course credits is assumed to have incurred one fifth of the costs for a 2-year degree, with a commensurate expenditure by the state. All figures exclude room and board expenditures.

Additional Unmeasured Impacts of the Program

There may be other consequences from the program that cannot be easily measured. These may include subjective assessments of how worthwhile the program was to participants or judgments about overall well-being and satisfaction later in life. Such benefits cannot easily be quantified and therefore they are omitted from the cost-benefit analysis. Insofar as there is a (weakly) positive correlation between subjective well-being and income/education (Frey & Stutzer, 2002), this omission is likely to bias the results toward finding no difference between the program and no-program group. Other financial and non-financial benefits may be mediated through the enhanced educational attainment of the program group (on the widespread and general benefits from education, see Wolfe & Zuvekas, 1997; on higher asset ownership, see above).

In particular, three factors should be noted that are not included in the cost-benefit analysis. (Inclusion in each case would widen the differences between the program group and no-program group.) First, there may be health status differences across the groups. Unadjusted cross-tabulations show several health advantages for the program group (see Chapter 6). From the perspective of the general public, many of these health status differences may be captured in differences in earnings or welfare receipt. (Health costs increase sharply as individuals age, raising reliance on Medicaid and Medicare.) For the individual, there may be genuine differences in quality of life.

The second factor to consider is the striking disparity between the program and no-program groups in mortality rates. Of the initial 58 program participants, 1 female and 1 male were deceased by age 40; of the 65 no-program group members, 2 females and 3 males were deceased. These mortality differences may be causal: Attanosio and Hoynes (2000) find a strongly positive correlation between low wealth and mortality, and life expectancies vary significantly across family backgrounds and education levels. In this analysis, the levels of earnings, criminal activity, and welfare receipt for these deceased individuals were given zero values across the age profiles.[15] However, no monetary values are included to compensate for loss of life directly.[16] Again, this produces a conservative estimate of the benefits of the program.

The third factor to note is the possibility of intergenerational program effects. These impacts may be especially important in a cost-

---

[15] An alternative approach is to treat these individuals as missing, and the most conservative approach is to impute missing values or zero values whenever this would bias downward the program effect. This latter approach was employed in initial testing to compare with the approach used in the final analysis. Because of discounting, these alternative mortality rate assumptions do not change the results substantially. The approach adopted in the tables is consistent with other policy evaluations.

[16] Imputing these costs is difficult (because of discounting); but they may influence the results substantially. From a meta-analysis of 33 studies, Mrozek and Taylor (2002) estimate the Value of a Statistical Life at $1.58–$2.64 million. Based on the relative probabilities across the program and no-program groups, the mortality impacts may be valued at $74,000 to $93,000 per person (undiscounted).

benefit framework: Impacts on the child of a parent at age 20 are discounted at a much lower rate than any earnings differences at age 40, for example. (A further motivation for looking at intergenerational effects is that they may alter societal inequities over the long term.) However, these effects are complex and differ across genders. They are therefore omitted from this analysis.

Cost-Benefit Analysis Results

Results for Participants and the General Public

The above analyses and related information in various chapters show considerable advantages to participation in the High/Scope Perry Preschool Project. These benefits should be compared to the program costs to produce a full cost-benefit calculation for the participants and for the general public. A third calculation is also made for the overall societal benefits, i.e., the sum of participant and general public benefits.

A range of estimates is produced to establish to what extent the benefits of the program exceed the costs. In the first instance, these estimates vary because different discount rates are applied. These different rates imply differences in the valuation of future benefits relative to the initial costs. In the sensitivity analysis, estimates vary because of changes in the assumptions underlying the cost calculations. In each case, tabulations are separated by gender and then averaged to derive the overall cost-benefit ratios.

Tables 7.7 to 7.9 report the cost-benefit analyses, with discount rates of 0%, 3%, and 7%. In each case, the top panel itemizes the program benefits. Some of these benefits—child care, educational investments up to age 27, and welfare receipt up to age 27—are taken directly from Barnett (1996). The remainder—educational investments after age 27, earnings, crime, and welfare receipt after age 27—are carried over from Tables 7.1 to 7.6. The middle panel reports the program costs. The final row reports benefits minus costs.

The first three columns of Tables 7.7–7.9 show the average net program benefits for participants. For the full sample, the program group individuals incurred some small educational costs over the age period 28 to 40, posted considerably higher earnings over their entire working life, and received somewhat lower welfare payments. The individuals do not bear the costs of crimes; they also did not bear any program costs. With a 0% discount rate, the result is a net benefit of $154,245 per person (final row, Table 7.7). Broken down by gender, the gains appear greater for program females: Whereas the average program male obtains net benefits of $127,250, the average program female gains $181,240. The program females accrue slightly larger advantages in lifetime earnings as well as positive welfare receipts after age 28. Applying a 3% discount rate, the overall gains from participation in the program average out at $63,267 (Table 7.8). When the discount rate is raised to 7%, the gains are still strongly positive at

Table 7.7

LIFETIME COST-BENEFIT ANALYSIS OF THE HIGH/SCOPE PERRY PRESCHOOL PROGRAM, DISCOUNT RATE = 0%

Source	Participants			General Public			Society (Participants and General Public)		
	Full Sample	Males	Females	Full Sample	Males	Females	Full Sample	Males	Females
PROGRAM BENEFITS									
Child care[a]	906	906	906	0	0	0	906	906	906
K–12 education[b]	0	0	0	11,917	16,594	7,239	11,917	16,594	7,239
Up to age 27[c]	0	0	0	(1,280)	1,254	(3,814)	(1,280)	1,254	(3,814)
Ages 28–40	(386)	84	(855)	(992)	(359)	(1,625)	(1,378)	(275)	(2,480)
Ages 41–65	0	0	0	0	0	0	0	0	0
Earnings									
Up to age 27	36,085	21,476	50,694	8,130	4,838	11,421	44,215	26,314	62,115
Ages 28–40	75,754	87,731	63,776	17,026	19,683	14,368	92,779	107,414	78,144
Ages 41–65	44,832	34,383	55,281	8,514	5,624	11,403	53,346	40,007	66,684
Crime									
Up to age 27	0	0	0	160,597	305,586	15,607	160,597	305,586	15,607
Ages 28–40	0	0	0	148,311	288,642	7,979	148,311	288,642	7,979
Ages 41–65	0	0	0	69,533	138,666	399	69,533	138,666	399
Welfare									
Up to age 27[d]	(4,808)	(5,792)	(3,823)	6,635	7,993	5,276	1,827	2,201	1,453
Ages 28–40	1,953	(4,984)	8,889	(2,710)	6,878	(12,297)	(757)	1,894	(3,408)
Ages 41–65	(91)	(6,554)	6,372	126	9,045	(8,793)	35	2,491	(2,421)
TOTAL BENEFITS	$154,245	$127,250	$181,240	$425,804	$804,444	$47,163	$580,049	$931,694	$228,403
PROGRAM COSTS[e]	0	0	0	15,827	15,827	15,827	15,827	15,827	15,827
NET BENEFITS	$154,245	$127,250	$181,240	$409,977	$788,617	$31,336	$564,222	$915,867	$212,576

Notes: All money values expressed in 2000 dollars. See earlier tables for sources.

[a] Barnett (1996, 28). [b] Barnett (1996, Table 13). [c] Barnett (1996, 36-38). [d] Barnett (1996, Table 27). [e] Barnett (1996, Table 4).

Table 7.8

LIFETIME COST-BENEFIT ANALYSIS OF THE HIGH/SCOPE PERRY PRESCHOOL PROGRAM, DISCOUNT RATE = 3%

Source	Participants			General Public			Society (Participants and General Public)		
	Full Sample	Males	Females	Full Sample	Males	Females	Full Sample	Males	Females
PROGRAM BENEFITS:									
Child care[a]									
K–12 education[b]	906	906	906	0	0	0	906	906	906
Up to age 27[c]	0	0	0	8,434	11,612	5,256	8,434	11,612	5,256
Ages 28–40	0	0	0	(719)	784	(2,222)	(719)	784	(2,222)
Ages 41–65	(160)	35	(354)	(412)	(149)	(674)	(571)	(114)	(1,028)
	0	0	0	0	0	0	0	0	0
Earnings									
Up to age 27	20,466	11,672	29,260	4,611	2,630	6,592	25,077	14,302	35,852
Ages 28–40	31,168	36,035	26,300	7,022	8,118	5,925	38,189	44,153	32,225
Ages 41–65	12,892	10,729	15,055	2,445	1,799	3,091	15,337	12,528	18,146
Crime									
Up to age 27	0	0	0	93,285	177,504	9,066	93,285	177,504	9,066
Ages 28–40	0	0	0	61,477	119,645	3,308	61,477	119,645	3,308
Ages 41–65	0	0	0	16,711	33,325	96	16,711	33,325	96
Welfare									
Up to age 27[d]	(2,793)	(3,364)	(2,221)	3,854	4,643	3,065	1,062	1,279	844
Ages 28–40	810	(2,066)	3,685	(1,117)	2,851	(5,085)	(308)	785	(1,400)
Ages 41–65	(22)	(1,575)	1,531	31	2,174	(2,113)	9	599	(582)
TOTAL BENEFITS	**$63,267**	**$52,372**	**$74,162**	**$195,621**	**$364,936**	**$26,305**	**$258,888**	**$417,308**	**$100,467**
PROGRAM COSTS[e]	**0**	**0**	**0**	**15,166**	**15,166**	**15,166**	**15,166**	**15,166**	**15,166**
NET BENEFITS	**$63,267**	**$52,372**	**$74,162**	**$180,455**	**$349,770**	**$11,139**	**$243,722**	**$402,142**	**$85,301**

Notes: All money values expressed in 2000 dollars. See earlier tables for sources.

[a] Barnett, 1996, page 28. [b] Barnett, 1996, Table 13. [c] Barnett, 1996, pp. 36-38. [d] Barnett, 1996, Table 27. [e] Barnett, 1996, Table 4.

Table 7.9

LIFETIME COST-BENEFIT ANALYSIS OF THE HIGH/SCOPE PERRY PRESCHOOL PROGRAM, DISCOUNT RATE = 7%

Source	Participants			General Public			Society (Participants and General Public)		
	Full Sample	Males	Females	Full Sample	Males	Females	Full Sample	Males	Females
PROGRAM BENEFITS:									
Child care[a]	862	862	862	0	0	0	862	862	862
K-12 education[b]	0	0	0	5,451	7,362	3,540	5,451	7,362	3,540
Up to age 27[c]	0	0	0	(279)	432	(989)	(279)	432	(989)
Ages 28–40	(64)	(11)	(116)	(135)	(49)	(220)	(198)	(60)	(336)
Ages 41–65	0	0	0	0	0	0	0	0	0
Earnings									
Up to age 27	9,933	5,334	14,532	2,238	1,202	3,274	12,171	6,536	17,806
Ages 28–40	10,138	11,718	8,557	2,284	2,640	1,928	12,422	14,358	10,485
Ages 41–65	2,668	2,406	2,930	505	411	599	3,173	2,817	3,529
Crime									
Up to age 27	0	0	0	46,807	89,064	4,549	46,807	89,064	4,549
Ages 28–40	0	0	0	20,114	39,145	1,082	20,114	39,145	1,082
Ages 41–65	0	0	0	2,837	5,658	16	2,837	5,658	16
Welfare									
Up to age 27[d]	(1,401)	(1,688)	(1,114)	1,934	2,330	1,538	533	642	424
Ages 28–40	265	(676)	1,206	(366)	933	(1,664)	(101)	257	(458)
Ages 41–65	(4)	(267)	260	5	369	(359)	2	102	(99)
TOTAL BENEFITS	$22,398	$17,678	$27,117	$81,396	$149,497	$13,294	$103,793	$167,175	$40,411
PROGRAM COSTS[e]	0	0	0	14,367	14,367	14,367	14,367	14,367	14,367
NET BENEFITS	$22,398	$17,678	$27,117	$67,029	$135,130	($1,073)	$89,426	$152,808	$26,044

Notes: All money values expressed in 2000 dollars. See earlier tables for sources.

[a] Barnett, 1996, p. 28. [b] Barnett, 1996, Table 13. [c] Barnett, 1996, pp. 36–38. [d] Barnett, 1996, Table 27. [e] Barnett, 1996, Table 4.

$22,398 (Table 7.9). This figure represents approximately 2% of total lifetime earnings.

The second set of columns in Tables 7.7–7.9 show the benefits to the general public. There are strong benefits from K–12 education savings in lower grade retention and special education placement; these outweigh the educational subsidies to higher college attainment over the ages 28 to 40. The net effect is lower educational expenditures and greater attainment for the program group. In terms of tax revenues, each age profile shows higher tax payments by the program group. However, the most important impact is the reduction in crime costs for the program group, particularly for the age profiles up to age 27 and from ages 28 to 40. These benefits are supplemented by lower welfare payments to the program group.

Using a 0% discount rate, set against the costs of the program at $15,827, the net benefit to the general public is $425,804 per participant (Table 7.7). As with the participant-level analysis, the program benefits vary by gender: General benefits per male participant are $804,444 whereas per female participant they are $47,163. This discrepancy arises because the crime savings for program males are substantial and welfare receipt for program females is higher. Table 7.8 shows the equivalent cost-benefit analysis with a 3% discount rate. This discount rate reduces the overall gains from the program, but the directional effects and gender relativities are unchanged. For the general public, the net benefits are high at $195,621; set against the costs, at a 3% discount rate, the program repays $12.90 for every dollar invested. Similarly, Table 7.9 uses a 7% discount rate to the streams of costs and benefits. The benefits remain positive at $81,396. Thus, for every dollar invested at a 7% discount rate, the yield to the general public is $5.67. Even at this discount rate, the program represents an investment that yields high returns.

The third set of columns in Tables 7.7–7.9 shows the overall impact on society. These represent the sum of benefits to the participants and society.

In addition to estimating net present value under alternative discount rates, we calculated the internal rate of return (IRR). The IRR is equal to the discount rate at which the net present value of costs and benefits are the same—i.e., it is the highest discount rate at which the program breaks even. For the *general public,* the estimated IRR from the program is 16.9%. The estimated internal rate of return for society as a whole is even higher, because it includes benefits to the participants as well—18.4%. Both rates are considerably above a critical threshold rate that might motivate investments in early childhood education programs and exceed rates of return calculated for other investments in education and training. These rates of return are more than double the historical rate of return to investments in the stock market (Siegel, 1998).

Sensitivity Analysis

The data available to estimate the cost-benefit ratio from investment in the High/Scope Perry Preschool Project are extremely rich, both in describing the circumstances of the participants and in following their lives over a long period of time. This gives confidence in estimating economic variables. Inevitably, however, a number of assumptions must be made about the economic consequences of the behaviors of the groups and about how livelihoods will change in the future. In this section, sensitivity analysis is performed to test how the results vary under different assumptions.

The sensitivity analysis focuses on plausible variations in the main determinants of the overall results, with each sensitivity analysis based on alternative data sources or citations. These sensitivity analyses are undertaken across the three discount rates. Thus, these analyses represent rederivations of the cost-benefit analyses reported above.

To motivate the sensitivity analysis, new assumptions are applied deliberately to understate and overstate the economic impact of the preschool program. Given that the program yields strongly positive benefits to participants, the primary focus is on how net benefits to society vary. This reanalysis yields what may be described as lower-level and upper-level estimates of the net present value of the program. This form of sensitivity analysis allows for the net benefits of the program to be bracketed. However, the main results are already based on conservative assumptions, so the lower-level estimates may be better described as "highly conservative" and the upper-level estimates as "less conservative," but not a measure of the maximum possible returns to the program.

To estimate the lower bound for the net present value, earnings, tax impacts, crime, and welfare receipts were recalculated. For the earnings calculations, a more conservative earnings profile was used. This profile has a lower fringe benefit rate and assumes no tax was applied to income up to a standard deduction of $4,750 (*www.irs.gov*), with a marginal tax rate of 15% applied above the standard deduction. For the crime burden calculations, criminal justice system costs were only applied to the number of arrests and not the number of crimes. For the welfare amounts, only female welfare receipt after age 40 was changed: this receipt was assumed to be a linear extrapolation of receipt during ages 28 to 40.

Similarly, to estimate the upper level for the net present value, earnings, welfare, crime, and tax impacts were recalculated. For the earnings calculations, a higher earnings profile was used (it assumes higher earnings growth beyond age 40). A more extensive calculation of welfare amounts was also assumed. For the crime analysis, the proportion of criminal justice system costs assumed to be allocated toward policing costs are estimated at 75% rather than 65.8% (the assumption applied above). Finally, the 25% tax rates applied by Barnett (1996) were used to calculate net tax revenues. In addition, deadweight loss estimates are factored into the analysis for both the crime and welfare costs. Deadweight losses arise because raising tax revenues for welfare payments and crime services imposes a distortion on the economic behavior of individuals. Based on a review of the evidence, this loss is conservatively assumed to be 15 cents per dollar of revenue raised (Fullerton, 1991). Both crime and welfare costs are increased by this factor.

Additional benefits are also introduced into this estimate, to see whether these alter the results. For the earnings profile, a 2% increase in productivity is assumed beyond age 40. This raises the returns, both in terms of earnings and tax contributions. A second potentially important benefit relates to health and the costs of health care.[17] These two items are included as a separate item in the upper-level sensitivity analysis.

Overall Conclusions and Policy Implications

As a summary, Table 7.10 presents the full distribution of returns, including the sensitivity analysis. These net benefits (i.e., total benefits minus costs) are broken down by gender; for participants, the public, and society; with different discount rates; and with lower, conservative, and upper range estimates. The cost-benefit analysis performed here shows strongly positive impacts from participation in the program and strongly positive gains for the general public in providing this program. Almost all the benefit estimates are strongly positive, significantly outweighing the costs of the program. Only under very restrictive assumptions (or high discount rates) do the returns become negative, and only then for the female subsample.

Figure 7.1 shows the results in terms of the distribution of benefits to the general public across the categories of education (including schooling), earnings, crime, and welfare disbursements (a 3% discount rate is applied). Clearly, the greatest impact is in terms of crime reduction, although the other benefits are substantial and the large crime reductions are not necessary to offset the costs of the program. Figure 7.2 compares the undiscounted lifetime earnings and lifetime crime costs of program and no-program males and program and no-program females. The biggest advantage is clearly due to the reduction in crime costs of males. Preschool program participants earned 14% more than they would have otherwise—$156,490 more per person in undiscounted 2000 dollars over their lifetimes. Male program participants cost the public 41% less in crime costs, $732,894 less per person in undiscounted 2000 dollars over their lifetimes.

Thus, the conclusion that the Perry Preschool Project was a sound investment is robust to the choice of discount rate and to variations in assumptions about the costs of crime, earnings, and welfare. Moreover, this conclusion supports the analysis undertaken by Barnett (1996). In fact, the empirical projections used in that analysis are very close to the actual outcomes from the program.

With regard to **policy implications,** this analysis reaffirms—and even strengthens—Barnett's (1996) conclusions: **The High/Scope Perry**

---

[17] For this analysis, differential rates of smoking are included (37% of the program males vs. 48% of the no-program males and 53% of the program females vs. 59% of the no-program females smoke). The average amount of health care spending per person per year in the U.S. is $2,500 (Cutler, 2002). One estimate is that smokers spend around 20% more on health care than those who have never smoked; an alternative cost estimate is that 8% of all health care spending is smoking-related (Hodgson, 1992). Thus, the annual additional health care cost of smoking ranges between $200 and $500 per year. Assuming health care costs are split between the individual and the taxpayer, these annualized amounts can be included as additional benefits.

Table 7.10

SENSITIVITY ANALYSIS FOR NET PROGRAM BENEFITS

Source	Participants			General Public			Society (Participants and General Public)		
	Full Sample	Males	Females	Full Sample	Males	Females	Full Sample	Males	Females
Lower-range estimates									
Discount rate = 0%	$143,498	$113,036	$173,960	$240,862	$479,601	$2,123	$384,360	$592,637	$176,083
Discount rate = 3%	57,454	46,714	68,194	99,750	199,999	(500)	157,204	246,713	67,694
Discount rate = 7%	20,038	15,876	24,200	32,136	69,795	(5,524)	52,174	85,671	18,676
Conservative-estimates									
Discount rate = 0%	154,245	127,250	181,240	409,977	788,617	31,336	564,222	915,867	212,576
Discount rate = 3%	63,267	52,372	74,162	180,455	349,770	11,139	243,722	402,142	85,301
Discount rate = 7%	22,398	17,678	27,117	67,029	135,130	(1,073)	89,426	152,808	26,044
Upper-range estimates									
Discount rate = 0%	199,244	189,897	208,590	550,702	1,036,543	64,861	749,946	1,226,440	273,451
Discount rate = 3%	70,953	63,687	78,218	237,468	449,590	25,346	308,421	513,277	103,564
Discount rate = 7%	22,495	18,263	26,727	88,298	172,228	4,367	110,793	190,491	31,094

Notes: For lower range and upper range estimates see Barnett, Belfield, & Nores (2004).
For conservative estimates, see Tables 7.7–7.9.

Figure 7.1

HIGH/SCOPE PERRY PRESCHOOL PROGRAM PUBLIC COSTS AND BENEFITS

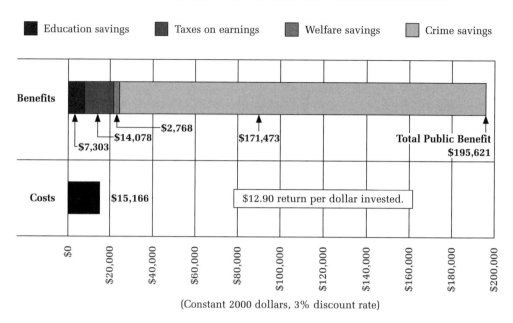

(Constant 2000 dollars, 3% discount rate)

Figure 7.2

LIFETIME EARNINGS AND CRIME COSTS BY PRESCHOOL EXPERIENCE
(2000 DOLLARS, 0% DISCOUNT)

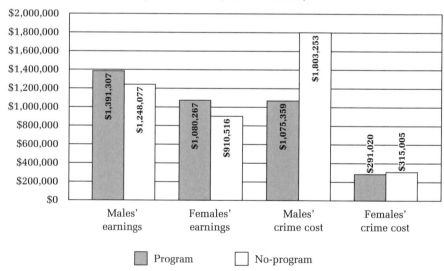

Preschool Project yields considerable returns both to the individual and society, with a very high rate of return. But would similar returns be anticipated under current economic conditions? Would similar returns be anticipated for public preschool programs for all children in poverty and for the population more generally?

To extrapolate as to the returns to investment in a similar program under current conditions requires predictions regarding the four main components of the cost-benefit analysis: education, earnings, crime, and welfare. For each component, it seems likely that the relationships reported in this analysis would be maintained or strengthened.

One important saving from the program was the reduction in expenditures for schooling up to age 18. Educational costs (including special education) have risen sharply over the last 2 decades, at a rate considerably beyond inflation (NCES, 2002a). Reasons for this trend may include enhanced opportunities for females outside of teaching (raising teachers' salaries) and the move towards smaller class sizes (Hanushek, 1998). Moreover, few technological changes in teaching have occurred, and along with flat standardized test scores and static dropout rates, productivity growth may not have kept pace with cost increases or with productivity growth in other industries (see Hoxby, 1999). Thus, it is plausible that the unit cost of schooling will keep rising. Preschool programs that subsequently reduce grade repetition and lower special education placement are likely to remain cost-effective.

Current earnings profiles also augur well for high returns to investment in preschool programs. For low-skill males, real earnings have increased relatively little since the 1970s; and education has grown in importance in determining wages (Carneiro & Heckman, 2003). Thus, a preschool program that raises education and skill levels may be an important way to raise economic well-being through enhanced employment prospects.

For males, the most important impact of the preschool program was in reducing criminal activity. This reduction may have been direct, in influencing predispositions towards crime, and indirect, in enhancing opportunities in the labor market. Following a similar pattern to schooling costs, policing and criminal justice system costs have been increasing beyond the rate of inflation within the last decade (Stephan, 1999). The growth in aggregate spending has been dramatic: In real terms between 1982 and 2001, police spending rose by 208%, judicial spending by 264%, and corrections spending by 343% (BJS, 2002a). Programs that raise economic status and reduce crime rates appear to be high-yield.

Finally, welfare costs are unlikely to impact adversely on the yield of future programs: Most recent reforms have reduced entitlements and tightened time limits for welfare (Blank & Ellwood, 2002). However, given that welfare differences between program and no-program groups were not large, subsequent changes to welfare reforms and entitlements are unlikely to have much influence on the overall returns to an investment in preschool programs.

The major determinants of how well our results will generalize to large-scale public preschool programs are the extent to which the characteristics of the preschool programs, children served, and broader context depart from those in this study. As is discussed elsewhere in the monograph, similar results depend on having a high-quality preschool program that effectively contributes to gains in social and emotional development as well as in cognitive development. The issue of context was discussed above in terms of changing economic circumstances. This leaves the question of the differences between the particular sample for this study, economically disadvantaged children generally, and the general population. Although much remains to be learned, existing research provides useful insights.

Many studies of preschool program impact have found sizeable effects for children from low-income families, regardless of ethnic background (Barnett, 2002). Studies tend to find smaller effects for less disadvantaged children. Nevertheless, even children from middle-income families have fairly high rates of school failure and dropout (more than 1 in 10) as well as substantially lower levels of cognitive and social skill levels at entry to kindergarten, compared to children from high-income families (Barnett, Brown, & Shore, 2004). Particularly useful is a recent evaluation of the impacts of Oklahoma's universal preschool program in Tulsa (Gormley, Gayer, Phillips, & Dawson, 2004). This study found substantial effects for all children, including those who qualified only for a reduced price school lunch and those who qualified for no lunch subsidy at all. As a whole, the evidence indicates that preschool programs yield the largest gains for children from lower-income families, but that gains for children who are not poor can still be quite substantial.

Given the size of the estimated benefits, the generalization of the results for crime is particularly important. It is reasonable to expect that even for low-income populations generally, impacts on crime might be smaller than in this study because of the very high levels of crime and arrest rates for this study's control group. However, it should be noted that the juvenile arrest rates in this study (15% preschool, 26% no-preschool) are extremely similar to those in the Chicago Child-Parent Centers study (17% preschool, 25% no-preschool). Even if the benefits from crime reduction from preschool programs for children in poverty generally were only one third those estimated in this study, they would still be quite large. Even more remarkably, if crime benefits were only 10% of what is estimated here (averaged across all children, perhaps), they would still by themselves pay for the preschool program (discounted at 3%).

In sum, the evidence presented here can inform public policy and indicates a compelling motive for wider public investment in highly effective preschool education.[18] It seems likely that the benefits per child would be smaller as the program expands to children who are less disadvantaged than those in this study, other things being equal. At the same time, there are reasons to believe that changes in the social context have increased the payoff to investing in preschool education. Finally, there are questions of general equilibrium (systemic) effects from wider provision of highly effective preschool education. Programs that reach most or all children in

---

[18] Inference for other countries must be performed with caution. In particular, differences from the U.S., in terms of how labor markets and criminal justice systems operate, must be appreciated.

a community might change classroom climate, teacher expectations, and the curriculum up through the grades. This could increase the productivity of education from kindergarten on, thereby leading to even larger gains. However, large-scale programs might produce lower returns if impacts on grade retention and special education are attenuated, or later benefits from crime reduction or increased earnings are diminished because a substantial portion of the population has higher education levels, skills, and abilities. Evidence with respect to these possibilities is not conclusive. For example, despite substantial increases in the educational attainment of the U.S. population in the 1990s, the returns to education increased.

VIII Paths From Preschool to Success at Age 40

This chapter presents a structural equation model that specifies the paths from preschool experience to educational attainment, earnings, and arrests by age 40. It replaces the age 27 terminal variables used earlier and otherwise updates earlier models (Schweinhart et al., 1993; Barnett et al., 1998). *Beginning with preschool experience and children's preprogram intellectual performance, it traces relationships presumed causal to children's postprogram intellectual performance, then to their school achievement and commitment to schooling, then to their educational attainment, then to their adult earnings and lifetime arrests.*

The purpose of this analysis is exploratory rather than confirmatory. It presses the limits of the data in two ways. First, it slightly exceeds the maximum parameters for a model permitted by a sample size of 123 study participants. According to Kline (1998), "If the subject/parameter ratio is less than 5:1, the statistical stability of the results may be doubtful," which translates to 25 parameters (variances, covariances, and paths). With 31 parameters, the model presented here takes full advantage of the sample size to explain findings established by its experimental design. In fact, the actual causal model is surely much more complex than the one presented, so this model offers no more than a simple outline of what is happening in the study. Given the wealth of data in the study, we first focused on variables that fit conceptually and temporally and that had been used in previous models. When possible, we combined similar variables to increase their reliability and to maintain the sample size by reducing missing data on variables.

Second, because the structural-equation model presented in this chapter assumes multivariate normality, the correlational analyses assume that the variables are normally distributed. We recognize, however, that most of these variables were not normally distributed. Skewness and kurtosis are two measures of how actual distributions differ from normal distributions. Skewness is a measure of the asymmetry of a distribution, whether it is the same to the left and right of center. Kurtosis is a measure of whether the data are peaked or flat relative to a normal distribution. Of the seven variables other than preschool experience, all but postprogram intellectual performance showed statistically significant evidence ($p < .05$) of combined skewness and kurtosis. Preprogram intellectual performance, achievement, earnings, and arrests were significantly skewed. Commitment to schooling, educational attainment, and arrests had significant kurtosis.

Comparison with the 1993 model. Like the model by Schweinhart et al. (1993), the model presented here includes preschool experience and postprogram intellectual performance, and replaces educational attainment by age 27, annual earnings at age 27, and arrests by age 27 with their age 40 counterparts. It includes preprogram intellectual performance rather than family socioeconomic status as a background variable because its inclusion tightens the focus on the contribution of preschool experience to intellectual performance. The model includes commitment to schooling rather than motivation because, while both variables assess the motivational effect of preschool experience, self-reported commitment to schooling had a higher correlation with preschool experience and taps how study participants see themselves, whereas teacher-rated motivation taps how teachers see the study participants. This model does not include years in mental impairment programs or literacy at age 19, as did the 1993 model, but does include achievement at age 14, which had a stronger correlation with preschool experience and is conceptually juxtaposed with commitment to schooling. Achievement at age 14 was excluded from the 1993 model because of missing data, but this time age 10 achievement data were used for the cases with missing age 14 achievement data.

Variables Considered But Not Selected for the Model

Other variables were considered but not selected for this model. The main reason is that the number of parameters included in the analysis had to be minimized due to the sample size. Although elimination of initial socioeconomic status and gender from the model reduces the amount of variance explained, it creates no major bias in preschool experience effects because neither of these variables is significantly correlated with preschool experience. Mental impairment treatment, grade repetition, mother's participation (included in the model by Barnett et al., 1998), and personal misconduct (included as "personal behavior" in the model by Barnett et al., 1998) were not included because their correlations with preschool experience and major outcomes were weaker than the variables included. Two other variables—gender-by-preschool-experience and childhood intellectual performance—were excluded only after lengthy deliberation.

Gender-by-preschool-experience (that is, the interaction term comprising program males, no-program males, program females, and no-program females) was not selected because it did not significantly affect the relationship between preschool experience and postprogram intellectual performance. Rather, it entered into the study later with significant differences between program females and no-program females on mental impairment treatment (8% vs. 36%), grade repetition (21% vs. 41%), and high school dropout (12% vs. 52%), as presented in Chapter 3. Mental impairment treatment and grade repetition are based on judgments made by teachers with the support of special education personnel. Apparently, the preschool program affected children's behavior in a way that influenced teachers' appraisals of girls, but not boys.

Childhood intellectual performance (Stanford-Binet IQs at ages 8, 9, and 10 averaged) was not selected, to keep the model parsimonious. This model differs from the one by Barnett et al. (1998), which included early and later IQ and achievement, but focused on only one terminal outcome—educational attainment—not earnings or crime. In the 1998 model, the temporary effect of preschool experience on IQ appears as a positive path between preschool and postprogram IQ, followed by a positive path from postprogram to childhood IQ and a negative path from preschool experience to childhood IQ. This pattern is another way of representing the notorious fadeout of the preschool effect on IQ, which failed to support the original hypothesis that preschool programs would lead to a permanent improvement in intellectual performance and thereby have long-term effects. Instead, in this study, childhood intellectual performance functions as a negative mediator, that is, as a damper on preschool program effects. As such, it does not exactly fit in a model of preschool program effectiveness. Further, in the 1998 model, childhood intellectual performance was only weakly related to later achievement (standardized beta weight = .11). The rise and fall of intellectual performance as a result of preschool experience probably says more about intellectual performance than about preschool program effectiveness. Intellectual performance appears to be sensitive to environmental stimulation (Schweinhart & Weikart, 1980). In the presence of a stimulating preschool program, it improves; in its absence, it declines. As program and no-program groups moved into the same school environment, their mean intellectual performance converged.

Variables Selected for the Model

We selected the following eight variables for the model:

1. **Preschool experience:** No preschool program or preschool program.

2. **Preprogram intellectual performance:** Stanford-Binet IQs (Terman & Merrill, 1960) at study entry, at age 4 for the oldest class, age 3 for the younger classes.

3. **Postprogram intellectual performance:** Stanford-Binet IQs (Terman & Merrill, 1960) after 1 and 2 years of the preschool program, at ages 4 and 5 averaged.

4. **Commitment to schooling:** Factor score for three items collected at age 15 from study participants—*schoolwork requires home preparation and days per week doing some homework;* and from their parents—*Is your child willing to talk about school? (Enjoys it, talks when asked, doesn't like to, or refuses).*

5. **Achievement:** California Achievement Tests (Tiegs & Clark, 1971) total standard scores at age 14 (age 10 if age 14 score missing).

6. **Educational attainment:** Years of schooling completed through age 40; grade of high school dropout, high school graduation = 12, associate's degree = 14, bachelor's degree = 16, and master's degree = 18. The Pearson product-moment correlation between this variable and the age 27 one was .856 (two-tailed $p < .01$, $n = 119$).

7. **Earnings:** Earnings in the past calendar year reported by study participants on the age 40 interview, including estimates from responses to related interview items. The Pearson product-moment correlation between this variable and the age 27 one was .582 (two-tailed $p < .01$, $n = 105$).

8. **Arrests:** Through age 40—total of juvenile arrests, arrests through age 27, and arrests from ages 28 to 40. The Pearson product-moment correlation between this variable and the age 27 one was .877 for arrests (two-tailed $p < .01$, $n = 121$).

Table 8.1 presents a correlation matrix of these eight variables, using Pearson product-moment correlations. Preschool experience was significantly correlated with postprogram intellectual performance, commitment to schooling, achievement, and arrests, but not with educational attainment and earnings because of differences in scaling between these variables and those presented in earlier chapters. Most of the variables in the matrix were significantly correlated with one another except for preprogram intellectual performance, selected to isolate the effect of preschool experience on postprogram intellectual performance. The strongest correlation in the matrix was between preschool experience and postprogram intellectual performance.

The Model

As Figure 8.1 shows, the model begins with preschool experience and children's preprogram intellectual performance, which influence their postprogram intellectual performance, which influences their school achievement and commitment to schooling, which influence their educational attainment, which influences their adult earnings and lifetime arrests.

Earnings and arrests appear in the model as continuous variables, despite the fact that their data are skewed. We considered collapsing them into four or seven categories, but found that they fit the model better as continuous variables. To see how much their skewness might be affecting the findings, we examined scatterplots of their relationships with educational attainment—their only connection to the rest of the model. For either variable, we identified four cases as outliers (cases with educational attainment of 16–18 years or over 40 arrests), then examined their Pearson product-moment correlations with educational attainment, with and without the outliers. For educational attainment and earnings, the correlations were .433 with the outliers and .407 without them. For educational attainment and arrests, the correlations were −.269 with the outliers and −.267 without them. We concluded that the model was not distorted by outliers in earnings and arrests.

The structural equation model was estimated with the Amos program, version 4.01 (Arbuckle, 1999). Of the eight observed variables in the model, two exogenous ones initiate the model—preschool experience and preprogram intellectual performance—and six endogenous ones continue the model—postprogram intellectual performance, commitment to schooling, achievement, educational attainment, arrests, and earnings. The model has six unobserved exogenous error terms, one for each of the endogenous variables, for a total of 14 variables in the model. It has 31 parameters and a sample size of 123, four cases per parameter, one less

Table 8.1

MATRIX OF PEARSON PRODUCT-MOMENT CORRELATIONS OF CAUSAL MODEL CANDIDATE VARIABLES

Variable	Cases	Preschool Experience	Preprogram IQ	Postprogram IQ	Commitment	Achievement	Educational Attainment	Earnings
Preschool experience	123							
Preprogram IQ	123	.080						
Postprogram IQ	123	.509**	.439**					
Commitment	97	.317**	.140	.481**				
Achievement	116	.263**	.177	.454**	.359**			
Educational attainment	119	.166	.191*	.415**	.429**	.452**		
Earnings	112	.109	.176	.308**	.346**	.224*	.433**	
Arrests	123	−.190*	−.122	−.226*	−.263**	−.267**	−.269**	−.277**

$*$ p (two-tailed) < .05; $**$ p (two-tailed) < .01.

Figure 8.1

A MODEL OF THE PATHS FROM PRESCHOOL EXPERIENCE TO SUCCESS AT 40

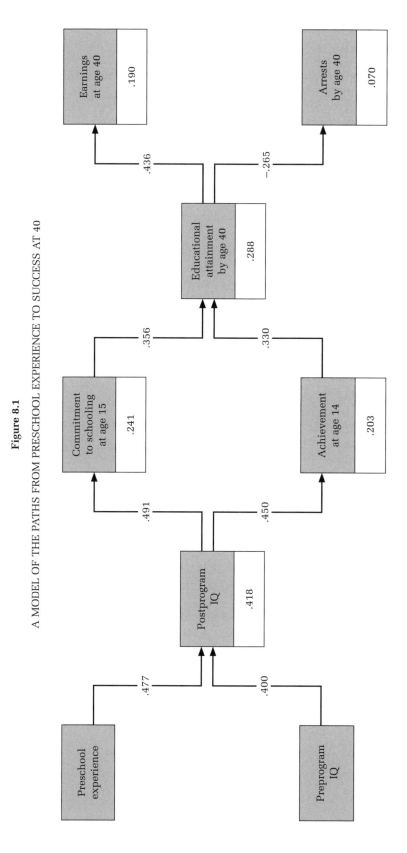

Note. Path coefficients are standardized regression weights, all statistically significant at *p* < .01; coefficients in each box are squared multiple correlations.

than the minimum recommended by Kline (1998). Thus, this analysis cannot and does not stand alone, but must be considered in the light of supportive theory and similar findings in other studies. Figure 8.1 presents the estimates of the standardized regression weights for each path. Five of the eight paths have weights over .400, and all were statistically significant at $p < .01$. This model meets the standards for goodness of fit: The probability of its chi-square statistic (24.639, with 19 degrees of freedom), which exceeds .100 when the model is a good fit for the data, was .173. The root mean square error of approximation (RMSEA)—for which less than .05 indicates a close fit, .05 to .08 indicates a fair fit, and over .10 indicates a poor fit—was .049, with a 90% confidence interval ranging from .000 to .099.

To determine whether gender affected the model, a pair of multi-sample analyses were performed on the 72 males and 51 females in the sample. For one analysis, all coefficients were allowed to vary between males and females; for the other, regression weights were constrained to be equal for males and females. The difference in the chi-square statistic between these nested models was 8.224, with a difference of 8 degrees of freedom. Its probability was greater than .3, indicating that the difference between models was not statistically significant. Constraining the coefficients to be equal did not significantly degrade the model. There is no evidence that the coefficients are different for males and females.

The following paragraphs consider the meaning and implications of each step in this path:

- **Preschool experience and children's preprogram intellectual performance influence their postprogram intellectual performance.** The primary effect of the High/Scope Perry Preschool Project was on children's postprogram intellectual performance, which was of course rooted in their preprogram intellectual performance. The relationship between children's preschool experience and their postprogram intellectual performance is actually stronger than the relationship between their preprogram and postprogram intellectual performance.

  The path from preschool experience to postprogram intellectual performance is the only path in the model that leads directly from preschool experience. The obvious, but probably incorrect, conclusion is that the preschool program's only effect was on children's intellectual performance. We agree with leading social scientists who have argued, despite mixed evidence, that high-quality preschool programs have important effects on the motivation and socioemotional development of participants (Carneiro & Heckman, 2003; Shonkoff & Phillips, 2000; Zigler & Butterfield, 1968) and earlier in this monograph proposed improvements in program participants' impulse control and anticipation of consequences as mediators between preschool experience and lower crime rates. The relationship between postprogram intellectual performance and program participants' commitment to schooling is the strongest in the model. This fact suggests that IQ tests tap children's commitment to schooling as well as their intellectual ability. Further, the direct measures of commitment and motivation in the study, in comparison with IQ tests, were not as valid, precise, or focused on an immediate preschool program effect. Self-reported commitment to schooling was not assessed until study participants were 15 years old—10 years after the preschool program. Motivation was assessed by teacher ratings when study participants were 6 to 9 years old, beginning a year after the preschool program and judged by teachers rather than reported by the study participants themselves.

- **Children's postprogram intellectual performance influences their school achievement and commitment to schooling.** Children's postprogram intellectual performance served as the gateway for preschool program effects on school achievement and commitment to schooling—two inseparable aspects of what it takes to succeed in school. Although the model does not represent this relationship, achievement and commitment interact with each other: High achievement leads to higher commitment, and higher commitment leads to higher achievement. The opposite also holds: Low achievement leads to lower commitment, and lower commitment leads to lower achievement. This pattern is the school application of social bonding theory, developed to explain how juvenile delinquency develops (Elliott, Ageton, & Canter, 2002). The idea is that a person's various bonds of commitment to social institutions keep them from committing delinquent acts.

  It should be noted, however, that it takes some years for high-quality preschool programs to exert their indirect effect on school achievement. The High/Scope Perry Preschool Project's strongest effect on school achievement was not apparent until participants were 14 years old, and probably was the result of a cumulative effect of children's stronger commitment to schooling resulting in more supportive treatment by school staff. It is also possible that program effects on participants' commitment to schooling and school achievement originated during the actual program, but could not be reliably and validly measured until children got older.

- **Children's school achievement and commitment to schooling influence their educational attainment.** School achievement and commitment to schooling together constitute successful adaptation to schooling, which culminates in educational attainment. Students drop out of school because of a weak commitment to schooling as a result of low achievement. Students graduate from high school and choose to participate in higher education because of a strong commitment to schooling as a result of high achievement or sheer tenacity.

- **Young people's educational attainment influences their adult earnings and lifetime arrests.** Those who stay in school longer get better paying jobs and commit fewer crimes. Much as postprogram intellectual performance serves as a gateway for preschool program effects, educational attainment, particularly high school graduation, is widely and properly viewed as the gateway to adult success. The positive effects of preschool experience on earnings and crime rates flow through schooling, not outside it.

IX Case Studies

In the past, when reporting the longitudinal results of the High/Scope Perry Preschool study, detailed personal information about specific cases has been included, in addition to the results exploring group differences in the full sample. The examination of specific cases adds greater depth to the study of the influence and interplay of the multiple factors affecting the lives of the study participants. Additional insight is gained from the study participants' expression, in their own words, of their struggles, their goals, and their values.

The case studies were first presented in depth in the age 19 report (Berrueta-Clement et al., 1984) and then again at age 27 (Schweinhart et al., 1993).[19] In those presentations, specific themes relating to the developmental stage of the study participants were explored in the lives of the 8 case study participants and discussed in relationship to the significant group differences obtained in the full analysis. Among the case studies, the individuals who were more or less successful were identified. At age 19, the case study themes related to *determinants* of success and included parental roles, attitudes toward money, role models, church and religion, sense of responsibility, and personality and goal orientation. In the lives studied, success was more likely for those whose parents supported schooling, who found positive role models for achievement, and who evidenced a sense of responsibility for other people or causes beyond themselves and their own personal gain.

When these same cases were reviewed at age 27, the themes that emerged were relevant to the challenges the young people faced as they strove to establish themselves as independent adults. The four themes—schooling, employment and earnings, criminal records, and relationship to the next generation—took into account their present status and future goals and served as *manifestations* of success in young adulthood. At that time, success was manifested by commitment to learning, involvement in meaningful and legitimate work roles, and desire to share positive values with the younger generation. Thus, positive educational experiences, a supportive environment, opportunities to achieve, and a sense of responsibility were early and consistent influences that appear to foster a successful life path.

As the study participants reach midlife, the indicators of a successful life remain essentially unchanged. Following are the four life themes that are explored at midlife:

- Education

- Employment and earnings

- Criminal records

- Family, health, and community life

This chapter begins with a presentation of the methodology of the case study research, followed by a narrative summary of the lives of each of

---

[19] The research and presentation of the case studies in previous volumes was done by Ann S. Epstein, a long-time High/Scope staff member. The authors gratefully acknowledge her contributions to this research and have drawn extensively from her previous work in the preparation of this chapter.

the 8 case study participants. In the final section, the relationship of the four themes to the participants' life success is discussed and some conclusions are presented.

Case Study Methodology

The 8 case study participants[20] were originally chosen to represent a range of backgrounds, experiences, and developmental paths. Those selected for the case studies did not constitute a random sample. When initially selected in their early 20s, participants were balanced across three dichotomies—program versus no-program, male versus female, and successful versus unsuccessful in terms of education, economic, and social-outcome variables. The goal was to investigate the benefits that could be obtained from experience, apart from the preschool program, and the barriers that even a high-quality preschool program had little chance of overcoming. The same 8 individuals were followed for the case study investigations at age 27 and at midlife. Although originally selected in terms of their life success or lack thereof, at each subsequent point of follow-up, it was not known whether their life paths would continue with the same patterns of success.

The database for the case studies is extensive. For the age 19 report, the sources for the case study data were the following:

- Family background information and home-visiting records from the preschool years
- Teacher ratings and comments from the preschool program and elementary grades
- Standardized test scores
- School records and psychological evaluations
- Interviews with study participants at age 15 and with their parents
- Interviews with study participants at age 19
- Open-ended follow-up interviews (shortly after the age 19 assessment) with the case study participants and their parents.

Additional data sources at age 27:

- Interviews with study participants at age 27
- School records
- Crime records
- Social service records

---

[20] All names have been changed to protect the identities of the study participants.

Interviews conducted when study participants were in their early 20s, as well as portions of the age 27 interviews, were audiotaped and transcribed, allowing for the use of extensive direct quotes.

Data sources for the midlife case study investigation included all of the above plus the following:

- A personal interview at approximately age 40
- Updates of criminal records
- Updates of social service records

Answers to a series of open-ended questions inquiring about life goals, values, and future plans were audiotaped at the end of all but 2 of the 8 interviews (Gerald Daniels and Marlene Franklin). The questions were asked and the answers recorded in writing for Gerald Daniels; for Marlene Franklin there are no answers recorded. The interviewer was the same man who interviewed the participants at age 27; he was unaware of their group status or that they were case study participants. The case study analysis and report preparation were done by a researcher who had no personal contact with the study participants.

When reading the case study presentations, it is important to remember that statistically valid conclusions cannot be drawn from the lives portrayed. As in previous monographs, the case studies presented here are meant to complement the statistical analyses presented in other chapters. The cases are presented to give life and depth to the study participants and as a source of hypotheses about the interrelationships among the complex factors at work in their lives.

Case Studies

Each of the case studies begins with a summary of the profile presented in previous monographs, first when the participants were in their early 20s, and again when they were in their late 20s. Following this summary is an update of each person's status at midlife. In the final section of this chapter, the case studies are examined from the perspective of the four life success themes: education; employment and earnings; criminal records; and family, health, and community life. The themes are derived from previous case study reports and the statistical analyses presented in earlier chapters.

Jerry Andrews (Program Group, Male)

Jerry came from a family in which the importance of education had been stressed for several generations. His mother was involved in the preschool program while Jerry attended, serving as a classroom aide and actively participating in home visits. Although his parents divorced when he was quite young, Jerry's uncles provided him with strong role models while he was growing up and encouraged him to attend college. Jerry's mother also acknowledged that his father, even after the divorce, motivated their son to excel academically. Jerry agreed, but also saw important influences in his life from outside his family—friends who shared his academic interests and the teachers and school counselors who encouraged him in his studies.

Living up to the family's educational values was important to Jerry. In high school he received an academic award for earning all A's in his senior year, and at age 20 he was enrolled in a preengineering program at a community college while working half-time as a packer at a large thrift store to finance his schooling. At that time, he planned to eventually enter the University of Michigan to obtain an engineering degree with a specialty in drafting.

When interviewed at age 27, Jerry had not fulfilled his educational goals, but they were still his central goals. He had completed 3 years of college at a community college and still planned to complete a bachelor's degree in engineering or architecture at a 4-year university in the next 2 or 3 years. At that time, Jerry was working 68 hours a week at two jobs—full-time as a mail carrier and part-time as a produce clerk at a supermarket—and saving as much money as possible to finance his schooling. He had never been married and did not have any children. He lived alone in a rented 4-room apartment, had close ties with family and friends, and thought he was "doing great." He believed he was an important and positive influence on those who knew him.

Jerry at midlife

By midlife, Jerry's life has changed considerably. When he was in his mid-30s, Jerry moved to Florida and married. He has 4 children, 2 of them born before he moved south. His children range in age from 1 year to 10 years. The 2 oldest children attend primary school and, according to Jerry, are "almost never a problem." When asked about his expectations for his children, Jerry said he expects them to attend college and hopes they will earn master's degrees.

Jerry's strong work ethic remains unchanged. He reports that he has been steadily employed for the past 15 years. He now works as a mail carrier 46 hours a week and also as a cabin service employee at the airport for 40 hours a week. Between the two jobs his monthly income is $4,880. Although Jerry did not return to school to complete his bachelor's degree as planned, he is currently studying to obtain his commercial driver's license and become a commercial truck driver. He has no further educational plans at this time.

In spite of his history as a hard worker, Jerry encountered financial difficulties in his late 20s and had to declare bankruptcy. His financial situation appears stable at this time. He reports a yearly income of $54,000 with an additional $13,000 from his spouse, who works in a grocery store. He owns the 11-room house where he lives with his wife and children, has two cars, a retirement plan, life insurance, credit cards, and health insurance. He states that he has never received money from the social service system.

Jerry is pleased with his life. He says he does not smoke, drink alcohol, or take illegal drugs, and is in excellent health. He gets along well

Table 9.1

PROFILE OF JERRY ANDREWS
PROGRAM GROUP, MALE

Variable	Status at Age 27	Status at Age 40
Schooling	3 years college completed; plans to complete B.A in engineering or architecture by age 40	3 years college completed; studying for commercial driver's license
Employment	Full-time mail carrier; part-time produce clerk	Works two full-time jobs: mail carrier and airport cabin service
Earnings	$2,600 per month	$54,000/year; spouse $13,000/year
Welfare	None	None
Marriage	Single, never married, not cohabiting	Married in mid-30s to current spouse
Children	None	4 children ranging in age from 2 to 10 years
Residence	Rented apartment	Owns home
Community involvement	None	None
Criminal record	None	One misdemeanor

with his birth family and people in general. Although he says religion is only somewhat important to him, his children attend a Catholic school. He says his main personal goal right now "is to make sure that I can keep them in that school 'cause they have a real good education system in there, and I think they'll come out a lot better . . .". The best aspect of his life right now is his family and "watching them grow." He takes pride in the fact that he is able to provide them with a safe environment and a good education. He sees no obstacles in his way and advises young people to take responsibility for their lives: "Find a goal that you want and do what it takes to achieve it. You really can't blame anybody if you don't."

Yvonne Barnes (No-Program Group, Female)

At age 20, Yvonne lived with her parents in the house where she grew up. Although she graduated from high school, her school records were dotted with academic problems and disciplinary incidents from the time she entered kindergarten. As early as first grade, a psychological report noted that Yvonne was highly anxious and withdrawn and had poor psychomotor coordination. Records also show that Yvonne had several stays in detention centers as a juvenile.

Yvonne described her school days as a time of "hanging out." She did just enough work to get by. At age 20, looking back, Yvonne regretted that she did not do better. She was determined to leave home and reported vague plans to get a job or enter college or enlist in the Army, but admitted that unless she changed her behavior, she would go nowhere.

At age 27, Yvonne presented a mixed picture of someone who was a hard worker, but also had a continuing history of social misconduct and run-ins with the law. She stated that she had a culinary arts certificate from the local community college and had worked in restaurants for the past 7 years. Her goal, at that time, was to open her own restaurant within the next 5 years. In addition to her full-time job as a cook, she worked part-time as a housekeeper at a hotel. Yvonne still lived with her mother and grandparents in a 6-room house, although she admitted that she did not get along with them and they were disappointed in her. She paid her share of the monthly rent and other bills.

Yvonne continued to get into trouble with authorities. Court records showed 15 misdemeanor incidents between the ages of 20 and 27, including several assault and battery charges, petty larceny, and drug possession. She had paid fines, and served time in jail and on probation. She had a history of psychiatric care in her mid-20s, but no specific diagnosis was on record. In spite of her troubled past, Yvonne insisted that she had turned her life around. At age 20, and again 7 years later, Yvonne maintained a belief in herself and her ability to do better.

Yvonne at midlife

At age 40, Yvonne lives alone in a 5-room apartment in a small rural community about 25 miles from Ypsilanti. She has never been married and reports no pregnancies. Her work history has been unstable; she reports that she has had 10 jobs in the past 15 years. Most of the jobs were as a cook, but her most recent employment was as a factory worker. She reports satisfaction with that job, where she earned $1,500 per month, but she was laid off recently. She currently earns $768 per month as a cook at a fast food restaurant and also reports receiving unemployment compensation at the rate of $232 per month. She says she has a savings account and life insurance, but no checking account or credit cards.

Yvonne says she is in fair health, but does not report any specific health problems. She does not have a regular doctor and says that she does not know where to go for medical care. In the past 15 years, she was without health insurance for more than 10 years, but now has Blue Cross/Blue Shield through her employer. She is overweight and smokes cigarettes. Her self-reported drinking and drug history shows some inconsistencies. She states that she drinks everyday, 10 drinks per day, but also says that only seven times in the past month has she had more than 5 drinks at one time. She admits to drug use—marijuana, cocaine, and crack—and reports that drug use has had a negative impact on her work, physical health, and finances. At the same time, she has never felt she needed treatment for drug use.

Her description of her personal life also shows confusion and inconsistency. Yvonne reports that she does not get along well with her family, but thinks she is doing better than they expected. Although she says she lives alone, she reports that her partner/roommate is giving her a hard time, along with her supervisor at work, friends, collection agencies, and members of her family. She says religion is very important to her and the one group she says she belongs to is a church, but that she never attends religious services.

When asked about her goals and plans for the future, Yvonne is somewhat at a loss: "Well, I'm hoping I can be in a good place to, uh . . . establish myself. So right now it's kind of hard to say, you know, why with the factory I'm workin' with is not going to be here very much longer, so I . . . might . . . my options are up, so I . . . I really don't know what to say." She would like to have "a real nice home . . . nice vehicle" and says she is trying to save money.

Records show that Yvonne has continued to have trouble with authorities—10 misdemeanors with charges including substance abuse, disorderly conduct, retail fraud, and various driving offenses. She has also been convicted of two felonies. One was a drug-related arrest 10 years ago for which she received 2 years probation. However, probation was revoked when she failed to report monthly, so she was sentenced to 6 months in jail with drug treatment. She was also convicted of a federal crime—tampering with a witness—and sentenced to 21 months of imprisonment and 3 years of supervised release. She reports spending a total of 5 years in jail or prison and 2½ years on probation. In spite of her

Table 9.2

PROFILE OF YVONNE BARNES
NO-PROGRAM GROUP, FEMALE

Variable	Status at age 27	Status at age 40
Schooling	Associate's degree in culinary arts	Unchanged; no further education plans
Employment	Full-time cook at restaurant; part-time housekeeper at hotel	Cook at fast-food restaurant 32 hours/week; recently laid off from factory work
Earnings	$1,500 per month	$784 per month
Welfare	None	None
Marriage	Single, never married, not cohabiting	Single, never married, unclear if cohabiting
Children	None	None
Residence	Lives with mother and grandparents	Rented apartment
Community involvement	Church; coaches girls' basketball	Talks with children about avoiding gangs and drug use
Criminal record	Juvenile detention center; 15 misdemeanor incidents: assault and battery, petty larceny, drug possession, car theft	5 years in jail or prison, 2 on probation; 10 misdemeanor incidents: drug possession, disorderly conduct, retail fraud, driving offenses; 2 felonies—drug-related, tampering with witness

difficulties, Yvonne maintains a positive outlook on life and would like to pass her philosophy on to the next generation. She says the best aspect of her life is "getting out and trying to help others" and that she talks to children in Detroit about avoiding gang activities: "First of all, I tell them to be who they are and to seek what's out there 'cause . . . we're put on earth to accomplish something out of life. . . . And number one is not to be gang related or be involved with drugs. That's what I would recommend for kids, to go out and be somebody in life instead of a gang buster or a crack head or . . . I wouldn't say crack head, I'd say drug abuser."

Calvin Charles (Program Group, Male)

In his early 20s, Calvin was interviewed in the state penitentiary where he was serving 18 months to 5 years for breaking and entering. A high school dropout after grade 10, Calvin had a history of resistance to authority and poor intellectual performance that persisted throughout his school years. By Calvin's own account at that time, he dropped out of school so he could make money in one illegal activity or another—larceny, drug dealing, stolen weapons. Calvin's parents encouraged him to stay in school, but by his early teens Calvin was making his own decisions and his parents expressed a sense of helplessness when it came to disciplining their son.

Calvin had no plans to change his means of support after his release from prison and, indeed, when interviewed at age 27, it was clear that his goal had not changed—making money by whatever means. At that time, he reported no legitimate source of income for the past 5 years. Although he stated that he was considering applying for a job at a fast-food restaurant, he admitted that his main money supply came from "hustling." He mentioned plans of getting his GED within the next 3 years and finding a job in construction, but at the same time said he preferred not to be tied down.

Calvin was married at age 21 and divorced 7 years later. At age 27, he said he was the father of 2 children, born when he was 17 and 27. He admitted to minimal involvement in their upbringing and had no specific expectations for them. He appeared to have no permanent address and said he "likes to move around a lot."

Calvin at midlife

Calvin admits to only one arrest in the past 15 years and gives no details. Public crime records show a different picture. According to records, Calvin has had arrests for two felonies in the past 15 years, both drug-related crimes. In addition, Calvin had seven misdemeanor incidents in the past 15 years, mostly driving offenses such as driving while under the influence and driving while his license was suspended. He served over 9 years in prison, from 1990 to 1999.

However by midlife, according to information gained in an interview with Calvin, his life had achieved considerable stability. He married again at age 33 and now lives in a rented apartment with his wife and 1 child. It is interesting to note that this marriage actually took place in 1991 while he was in prison. Calvin works as an assistant manager at a local discount store where he has worked for about 6 months, his first employment since his release from prison. He reports working 50–60 hours per week and making $1,800 per month. In addition, he makes a little extra money fixing and selling cars. Calvin reports that he has had four jobs in the past 15 years and has been unemployed for 9 of the past 24 months. His wife works full-time as a cashier, and Calvin reports their combined yearly income is almost $60,000 and that they have a retirement account, life insurance, and credit cards. Calvin denies receiving any social service payments in the past 15 years, although records show that he received cash and food assistance for at least 2 years.

Calvin says that he is in very good health, although he is obese and has been diagnosed with high blood pressure and arthritis. He receives care from a regular physician and has health insurance through his employer. Calvin is a smoker, but says he doesn't use alcohol. He admits to taking pain killers without a prescription and using marijuana and cocaine. He has been in drug treatment two times, both court-ordered.

Calvin's childrearing history is somewhat puzzling. At age 40, he reports that he has 5 children, born when he was 17, 23, 27, 28, and 29 years old; however, at age 27, he only admitted to having 2 children. He

Table 9.3

PROFILE OF CALVIN CHARLES
PROGRAM GROUP, MALE

Variable	Status at Age 27	Status at Age 40
Schooling	Dropped out of high school in grade 10; 3 years of special education	Unchanged; no further education plans
Employment	None within the last 5 years; "hustling"	Works 50–60 hr/week as an assistant manager of a retail store; makes extra money selling and fixing cars
Earnings	$1,500 per month, obtained illegally	$1,800 per month
Welfare	None	Cash and food assistance in 2 of the past 15 years
Marriage	Divorced after 7 years of marriage	Remarried for 9 years
Childrenaged	2 children born when he was 18 and 27	5 children, ages 24, 19, 15, 13, and 12
Residence	No permanent address	Rented apartment
Community involvement	None	None
Criminal record	1-year jail term and 2 years probation for breaking and entering; arrest for attempted murder; assault; drug possession; theft	Convicted of two drug-related felonies; served 9 years in prison; seven misdemeanors: driving offenses

also says he has had a major role in raising all of his children, contrary to his admission at age 27 that he did not have a major role in raising any of his children. He admits his oldest child, a daughter in her mid-20s, is not turning out as well as he expected. She is a high school graduate, never married, and has 3 children. She works full-time as a housekeeper at a hotel and receives some public assistance. She has been arrested once for nonpayment of traffic tickets. On the other hand, Calvin's next oldest child, a 19-year-old son, is turning out better than he expected. His son is employed full-time at a restaurant, is single, and has no children. Calvin expects that he will graduate from a 4-year college some day.

Calvin's goals for his future are optimistic. He wants to be a store manager and maybe even own his own store, but when asked about his plans to achieve these goals he is vague and says he is "trying to learn all I can and working hard." He says he has two or three other goals, but refused to divulge them on tape. Calvin believes there are no obstacles in his way, "the doors are wide open," and says his philosophy is to "try and try again . . . don't let nothin' get in [your] way." He is thankful that "I'm still here, and I'm healthy."

Gerald Daniels (No-Program, Male)

At age 24, Gerald was proud to have attended a Big Ten university on a full athletic scholarship. He attributed his success to a supportive family, positive role models throughout his school years, and his own sense of importance and determination. Although he was a good student in high school, Gerald admitted that sports were always more important to him than academics and, in fact, he did not complete his degree, but was dismissed from college for academic reasons during his final year.

When interviewed at age 27, Gerald expressed his intention to return to school and complete the few credits necessary for a degree in criminal justice. He was working full-time in a semiskilled position as a lathe operator on an assembly line at an automotive supply factory. He had worked there steadily for 3 years and was saving money. Still ambitious, he wanted to move up at work and had applied for a skilled-trades job as a machine operator. He had never been married and had no children.

Although he expressed regret about his incomplete academic career, determination to hang in and to overcome setbacks was still characteristic of Gerald's philosophy of life. He expressed appreciation for the positive influence that his family and his coaches had on his life, and tried to pass along a positive influence to others by volunteering as a Big Brother and in the Fellowship of Christian Athletes.

Gerald at midlife

Gerald's lifestyle at age 40 is much the same as it was at age 27. He has never married, has no children, and lives with his brother in his brother's house. When asked about his education, Gerald said that he completed his degree in 1980, although records show he was dismissed for academic reasons before his last semester was completed. He indicated no further educational plans at this time.

Although he is dissatisfied with the job and the pay, Gerald continues to work for the automotive industry as a semiskilled production worker. He only has had two other jobs in the past 15 years, both factory work. He stayed with the company he was working for at age 27 for 14 years, until the plant closed. In that time he moved up the pay scale from $12 to $17 per hour, but it is unclear if he attained his goal of a skilled labor position. Now he works more than 40 hours per week and makes about $32,000 per year—not much more money than he made at age 27. He knows that in order to achieve his goal of buying a house, he needs to make more money. His plan to achieve that goal is to find another job and save money.

In spite of his job frustration, Gerald's life is stable. He has a retirement plan, and life and health insurance, but no credit cards. He is in very good health and has a regular doctor. He smokes and uses alcohol in moderation. Gerald admits to using marijuana occasionally, but expresses regret that he lost a brother to drug abuse. Records show five misdemeanor citations—several for driving offenses and one for secondary retail fraud. Sentences for the crimes included fines and a few days spent in jail. When interviewed, Gerald did not admit to any crimes.

Clearly, Gerald's life has not taken the path he predicted at age 27 when he hoped, in the long run, to return to school and obtain a master's degree and, in the short run, to obtain a more skilled factory job. Although

Table 9.4

PROFILE OF GERALD DANIELS
NO-PROGRAM GROUP, MALE

Variable	Status at Age 27	Status at Age 40
Schooling	Completed 3.5 years college in criminal justice on athletic scholarship; plans to complete a bachelor's degree and a master's degree by age 30	Says he completed bachelor's degree in 1980; but no degree on record; no further education plans
Employment	Full-time lathe operator	Full-time factory production worker
Earnings	$2,200 per month	$2,300 per month
Welfare	None	None
Marriage	Single, never married, not cohabiting	Single, never married, not cohabiting
Children	None	None
Residence	Owns home	Lives in brother's house
Community involvement	Big Brother; Fellowship of Christian Athletes	Youth football
Criminal record	None	Five misdemeanor offenses: driving offenses, secondary retail fraud; a few days in jail

he didn't address the issue, it is probable that factory closings and a short period of unemployment caused him financial setbacks and may have resulted in the loss of the house he owned when interviewed previously. In spite of the setbacks, Gerald continues to have a positive, if less ambitious, outlook. He gets along very well with his family and says that the best aspects of his life are his health and his family. He continues to participate in his community by voting in local and national elections, participating in community meetings, and volunteering to help with youth football.

Bonita Emerson (Program Group, Female)

By age 27, Bonita had achieved her educational goals and was working full time as a second grade teacher. She had obtained both bachelor's and master's degrees in special education and planned to continue to take graduate-level courses to further her learning. Bonita gave credit to her strong and supportive family for "pushing" her to get a good education. An aunt who lived with the family for several years when she was growing up served as powerful role model for Bonita and kindled in her a desire to be a teacher and to dedicate herself to helping the African American community.

As a young teacher in her early 20s, Bonita was inspired by the promise of education as an ideal organizing force for African Americans to help themselves, and she believed strongly that parents' involvement in their children's schooling was the primary mechanism for bringing about lasting improvements. However, after several years of teaching in her community, Bonita had become somewhat dissatisfied with the local school system, which served a predominantly low-income population. She perceived inequalities in the funding mechanism that used property taxes as the tax base for schools.

Bonita was married at the age of 25. Her husband was also a college graduate and, together, their monthly earnings were $5,000. They were renting an apartment and saving money to buy their own home and start a family within the next 5 years. Bonita remained close to her family and the aunt who inspired her to become a teacher. She felt fortunate to have had such positive role models in her youth, but also recalled school counselors who tried to discourage her ambitions and those of other young black students. Bonita saw herself as an important role model for her students as well as other adults around her. She remained active in her church, teaching Sunday school, and was also active in several African American organizations, such as the National Association for the Advancement of Colored People.

Bonita at midlife

At age 40, Bonita's priorities have shifted from a focus on community activism to her personal life. Her marriage ended after a painful period of confronting her spouse's drug abuse. The marriage lasted 10 years, and the couple adopted a child about a year before they were divorced. Now Bonita lives in her own home with her son, who attends kindergarten.

Table 9.5

PROFILE OF BONITA EMERSON
PROGRAM GROUP, FEMALE

Variable	Status at Age 27	Status at Age 40
Schooling	Bachelor's and master's degrees in special education; endorsement in K–12 learning disabled	Unchanged; no further educational plans
Employment	Full-time teacher of second-third grade	Full-time teacher consultant
Earnings	$2,200 per month; spouse, $2,800 per month	$4,750 per month
Welfare	None	None
Marriage	Married since age 25	Divorced at age 35; actively looking for a mate
Children	None	5-year-old adopted son
Residence	Rented apartment	Owns home
Community involvement	Church; teaches Sunday school; member of national and local African American organizations	Church, volunteer work
Criminal record	None	None

She continues her parents' tradition of stressing the importance of a good education and expects her son to attend college and, ultimately, to obtain a master's degree.

Bonita has worked for the school system for the past 15 years, has moved up the career ladder, and has no future educational plans for herself. She is now employed as a teacher consultant and says her salary is $4,750 per month. Her financial situation is stable and she manages her money carefully; she has a retirement plan, mutual funds, life insurance, a checking account, and credit cards. Bonita reports that her health is very good; she has health insurance through her employer and has a regular physician. She does not smoke, drink, or use illegal drugs.

Although she has had to deal with some setbacks in life, Bonita continues to have a confident, proactive approach to problem solving. When asked about future plans, she says she plans to continue teaching, lose weight, and remarry. In pursuit of the last goal, Bonita is letting everybody know she is looking for a mate and has even joined an Internet dating service. Her positive self-image and determination are evident when she laughs and says, "I'm just a wonderful person, and I'm looking for a strong brother who will be with me. . . . I get so caught up in my work and parenting that, you know, sometimes I don't have time for social events. But I'm gonna have time. I'm gonna change some things."

Marlene Franklin (Program Group, Female)

The youngest of 5 children, Marlene was the only one of her siblings to graduate from high school. She excelled at athletics in school, but was a poor student. In spite of her poor grades, she enrolled in a 2-year secretarial program at the local community college after graduation but dropped out after a year. According to her mother, her schooling was derailed when Marlene began running around and rushed into starting a family. At the age of 22, she had 2 children, aged 1 and 2, and was in the middle of divorce proceedings after 3 years of marriage. Marlene attributed the breakup of her marriage to her husband's dissatisfaction with her use of marijuana. Although she wanted to do a good job of raising her children, she was unemployed, receiving AFDC and Food Stamps, and was confused about the direction she wanted her life to take.

Surprisingly, at age 27, Marlene was still married and living with her husband and their 2 daughters in a subsidized rented apartment. She was concerned about the drugs and violence pervasive in her apartment complex, but, as before, confused about how to better her situation. Marlene had been employed for the past 5 years as a full-time housekeeper in a convalescent home. She was somewhat dissatisfied with the pay, routine work, and lack of opportunity for advancement, but other than reading the want ads, she was not actively seeking a new job. Her husband was employed as a university custodian and their combined monthly income totaled $2,170. She said she had received welfare for 2 out of the last 10 years.

Marlene still smoked marijuana, but had no record of drug-dealing or other criminal activity. Her life was taken up with work, childrearing, and partying with friends. She said she had minimal involvement with her children's schooling and rarely helped them with their homework. According to Marlene, the girls were doing average scholastically and not getting into trouble at school. She expected them to graduate from high school, get jobs, or perhaps attend a community college or technical school. In spite of her frustration with their living situation, Marlene expressed satisfaction with her life and had no concrete plans to change her direction.

Marlene at midlife

At age 40, Marlene has 5 children, ranging in age from 2 to 20 years. She and her husband divorced after 12 years of marriage, and her 2 youngest children were born out of wedlock. She lives in a subsidized townhouse with her children, grandchildren, and sister. The grown children contribute to housing costs.

Marlene says her 2 oldest children have not turned out as well as she expected. Both of them got into trouble occasionally at school and were suspended from school at times. Her oldest child dropped out of high school in grade 11 to have a baby. She is currently employed as a cashier, receives welfare, and is studying to complete her GED. She has never been married and is pregnant with her second child. Marlene's second oldest, a 19-year-old daughter, followed a similar path—dropping out of school in grade 10 to have a child. She also has never been married, works as a cashier, and receives welfare. Marlene says that her children have used crack. However, in spite of their past difficulties, she remains hopeful that both daughters will eventually graduate from high school and attend community college.

Marlene herself is not working now and has been unemployed for 12 out of the last 24 months, although she says she is looking for work. She reports that she has had four jobs in the last 15 years, most of them in housekeeping. She claims that her past month's earnings were $1,000 and her past year's earnings were $10,400, but the source of the income is unclear given her lack of employment. Marlene has no retirement savings, life insurance, checking account, or credit cards. She says she is not on welfare, but acknowledges receiving Food Stamps for 1 year of the past 15. Marlene says she is in very good health and has a regular doctor, but has had no health insurance since her divorce. She acknowledges that she smokes, drinks at least 3 drinks 10 days per month, and uses marijuana.

Marlene has had some trouble with the law in the past 15 years. Records show six misdemeanor incidents for crimes such as driving with a suspended license, driving while under the influence, and possession

Table 9.6

PROFILE OF MARLENE FRANKLIN
PROGRAM GROUP, FEMALE

Variable	Status at Age 27	Status at Age 40
Schooling	High school graduate; enrolled in secretarial program at community college, but dropped out	Unchanged; no further educational plans
Employment	Full-time housekeeper in convalescent home	Unemployed, looking for work; has worked in housekeeping, and in warehouse
Earnings	$1,000 per month; spouse, $1,170 per month	$1,000 in past month; $10,400 in past year; source of income unclear
Welfare	AFDC and General Assistance for 6 months in the last 5 years	Food Stamps for 1 year in past 15 years
Marriage	Married since age 20	Divorced at age 32; single, not cohabiting
Children	2 children born when she was aged 20 and 21	5 children, ages 20, 19, 10, 8, and 2
Residence	Subsidized apartment	Subsidized apartment
Community involvement	None	Voted in last election; no volunteer work
Criminal record	None	Six misdemeanor incidents; possession of marijuana, driving under the influence; sentenced to jail time, fines, drug treatment

of marijuana. As a result of the drug possession, she spent 38 days in jail, paid a fine, and was ordered to undergo drug treatment. When asked, she admits to two arrests and some jail time, but denies ever having or needing drug treatment.

The confused approach to life that has previously characterized Marlene's life is still evident at age 40. She says she gets along fairly well with her birth family, but is not doing as well as they expected and feels helpless in dealing with her problems. Although she says that religion is very important to her, she never attends religious services. She also admits to no involvement in her community.

Dwight Gaines (No-Program Group, Male)

Dwight graduated from high school on time after receiving a great deal of individualized academic help. Although his teachers noted that he was a sociable child who tried hard to learn, his achievement was poor. In the fifth grade, he was certified as learning disabled and spent the next 4 years in special education. His school problems were exacerbated by a chaotic home life. Dwight's parents were separated, his mother was on welfare, and he was raised by various members of his extended family.

From an early age, Dwight's overriding interest in life was making money. During his school years, he earned money at odd jobs such as cutting grass or washing dishes. He tried selling marijuana in high school, but after his mother found out and "flushed the joints down the toilet," he no longer pursued illegal means of making money. After high school graduation, he worked in a series of unskilled jobs, but none lasted for long and he spent periods of time unemployed.

Dwight married at age 23 and, when interviewed at age 27, he reported he had 4 children—1 child born when he was 16 and 3 children with his present wife. At that time, money was still a central issue in his life. He was employed as a cook in a fast-food restaurant and also did some hauling with his truck. Between the two jobs he estimated he brought in about $1,000 per month; his wife, a nurse's aide, earned $2,000 per month. Their income was supplemented by Food Stamps and Aid for Families with Dependent Children, which Dwight received for raising his first child. He and his wife rented a large house where they lived with the 4 children.

Dwight's biggest challenge was finding ways to earn money. He was away from home a lot trying to line up jobs, a fact that frustrated his wife. He reported only moderate involvement in raising his children and his ties with his birth family were marginal. He was dissatisfied with his current work situation and looking for another job. He thought he might study auto mechanics at home and become a truck driver. He also mentioned vague plans to go back to school and earn an associate's degree within the next 10 years.

Dwight at midlife

At midlife, Dwight's income and job situation have improved, but the stability of his family life has eroded. He has been separated from his wife for 4½ years and lives with a sibling and nieces and nephews in a rented apartment—6 people in 4 rooms. Curiously, he reports having a major role in raising only 1 child, a 15-year-old daughter. His daughter is in ninth grade and lives with her mother. According to Dwight, she is turning out better than he anticipated and he expects that she will complete up to 2 years of college.

Dwight has worked as a grocery store produce worker for the past 8 years and says he earns $1,725 per month. He has had five jobs over the past 15 years—all unskilled. He now has a savings account and a checking account, but no credit cards or life insurance. He voluntarily pays $125 per month in child support and also pays the full rent on the apartment where he lives. Although his present financial situation is stable, he acknowledges receiving welfare for 10 of the past 15 years.

Dwight claims that he is in fair health and that back problems have occasionally stopped him working for a week or more. Additional health problems include obesity, diabetes, and heart problems. He has regular medical care paid for by the health insurance provided by his employer. He says he is a nonsmoker and doesn't drink alcohol, but occasionally uses marijuana.

Table 9.7

PROFILE OF DWIGHT GAINES
NO-PROGRAM GROUP, MALE

Variable	Status at Age 27	Status at Age 40
Schooling	High school graduate; 4 years of special education; hopes to complete associate's degree by age 37; taking home-study program to earn truck driver's license	Unchanged; no further educational plans
Employment	Full-time cook at fast-food restaurant; hauling with his own truck	Full-time produce worker at grocery store
Earnings	$1,000 per month; spouse, $2,000 per month	$1,725 per month
Welfare	AFDC and Food Stamps	Received welfare 10 of the past 15 years
Marriage	Married since age 23	Separated at age 34; single, not cohabiting
Children	1 child born out of wedlock when he was 16; 3 children born when he was aged 23 to 27	Reports only one 15-year-old daughter
Residence	Rented house	Rented apartment
Community involvement	None	None
Criminal record	None	Two misdemeanors; driving offense and fishing without license

Although he likes his present job, Dwight still has dreams for the future. He is looking into having his own "barbeque shack;" however, he continues to be frustrated by the need for more money. He has inquired about obtaining loans and investing with friends, but says he needs more time. He would also like to own his own house. In spite of financial frustration and family problems, he maintains a positive outlook: "I'm a 'people' person. I've helped quite a few people, you know, in my life, and that makes me happy when I can get out and do something else for somebody else." He would advise young people starting out today to "keep your head up, don't let, you know, the small things get next to you . . . try to make the best out of everything."

Gloria Henderson (No-Program Group, Female)

At age 20, Gloria was in her third year of college at a local 4-year state university. Gloria saw schooling as the most promising means for a young black woman like herself to achieve her goals, and it was clear that her respect for education came from the strong influence of the prominent women in her life—her mother and both of her grandmothers. When Gloria was in junior high school, her mother returned to college to complete her bachelor's degree, and her determination to finish her degree while raising 3 children had a profound effect on her daughter.

During Gloria's senior year in high school, she became pregnant and gave birth to a daughter. Instead of becoming an impediment to her education, Gloria's daughter became a key motivating factor. With the help and support of her mother and grandmothers, Gloria returned to school immediately and managed to graduate from high school with her class. She was determined to achieve her full potential: "Even if it takes me 20 years to get out of school, you can bet I'll have what I want."

Although family and financial obligations meant that she was unable to continue with college as planned, at age 27, Gloria was the same determined and independent young woman she was at age 20. She earned an associate's degree in criminal justice, but dropped out before completing her third year of college. She expected to resume her schooling and complete a bachelor's degree within the next 3 years. In the meantime, she was working full-time as a supervisor of computer operations at a large state university, earning $19,000 annually. She maintained a savings account and investments, but admitted to some financial struggles.

She and her boyfriend of 3 years had a daughter together and within the next 5 years Gloria hoped to marry him and own a house. She was strongly motivated to create a positive atmosphere for her children and provide for their future. In addition to family and work obligations, she was active in her church and other community organizations. She expressed concern about the well-being of African Americans as a group and believed that after she earned a degree in criminal justice, she could make a greater contribution to the community.

Gloria at midlife

At age 40, Gloria continues to have a positive outlook and her determination to achieve her goals is unchanged. She was married at age 31, and she and her husband had another daughter soon after. Her children are now aged 21, 12, and 8. She and her family are living temporarily with her mother while they finish building their own home.

Gloria's oldest daughter lives on her own with her 2-year-old child. She received average grades and graduated from high school on time, but was occasionally a problem while in school. At present she is single and employed full-time in housekeeping, and Gloria hopes she will continue her education and attend a 2-year college. She has never received welfare. Gloria reports that her 12-year-old daughter is seldom a problem and Gloria maintains a close relationship with her, helping her with homework and talking over problems together. Although she receives special education and tutoring in reading at school, Gloria hopes that someday her daughter will be able to obtain a master's degree.

Gloria is currently enrolled at a local business college and expects to complete a B.A. in human resource management next year. She would like to continue her education and pursue a master's degree, but realizes her ability to do so will depend on her work load and family responsibilities: "Right now my kids are my first priority." She has worked as an assembler at a factory full-time for the past 6 years and, although she is dissatisfied with the work, she is pleased with her earnings. She and her spouse, a

Table 9.8

PROFILE OF GLORIA HENDERSON
NO-PROGRAM GROUP, FEMALE

Variable	Status at Age 27	Status at Age 40
Schooling	Associate's degree in criminal justice; dropped out of 4-year college but plans to get B.A. by age 31	Enrolled in business college; expects to complete B.A. in 1 year; considering pursuing Master's degree
Employment	Full-time supervisor of computer facilities at a university	Full-time assembler at a factory
Earnings	$1,580 per month	$5,000 per month; spouse, $5,000 per month
Welfare	6 months in past 10 years	None
Marriage	Single, never married, not cohabiting; steady 3-year relationship with man she plans to marry	Married since age 31
Children	2 children born out of wedlock when she was 18 and 27	3 children, ages 21, 12, and 8
Residence	Rented apartment	Building a house with her husband; living temporarily with her mother
Community involvement	Church; community organizations; cheerleader coach for Junior Little League	Sexual assault counselor; volunteer at children's school
Criminal record	None	None

machine operator, each earn $5,000 per month. They have life insurance, investments in mutual funds, a checking account, and credit cards.

Gloria enjoys very good health, has a regular doctor, and has health insurance through her employer. She reports that she does not smoke, drink alcohol, or use drugs. Religious faith is important to Gloria, and although she doesn't attend services regularly, she is thankful for the opportunities she has had: "My kids can tell you I pray from point A to point Z." She continues to be active in her community, as a sexual assault counselor, and at her children's school functions.

Gloria is determined to continue to move up the employment ladder. Her long-term employment goal is to work on the international staff of the United Auto Workers, and she is currently interviewing for a position that would move her closer to that goal. While she is proud of her professional accomplishments and looks forward to future achievements, she is emphatic that the best aspect of her life is her family: "My kids always make me feel good about myself . . . [my husband's] nothing but a blessing to my life." She credits her husband for teaching her about financial planning to achieve material goals and continues to recognize the importance of the support she received from her mother and grandmothers.

Case Study Themes and Conclusions

While the detailed case study narratives personalize the findings presented in previous chapters, it is also helpful to summarize the case study information in terms of organizing themes. In previous monographs presenting Perry Preschool study longitudinal findings, the themes have been connected to the variables that accounted for success in the full-sample study. As the study participants age, the details supporting the themes of success change somewhat, but the themes themselves and the trajectories of individual lives remain remarkably consistent. Table 9.9 presents these indicators of success at midlife for the case studies according to the following four organizing themes:

- **Education**—special education, high school completion, and post-secondary attainment

- **Employment and earnings**—work, earnings, use of public assistance, home ownership

- **Criminal records**—misdemeanors, felonies, incarcerations

- **Family, health, and community life**—marital status, single parenthood, health, drug abuse history, community involvement

Although the themes presented are directly connected to the variables that account for some of the group differences presented elsewhere in the monograph, it is important to remember that the case study analysis does not involve statistically valid tests of the variables examined. The deliberate selection of both successful and unsuccessful cases from

Table 9.9

CASE STUDY INDICATORS OF SUCCESS

	Case Study[a]							
Indicators of Success	G.H. (NP, F)	B.E. (P, F)	J.A. (P, M)	G.D. (NP, M)	Y.B. (NP, F)	D.G. (NP, M)	M.F. (P, F)	C.C. (P, M)
Education								
No special education	1	1	1	1	1	0	1	0
High school diploma	1	1	1	1	1	1	1	0
1–2 years of college	1	1	1	1	1	0	0	0
3–4 years of college	1	1	1	1	0	0	0	0
Bachelor's degree	0	1	0	0	0	0	0	0
Master's degree	0	1	0	0	0	0	0	0
Employment and Earnings								
Full-time employment	1	1	1	1	0	1	0	1
Earning $3,000+ per month	1	1	1	0	0	0	0	0
No public assistance	1	1	1	1	1	0	0	0
Home ownership	1	1	1	0	0	0	0	0
Criminal records								
No misdemeanors	1	1	0	0	0	0	0	0
No felonies	1	1	1	1	0	1	1	0
No incarcerations	1	1	1	0	0	1	0	0
Family and community life								
Married	1	0	1	0	0	0	0	1
Never divorced	1	0	1	1	1	0	0	0
Not single parent	1	0	1	1	1	0	0	1
Good health	1	1	1	1	0	0	1	0
No history of drug/alcohol abuse	1	1	1	1	0	0	0	0
Community involvement	1	1	0	1	1	0	0	0
Success score (0–19)	17	16	15	12	7	4	4	3

Note. Each indicator of success is scored 1 for present or 0 for absent.

[a] Initials of persons studied, with information in parentheses as follows: P = program group; NP = no-program group; M = male; F = female.

the program group and the no-program group means the cases cannot be used to compare program outcomes. Instead, examination of the pattern of specific lives over time offers insight into the interplay of factors that affect decision making and resulting life paths.

The life courses of the 8 case study participants have been remarkably stable over time. Individuals who were successful early in life continue to be successful at midlife, and individuals who encountered failure in school and work, or engaged in criminal activity early on, continued to follow that pattern. At age 19, each case was assigned a plus (+) or a minus (–) to indicate success based on six themes deemed important at that age: parental support for education, attitudes about money, positive role models in their lives, the role of church or religion in their lives, their sense of responsibility, and their goal orientation (Berrueta-Clement et al., 1984). The 4 individuals who received a plus score at that time were Jerry Andrews, Bonita Emerson, Gerald Daniels, and Gloria Henderson. For the age 27 case study analysis, individuals were given a 1 or 0 to indicate their status on each of 14 different success indicators grouped in four areas: schooling, employment and earnings, criminal records, and their relationship to the next generation (Schweinhart et al., 1993). Each individual then received a summary score. The four individuals with the highest scores at age 27 are the same as those who received + scores at age 19.

At midlife, success scores were computed in a manner similar to that used at age 27. A 1 or a 0 was assigned to indicate individual status on each of 19 indicators grouped under the four themes (see Table 9.9). The 4 individuals with the highest scores were the same as those with the highest scores at ages 27 and 19. It is interesting to note that the dichotomy between the 4 individuals scoring highest and those scoring lowest widens over time. That is, the mean of the 4 highest scores at age 27 was 11 (out of a possible 14); the mean of the 4 lowest scoring individuals was 5. At midlife, the mean of the 4 highest scores was 15 (out of a possible 19); the mean of the 4 lowest scoring cases was 5. This informal analysis on a small selected sample suggests the hypothesis that those who achieve success early in life are on a path to ever increasing success as their lives continue, while those who experience early failure are likely to experience more of the same.

Education

The variables used to measure success in education at midlife are identical to those employed at age 27. There have been no changes in individual educational status since that time. At age 27, 4 of the case study participants planned to further their education and complete college degrees; by midlife, no one had carried out these plans. However, when interviewed at midlife, 2 of the participants were enrolled in educational programs (Jerry Andrews and Gloria Henderson), while the others had no further educational plans.

As reported at age 27, comparing those with the four highest to those with the four lowest total scores illustrates that the more successful adults clearly had an educational advantage over the less successful adults (75% vs. 25% of possible positive indicators on the six schooling variables). All but 1 of the less successful adults ended their education with high school, either dropping out or barely making grades for graduation. The 4 more successful adults had completed some college, although only 1 had obtained a bachelor's (and a master's) degree. In most cases, financial constraints interfered with educational aspirations. Without family resources to help defray education costs, participants were obligated to work full-time and save money to accrue the necessary funds. As they began to form families of their own, other needs prevailed.

The age 27 report also notes that, like the results for the full-sample statistical analysis, the case study sample females completed more schooling than males (63% vs. 38% of possible positive indicators). Overall, women in the case study sample had higher educational attainment than men, whether the females were successful or not. Moreover, in the unsuccessful group, the males but not the females required special education services in elementary and junior high school. Their stories indicated that, for females:

> School was the place to be as they were growing up. They could "hang out" and socialize even if they were not paying attention to academic matters. For males, the action was elsewhere—on the street earning money through legal or illegal means. Perhaps females felt that school offered more freedom and opportunity than home; males found that if they had no interest in learning, then school constrained them from exercising their other options (Schweinhart et al., 1993, p. 217).

Employment and Earnings

The striking feature of the economic status of the case study participants at midlife is how little progress most of them have made in their earning power since early adulthood. At age 27, 3 of the 8 individuals were earning at least $2,000 per month. Over a decade later, the number of participants earning more than $2,000 per month had only increased by 1 in spite of economic inflation of 37% over that time period, reducing the value of $2,000 to $1,460 in constant dollars (*Economagic.com*, 2004). In effect, most of the case study participants have actually lost earning power. The country was in a recession when the participants were most recently interviewed and some of their job histories reflect the overall economic condition. Two of the 8 case study participants had lost jobs due to factory closings in recent months and are now working for lower wages. A third was unemployed and looking for work.

As was the case at age 27, none of the 4 most successful case study participants had a record of using public assistance in the past 15 years. However, all but 1 of the less successful participants had received some type of assistance, 1 more than at age 27. On the other hand, home ownership increased among the case study participants. As young adults, only 1 of the case study participants owned a home; at midlife, 3 of the 4 most successful participants reported home ownership. Interestingly, the one participant who owned a home at age 27 (Gerald Daniels), no longer owns a home and now lives with his brother. He also reports recently being laid off from his job and earning a lower wage than he did previously.

Criminal Records

At midlife, 6 of the case study participants have records of misdemeanor incidents, 4 more than at age 27; however, only 2 of them had felony records, the same 2 participants who had felony records at age 27. Surprisingly, 4 of the 8 case study participants spent some time in jail or prison (as compared to 41% of the total sample), including 1 of the 4 most successful. The length of incarceration varied from a few days to several years (for those who were convicted of felonies).

At age 27, only 2 of the case study participants had criminal records (Yvonne Barnes and Calvin Charles)—these same 2 individuals have the most serious criminal records at midlife. The conclusions reached in the age 27 case study analysis of crime appear to be just as valid today:

> Patterns of problem behavior appeared to become established early. The [two] cases with adult criminal records also had school records citing repeated instances of assaults on peers, destruction of school property, and defiance of teachers. In these lives, unruly behavior in childhood was notably linked with academic difficulties. But children who struggle with learning do not automatically turn to delinquent acts. What distinguished these two was a sense that their parents felt helpless to influence their children's behavior. Carrying out the parental roles of teacher and disciplinarian seemed beyond the personal control of the adults responsible for these youngsters. (Schweinhart et al., 1993, p. 218)

Family and Community Life

Lifelong patterns that characterize marriage and family are difficult to establish in the case study sample. At midlife, 3 of the case study participants are married and 6 have children they are raising, 3 as single parents. Interestingly, the 3 participants who were married at age 27 have all subsequently been divorced and none of them have remarried. Neither marriage nor their own single parenthood appears to be related to success in this small sample, although 3 of the 4 most successful case study participants have never been divorced, in contrast to 1 of the 4 least successful cases. At midlife, 3 of the 4 most successful participants said they were involved in their community, compared to only 1 of the 4 least successful participants. This pattern is similar to that found at age 27 when all 4 of the most successful participants saw themselves as positive role models for the next generation, a feeling shared by only 2 of those least successful.

In the midlife interview, a number of questions were asked about the participants' health—including questions about chronic diseases, such as high blood pressure and diabetes, and drinking and drug use habits. The participants were also asked to state their height and weight. Although the precision of the data may be questioned given that it was self-reported, a clear pattern emerged in the case studies. All of the most successful participants reported that they were in good health and had no history of alcohol or drug abuse. In contrast, only 1 of the least successful participants reported being in good health, and all 4 had a history of alcohol or drug abuse. Although the analysis cannot be conclusive, the pattern is striking and suggests the need for further inquiry into the nature of the links between early support and education and subsequent drug use and poor health. Does early support and education help the individual develop a level of self-esteem that fosters positive decision making in the face of the temptations of the drug culture? Do those who have negative educational experiences turn to drugs seeking positive experiences? What is the nature of the link between chronic drug use and poor health?

Conclusions

These case studies provide a fascinating glimpse into the lives of individuals struggling to move from a background of poverty into the mainstream of society. It is instructive and sobering to contemplate the seemingly profound influence of early support and positive educational experiences. Earlier in life, the participants differed sharply in their goals—some were positive that the route to success was through education, while others were seeking ways to make money, by whatever means. These early attitudes shaped the paths of their individual lives. All of them encountered difficulties and detoured to some degree from their original plans. Financial setbacks and personal struggles were the norm, but the most successful participants were able to face their difficulties and adjust their plans in positive and realistic ways. The least successful made negative choices and decisions, which led them to crime and substance abuse and ultimately eroded their health and well-being. However, in spite of their divergent paths, at midlife, their goals and values were strikingly similar. Each of them craved a comfortable living situation and valued relationships with family and friends.

X Summary, Frequently Asked Questions, and Conclusions

This chapter summarizes the design and findings of the High/Scope Perry Preschool study. Then it presents conclusions from the study. It ends with answers to frequently asked questions, thereby taking advantage of the rich discussion that has surrounded this study for over 4 decades.

Summary

The High/Scope Perry Preschool study is a scientific experiment that has identified both the short- and long-term effects of a high-quality preschool education program for young children living in poverty. From 1962 through 1967, David Weikart and his colleagues in the Ypsilanti, Michigan, school district operated the High/Scope Perry Preschool Project for young children to help them avoid school failure and related problems. They identified a sample of 123 low-income African American children who were assessed to be at high risk of school failure and randomly assigned 58 of them to a group that received a high-quality preschool program at ages 3 and 4 and 65 to a group that received no preschool program. Because of the random assignment strategy, children's preschool experience remains the best explanation for subsequent group differences in their performance over the years. Project staff collected data annually on both groups from ages 3 through 11 and again at ages 14, 15, 19, 27, and 40, with a missing data rate of only 6% across all measures. After each period of data collection, staff analyzed the information and wrote a comprehensive official report.

This monograph is the eighth that the study has produced over the years. The findings of program effects through age 40 span the domains of education, economic performance, crime prevention, family relationships, and health. Key findings for education, economic performance, and crime prevention are summarized in Figure 10.1.

Education

The program group significantly outperformed the no-program group on highest level of schooling completed (77% vs. 60% graduating from high school; Table 3.1, pp. 52–53). Specifically, a much larger percentage of program than no-program females graduated from high school (88% vs. 46%). This difference was related to earlier differences between program and no-program females in the rates of treatment for mental impairment (8% vs. 36%) and grade repetition (21% vs. 41%; Table 3.2, pp. 56–57). The program group also significantly outperformed the no-program group on various intellectual and language tests from their preschool years up to age 7 (Table 3.3, p. 61); on school achievement tests at ages 9, 10, and 14; (Table 3.4, p. 62) and on literacy tests at ages 19 and 27 (Table 3.5, p. 64). At ages 15 and 19, the program group had significantly better attitudes toward school than the no-program group (Table 3.6, p. 68), and program-group parents had better attitudes toward their 15-year-old children's schooling than did no-program-group parents (Table 3.7, p. 69).

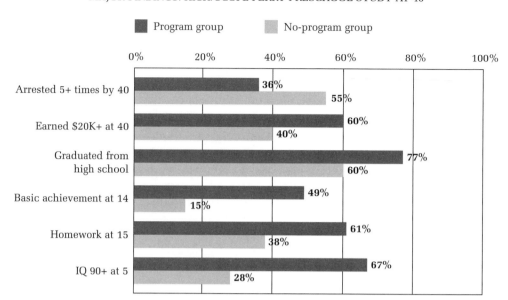

Figure 10.1

MAJOR FINDINGS: HIGH/SCOPE PERRY PRESCHOOL STUDY AT 40

Economic Performance

Significantly more of the program group than the no-program group were employed at age 40 (76% vs. 62%; Table 4.1, pp. 74–75), which continues the trend from age 27 (69% vs. 56%). At age 40, more program males than no-program males were employed (70% vs. 50%), although at age 27 more program females than no-program females were employed (80% vs. 55%). The program group also had significantly higher median annual earnings than the no-program group at ages 27 and 40 ($12,000 vs. $10,000 at age 27 and $20,800 vs. $15,300 at age 40) and higher median monthly incomes at both ages ($1,020 vs. $700 at age 27 and $1,856 vs. $1,308 at age 40). There was a consistent tendency for a smaller percentage of the program group than the no-program group to receive regular income from family or friends, which was statistically significant at age 27 (2% vs. 16%).

Rather than paying rent, receiving a subsidy, living with others, or being incarcerated, the program group had significantly more stable dwelling arrangements at ages 27 and 40—that is, more of them owned their own homes (27% vs. 5% at age 27, 37% vs. 28% at age 40; Table 4.2, pp. 78–79). At age 40, program males paid significantly more per month for their dwelling than did no-program males. Significantly more of the program group than the no-program group owned a car at age 40 (82% vs. 60%), especially males (80% vs. 50%), as they had at age 27 (73% vs. 59%). Indeed, at age 27, a significantly larger proportion of the program group than the no-program group had a second car (30% vs. 13%), especially males (36% vs. 15%). At age 40, significantly more of the program group than the no-program group had savings accounts (76% vs. 50%), especially males (73% vs. 36%).

While the evidence of less use of social services by the program group than by the no-program group is strikingly consistent across various indicators of social services usage, the evidence of a significant group difference in use of social services on individual indicators is equivocal. By age 40, fewer members of the program group than the no-program group reported receiving social services at some time in their lives (71% vs. 86%; Table 4.3, pp. 82–83), but this difference was not significant. At age 27, significantly fewer of the program group than the no-program group reported receiving social services at some time in the previous 10 years (59% vs. 80%). Among the individual categories of social services, the only significant differences between the program group and the no-program group involved family counseling at ages 34 to 40 (13% vs. 24%) and General Assistance from ages 23 to 27 (10% vs. 23%).

Crime Prevention

The study presents strong evidence that the Perry Preschool program played a significant role in reducing overall arrests and arrests for violent crimes as well as property and drug crimes and subsequent prison or jail sentences over study participants' lifetimes up to age 40. The program group had significantly fewer lifetime arrests than the no-program group (36% vs. 55% arrested 5 or more times; Table 5.1, p. 86) and significantly fewer arrests for violent crimes (32% vs. 48% ever arrested), property crimes (36% vs. 58% ever arrested), and drug crimes (14% vs. 34% ever arrested). Significant group differences in various types of crime occurred at various times of life—crimes other than violent, property, or drug crimes in adolescence (3% vs. 11%); total arrests (7% vs. 29% with 5 or more arrests) and drug crimes (9% vs. 25%) in early adulthood up to age 27; and violent crimes (14% vs. 31%) and property crimes (15% vs. 32%) in midlife from ages 28 to 40 (Table 5.1, p. 86). Consider also that by age 40, compared to the no-program group, the program group had significantly fewer arrests for property felonies (19% vs. 32% ever arrested; Table 5.3, p. 91), drug felonies (7% vs. 28%), violent misdemeanors (19% vs. 37%), and property misdemeanors (24% vs. 41%); significantly fewer arrests for property felonies by age 27 (14% vs. 26%); and significantly fewer arrests from ages 28 to 40 for violent felonies (2% vs. 12%), drug felonies (3% vs. 15%), and property misdemeanors (10% vs. 28%). By age 40, compared to the no-program group, the program group had participated in significantly fewer of 3 of the 78 types of crimes cited at arrest—dangerous drugs (3% vs. 20%), assault and/or battery (19% vs. 37%), and larceny under $100 (9% vs. 22%, Table 5.4, pp. 93–96). These types of crimes had significant group differences by age 27; assault and/or battery also had a significant group difference at ages 28 to 40. Moreover, the program group was sentenced to significantly fewer months in prison or jail by age 40 (28% vs. 52% ever sentenced; Table 5.5, p. 99), specifically from ages 28 to 40 (19% vs. 43%). Also, from ages 28 to 40, the program group was sentenced to significantly fewer months in prison for felonies (7% vs. 25%) and had served significantly fewer months in prison overall (9% vs. 21% ever served).

Health, Family, and Children

More program than no-program males raised their own children (57% vs. 30%; Table 6.2, pp. 111–112) and had second marriages (29% vs. 8%; Table 6.1, p. 108). The two oldest children raised by program-group members did not differ significantly from the two oldest children raised by no-program group members in education, employment, arrests, or welfare status. At age 40, more of the program group than the no-program group said they were getting along very well with their families (75% vs. 64%; Table 6.6, p. 119). Fewer program than no-program males reported using sedatives, sleeping pills, or tranquilizers (17% vs. 43%; Table 6.11, p. 127), marijuana or hashish (48% vs. 71%), or heroin (0% vs. 9%).

Cost-Benefit Analysis

In constant 2000 dollars discounted at 3%, the economic return to society of the Perry Preschool program was $258,888 per participant on an investment of $15,166 per participant—$17.07 per dollar invested (Table 7.8, p. 148). Of that return, $195,621 went to the general public—$12.90 per dollar invested (as compared to $7.16 in the age-27 benefit-cost analysis), and $63,267 went to each participant—$4.17 per dollar invested. Of the public return (see Figure 10.2), 88% ($171,473) came from crime savings, 4% ($7,303) came from education savings, 7% ($14,078) came from increased taxes due to higher earnings, and 1% ($2,768) came from welfare savings. Preschool program participants earned 14% more per person

Figure 10.2

HIGH/SCOPE PERRY PRESCHOOL PROGRAM PUBLIC COSTS AND BENEFITS

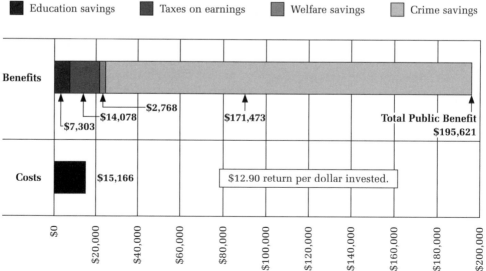

(Constant 2000 dollars, 3% discount rate)

than they would have otherwise—$156,490 more over their lifetimes in undiscounted 2000 dollars (Figure 7.2, p. 154). Male program participants cost the public 41% less in crime costs per person—$732,894 less in undiscounted 2000 dollars over their lifetimes (Figure 7.2).

Interestingly, 93% of the public return was due to the performance of males and only 7% to females, (Table 7.8, p. 148). This difference is due to the fact that compared to females, males committed substantially more crimes, but program males committed substantially fewer crimes than no-program males. This finding stands in stark contrast to the earlier finding that 84% of the program females, but only 32% of the no-program females, graduated from regular high school. Because education is itself an investment, it is not surprising that education cost more for program females, but it is disconcerting that the greater educational attainment of program than no-program females did not have a stronger impact on their earnings, as compared to males for whom program and no-program high school graduation rates were not significantly different. The return to society on program investment due to earnings was $86,233 for females as compared to $70,093 for males, only 21% more. We can surmise that program females did not earn more because wage growth for low-skilled jobs has been very low in recent decades; not all females participate in the labor market; and we omitted the benefits of education on household production and family behaviors.

The cost-benefit analysis is reasonably conservative in two respects. One is the omission of benefits that are hard to monetize, such as family, health, and wealth benefits. The other is the conservative assumptions about the earnings profiles and the unit costs of crimes; where multiple data sources were available, we typically chose the source that yielded smaller differences between program and no-program groups.

Path Model

A path model of the study (see Figure 10.3) suggests how preschool experience affects participants' success at age 40. Beginning with pre-school experience and children's preprogram intellectual performance, the model traces cause-effect paths to children's postprogram intellectual performance, then to their school achievement and commitment to schooling, then to their educational attainment, then to their adult earnings and lifetime arrests.

Frequently Asked Questions

Because the long-term High/Scope Perry Preschool Project study is well known and respected and stands at the fulcrum of decisions about public investment in early childhood programs, it has attracted many questions over the years that deserve thoughtful answers. Many of the questions and answers that follow involve the study's internal and external validity. Its internal validity is the extent to which its two groups are the result of simple random assignment and thus accurately reflect the impact of a

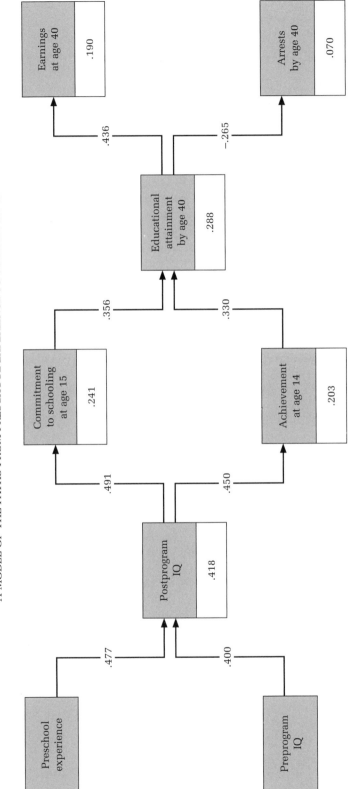

Figure 10.3

A MODEL OF THE PATHS FROM PRESCHOOL EXPERIENCE TO SUCCESS AT 40

Note. Path coefficients are standardized regression weights, all statistically significant at *p* < .01; coefficients in each box are squared multiple correlations.

good preschool education program experience against the impact of no preschool education program experience. Its external validity is the extent to which its study participants and treatment resemble the children and programs to which it is generalized.

Don't the departures from random assignment challenge the internal validity of the findings?

The internal validity of the High/Scope Perry Preschool study is very strong because its design is based on random assignment of children to program and no-program groups. For this very reason, its departures from strict random assignment have received intense scrutiny. These departures and their effects on major outcomes are examined at length in Chapter 2 of this monograph. First, the outcome analyses in this monograph were adjusted for seven background covariates: five that had statistically significant relationships with preschool experience and one or more of the key outcome variables; one (mother's employment) that had a statistically significant relationship with preschool experience due to the random-assignment departure of assigning some children of employed mothers to the no-program group; and another variable (father at home) that had a nearly statistically significant relationship with monthly earnings at age 40 as well as general policy relevance. Second, because younger siblings were assigned to the same group as their older sibling, we analyzed major outcomes with subsamples that included only one sibling per family. Third, because the sample consisted of five classes of children, we analyzed major outcomes using classes as covariates. The findings for the major outcomes were the same regardless of which of these analyses were used.

Isn't the sample size too small to generate scientific confidence in the findings?

Statistical significance testing takes sample size into account. To achieve statistical significance, group differences must become larger in magnitude as sample sizes become smaller. Indeed, a problem with very large samples is that educationally trivial group differences can achieve statistical significance. If the High/Scope Perry Preschool study sample were truly too small, none of its findings would have achieved statistical significance, and it would never have become influential.

How can the study be generalized to other programs?

Because few programs are evaluated by longitudinal studies involving random assignment of study participants, it is desirable to be able to generalize the results of such studies as broadly as possible. The external validity or generalizability of the study findings extends to those programs that are reasonably similar to the High/Scope Perry Preschool program. *A reasonably similar program is a preschool education program run by teachers with bachelor's degrees and certification in education, each serving up to 8 children living in low-income families. The program runs 2 school years for children who are 3 and 4 years of age with daily classes of 2½ hours or more, uses the High/Scope model or a similar participatory education approach, and has teachers visiting families or scheduling regular parent events at least every 2 weeks.* Each term in this treatment definition is examined further below:

- *A preschool education program*—a care and education program that contributes to young children's development.

- *Run by teachers with bachelor's degrees and certification in education*—The teachers in the Perry Preschool Project were certified to teach in elementary and special education; of all their education, the early childhood training was obviously the most relevant to their classroom practices.

- *Each serving up to 8 children*—The Perry Preschool Project had 4 teachers for 20 to 25 children, typical for special education classes (Kakalik, Furry, Thomas, & Carney, 1981). The equally successful classrooms in the subsequent High/Scope Preschool Curriculum Comparison study (Schweinhart & Weikart, 1997a, 1997b) had 2 teachers for 16 children, a ratio of 1 to 8. In general practice, High/Scope preschool classrooms appear to operate successfully with 2 adults and up to 20 children (Epstein, 1993).

- *Children living in low-income families*—Children were selected for the study because their parents had low educational attainment (high school graduation or less) and low occupational status (unemployed or unskilled), and their homes had fewer than 3 rooms per person. These families were of lower socioeconomic status than most U.S. residents at the time of the study. The study does not suggest a sharp cutoff point for program eligibility.

- *Offering 2 school years at 3 and 4 years of age*—The study presents no evidence that the program would have had similar effects if it had served children at earlier (infancy–3 years) or later ages (elementary school years). The preponderance of evidence shows children should attend a similar program for 2 school years (October through May for the Perry Preschool group); one year is enough only if one accepts a generalization from the 13 program-group members in the initial class, who attended the program for 1 school year and experienced the same effects as did the 45 program-group members in the other classes, who attended the program for 2 school years. This study, by itself, offers only weak evidence to support the limitation of many state preschool programs to only serving 4-year-old children. The better argument for this policy is the inequity inherent in serving some children for 2 school years when, as a result, other eligible children are not served at all, because the 3-year-olds served have taken the places of additional 4-year-olds.

- *With daily classes of 2½ hours or more*—The program runs at least 2½ hours a day, 5 days a week. A few minutes less should not matter, nor should hours more: Even a full, 9-hour-a-day program, if it meets all the other standards of quality, should produce similar if not greater effects.

- *Using the High/Scope educational model or a similar participatory education approach*—The High/Scope educational model was developed and used in the program (Weikart, Deloria, Lawser, & Wiegerink, 1970; Hohmann, Banet, & Weikart, 1979; Hohmann & Weikart, 1995, 2002). In this model, the classroom is arranged and the day is scheduled to support children's self-initiated learning activities along with small-group and large-group activities. Teachers help children as they plan, carry out, and review their own activities. Teachers plan ways to engage children in numerous key experiences in child development covering the areas of personal initiative, social relations, creative representation, movement and music, logic and mathematics, and language and literacy. Teachers study and receive regular training in the educational model and receive support in its use from a supervisor who knows the model and assists in its implementation.

- *With teachers visiting families at least every 2 weeks*—The program included weekly home visits, which might be reduced to every 2 weeks, or changed to an equivalent form of substantial outreach to parents, such as parent group meetings in which staff acknowledge and support parents as partners in the education of their children and model principles of active learning for them. The key is not to require a certain frequency of home visits or meetings, but to ensure that the basic message and lessons of a strong partnership with parents are clearly and repeatedly communicated. Sometimes, issues including the safety of home visitors in the community call for creative solutions to this challenge.

The study provides scientific evidence that its findings apply to reasonably similar programs. Program similarities, however, are defined somewhat more liberally than the actual program characteristics to allow for necessary and reasonable variations—serving up to 8 children rather than 5 or 6, serving children living in low-income families rather than only families living in poverty, home visits (or regular parent meetings and events) every 2 weeks rather than every week. These characteristics are structural, that is to say, they are relatively easy to name, count, legislate, regulate, and monitor. One of them, use of the High/Scope educational model, is structural in its simplest meaning, but encompasses process characteristics as well, that is, what actually happens in the classroom, such as the nature of teacher-child interaction. Programs with similar features can expect similar results. In program provision, it's not what you *say* you do but what you *actually* do that counts.

Were the findings due to curriculum or other aspects of the program?

The High/Scope Preschool Curriculum Comparison study (Schweinhart & Weikart, 1997a, 1997b), which immediately followed the High/Scope

Perry Preschool Project, suggests that the curriculum had a lot to do with the outcomes. The comparison study found that young people born in poverty experienced fewer emotional problems and felony arrests if they attended a preschool program that used the High/Scope model or a traditional Nursery School model rather than a Direct Instruction model.

Since 1967, the study has followed the lives of 68 young people born in poverty who were randomly assigned at ages 3 and 4 to one of three groups, each experiencing a different curriculum model:

- In the **Direct Instruction model,** teachers followed a script to directly teach children academic skills, rewarding them for correct answers to the teacher's questions.[21]

- In the **High/Scope model,** teachers set up the classroom and the daily routine so children could plan, do, and review their own activities and engage in active learning key experiences in child development individually, in small groups, and in whole-class groups.

- In the **traditional Nursery School model,** teachers responded to children's self-initiated play in a loosely structured, socially supportive setting.

Program staff implemented the curriculum models independently and to high standards in 2½-hour classes held 5 days a week and conducted 1½-hour home visits every 2 weeks, when children were 3 and 4 years old. Except for the curriculum model, all aspects of the programs were nearly identical. The findings presented here are corrected for differences in the gender makeup of the groups.

By age 23, the High/Scope and Nursery School groups had 10 significant advantages over the Direct Instruction group, but the High/Scope and Nursery School groups did not differ significantly from each other on any outcome variable (Schweinhart & Weikart, 1997b). The High/Scope and Nursery School groups both had two significant advantages over the Direct Instruction group at age 23:

- Only 6% of either group needed treatment for emotional impairment or disturbance during their schooling, as compared to 47% of the Direct Instruction group.

- More of the High/Scope group (43%) and the Nursery School group (44%) had done volunteer work, as compared to only 11% of the Direct Instruction group.

The High/Scope group had six additional significant advantages over the Direct Instruction group:

- Only 10% had ever been arrested for a felony, as compared to 39% of the Direct Instruction group.

---

[21] This 1960s model has undergone subsequent development, and current versions differ somewhat from the one in this study.

- None of the High/Scope group had ever been arrested for a property crime, as compared to 38% of the Direct Instruction group.

- At age 15, 23% of the High/Scope group reported that they had engaged in 10 or more acts of misconduct, as compared to 56% of the Direct Instruction group.

- Fewer of the High/Scope group (36%) said that various kinds of people gave them a hard time, as compared to 69% of the Direct Instruction group.

- With regard to marriage, 31% of the High/Scope group had married and were living with their spouses, as compared to none of the Direct Instruction group.

- Of the High/Scope group, 70% planned to graduate from college, as compared to 36% of the Direct Instruction group.

The Nursery School group had two additional significant advantages over the Direct Instruction group:

- Only 9% of the Nursery School group had been arrested for a felony at ages 22–23, as compared to 34% of the Direct Instruction group.

- None of the Nursery School group had ever been suspended from work, as compared to 27% of the Direct Instruction group.

Through age 10, the main finding of the Preschool Curriculum Comparison study was that the overall average IQ of the three groups rose 27 points—from a borderline impairment level of 78 to a normal level of 105 after 1 year of their preschool program—and subsequently settled in at an average of 95, still at the normal level. The only curriculum group difference through age 10 was measured as the preschool programs ended: The average IQ of the Direct Instruction group was significantly higher than the average IQ of the Nursery School group (103 vs. 93). Throughout their school years, curriculum groups did not differ significantly in school achievement, nor did their high school graduation rates differ significantly. The conclusion at that time was that well-implemented preschool curriculum models, regardless of their theoretical orientation, had similar effects on children's intellectual and academic performance. However, time has proved otherwise. Tightly scripted, teacher-directed instruction, although touted by some as the surest path to school readiness, instead seems to purchase a temporary improvement in academic performance at the cost of a missed opportunity for long-term improvement in social behavior.

Does the High/Scope Perry Preschool study apply to Head Start and state preschool programs?

Because of the demand for knowledge of the lasting benefits of preschool education programs, there has been a tendency to generalize the High/Scope Perry Preschool study's findings beyond reasonably similar programs. Several of these generalizations deserve discussion here.

The most common generalizations of the High/Scope Perry Preschool study findings relate to the national Head Start program. Indeed, news reports have often imprecisely referred to the Perry Preschool Project as a Head Start program (see discussion by Woodhead, 1988). News reporters would argue that this conflation of terms is a useful convenience to simplify the story in that both the Perry Preschool program and Head Start serve young children living in poverty and began in the U.S. in the 1960s. Nonetheless, Head Start, as nationally defined by its Program Performance Standards (U. S. Administration for Children and Families, 2001), clearly does not meet the standard of reasonable similarity with the Perry Preschool program for generalization purposes:

- Most Head Start teachers do not have a bachelor's degree. In 2000, only 28% of Head Start teachers had a bachelor's degree, while 19% had an associate's degree, 32% had some college experience but no degree, and 74% had a Child Development Associate credential or state-awarded preschool certificate (Zill et al., 2003). Teacher salaries in Head Start average $21,000—about half of the average of $43,000 for public school teacher salaries (National Institute for Early Education Research, 2003)—while teacher salaries in the High/Scope Perry Preschool Project were at public school teacher salary levels at the time of the program, with a 10% bonus for participation in a special program.

- Head Start does serve most but not all participating children for 2 or more program years. In FY 2003, for example, 34% of Head Start children were 3 years old, 53% were 4 years old, 5% were 5 or older, and 8% were under 3 (U. S. Administration for Children and Families, 2004b). In FY 2002, 36% of Head Start children were 3 years old, and it is reasonable to assume that these children continued in Head Start as 4-year-olds in FY 2003, so that most of the 4-year-olds in Head Start in FY 2003 (36% among the 53%) had been in the program the previous year. We can therefore surmise that in FY 2003 only 17% of Head Start 4-year-olds attended the program for only 1 year.

- Only 20% of Head Start programs report using the High/Scope educational model, while 39% report using the Creative Curriculum model, and 41% report using some other curriculum approach (Zill et al., 2003). The Creative Curriculum model has goals similar to the High/Scope model, but emphasizes different practices to attain these goals (Dodge, Colker, & Heroman, 2002).

- Head Start Program Performance Standards require only 2 home visits a year.

The Head Start Family and Child Experiences Survey (FACES) found that children gained 4 points in standard scores on the Peabody Picture Vocabulary Test during their Head Start year (Zill et al., 2003). Children in the High/Scope Perry Preschool Project gained 8 points in their first year and a total of 14 points in 2 years. In other words, on average, Head Start programs are achieving some success, but could be doing more to help children reach their potential.

Forty states now invest in state preschool programs for young children living in poverty or otherwise at special risk of school failure (Barnett et al., 2003; National Prekindergarten Center, 2003). As these programs have developed, especially in the past 2 decades, policymakers have paid attention to program quality, thereby acknowledging the argument from the High/Scope Perry Preschool study and similar studies that only high-quality preschool programs for poor children are known to have long-term benefits for participants and a strong return on public investment. However, politics is the art of compromise, and the high quality of the High/Scope Perry Preschool program (as defined earlier) is seldom achieved in state preschool programs (Gilliam & Zigler, 2004).

The simple scientific conclusion is that the findings of the High/Scope Perry Preschool study do not apply to typical Head Start or state preschool programs, but may apply to exemplary ones and could apply to typical ones if policymakers and administrators chose to implement the standards of high quality described here. It is important to get this point just right, neither overstating nor understating the Perry Preschool Project study's generalizability. While the findings do not apply to typical Head Start programs as they exist today, it is not because the Perry Preschool program studied was an unattainable ideal run by super-educators, the likes of which will never be seen again. To borrow a phrase from Lisbeth Schorr, the programs and findings presented in the Perry Preschool study monographs are completely and realistically "within our reach" (Schorr, 1989, p. *i.*).

Does the study apply to child care programs?

Several studies of U.S. child care centers have concluded that their quality is unacceptably low (Cost, Quality, & Child Outcomes Study Team, 1995; Whitebook, Phillips, & Howes, 1993). In terms of the quality criteria listed here, child care programs have certain seemingly insurmountable financial problems. Unlike Head Start and state preschool programs, which are fully paid for by the government, an estimated 60% of child care costs are borne by the participating families (Stoney & Greenberg, 1996). While child care programs can certainly aspire to be genuine preschool education programs and maintain a ratio of no more than 8 children per teacher, the need for child care includes, but also extends well beyond, 3- and 4-year-old children. By definition, these programs could serve all children whose parents are employed or in school, a definition that includes but is not limited to low-income children.

For the most part, the average pay for child care teachers is less than half that of public school teachers ($43,000). The average annual wage for child care workers in 2002 was $23,820 in local government programs, $18,279 in state and federal programs, $15,155 in private programs, and $11,507 for self-employed child care workers (National Child Care Information Center, 2004a). It should come as no surprise that only one state, Rhode Island, requires child care teachers to have bachelor's degrees, and only 15 states have any educational requirements at all for child care teachers (National Child Care Information Center, 2004b).

The High/Scope educational model widely influences teaching practices in child care programs; but the meager funds available for training in these programs mean that few providers actually receive much training in the High/Scope model. Daily classes certainly do run more than 2½ hours, and there is no reason to think that their additional duration, per se, prevents program staff from delivering as much or more quality education as programs of shorter duration. Teachers do not provide regular home visits to families, but that would not be the correct standard to use in these cases. Rather, the child care programs' challenge is to develop teacher-parent relationships of mutual respect and understanding that are of the same quality as those that result from biweekly home visits or regularly scheduled parent meetings.

Does the study apply to open-enrollment preschool programs?

The relatively new open enrollment preschool programs have also been linked to the High/Scope Perry Preschool study findings. These programs are sometimes called universal and, other than age and residence requirements, have no demographic restrictions (such as poverty) on program enrollment. The findings of the High/Scope Perry Preschool study and similar studies would apply only to children served by these programs who are reasonably similar to children living in poverty or otherwise at risk of school failure.

It is important to keep in mind, however, that poverty is not an inherent trait of children but rather a socioeconomic extreme of settings in which they live. A good preschool program offers a productive early childhood educational environment, while early childhood poverty by and large offers an unproductive early childhood educational environment. So the longitudinal preschool studies provide evidence that *the degree of educational productivity in early childhood settings has a large influence on young children's subsequent lives.* All young children spend their time in settings that vary in their educational productivity, so the findings apply in this way to all children. But if it is a setting's educational productivity that matters, early childhood programs are not *inherently* more educationally productive than children's homes, nor are children's homes *inherently* more productive than early childhood programs. Young children from educationally productive homes who attend less educationally productive early childhood programs would suffer negative effects on their development. The survey of existing preschool settings in the previous paragraphs gives reason to be seriously concerned about this reverse application of the findings of the longitudinal preschool program studies.

Does the study apply to early childhood programs in other countries?

As the characteristics of a country's children and programs diverge from the characteristics of the Perry Preschool Project's children and program, applications become less certain. Generalization of the study to other industrialized countries, such as Great Britain, seems probable, but generalization of the study to less industrialized countries requires greater caution. The challenge of such applications becomes clear as one considers the practical ranges of outcome variables in various countries. Improving the high school graduation rate, for example, is a reasonable goal in industrialized countries, but not in some less industrialized countries. One might reasonably argue, however, that a high-quality preschool program would improve children's educational performance in less industrialized countries, but that this effect would be expressed in ways other than an improved high school graduation rate. For example, the Turkish Early Enrichment Project (Kağitçibaşi, Sunar, & Bekman, 2001) found evidence of long-term program effects on children's educational success and social adjustment in a very different culture. Cost-benefit analysis is particularly sensitive to such differences between countries.

Did the Perry Preschool program occur too long ago to apply to current programs?

The Perry Preschool Project operated from 1962 through 1967. The rapid pace of technological change in modern society—including the advent of widespread use of computers, worldwide electronic communication, and increased long-distance transportation, among other advances—is unprecedented in history. But there is no compelling reason to assume that this rapid pace of technological change would alter basic principles of human behavior and education. Throughout most of the history of the world, few would have regarded half a century or even a century as a sufficient amount of time to permit profound changes in traditions, let alone profound changes in human nature that would affect how children respond to an educational program. Indeed, education and the social sciences in general are quests for *timeless* principles, not for principles that must be rediscovered once or twice a decade. The argument that the findings of such studies have limited applicability to the present because of rapid change is quite similar to a belief that because each human experience is unique, scientific generalization is impossible. A current manifestation of this belief is the postmodernism movement (Dahlberg, Moss, & Pence, 1999). Postmodernism is essentially a nonscientific movement—even antiscientific. In contrast, the scientific approach adopted in the High/Scope Perry Preschool study is the logical application of the principle that similar experiences have similar effects on human development—what might be called the principle of external validity or generalizability.

Does the evidence of the effectiveness of the High/Scope educational model come only from programs run decades ago?

No. The Head Start FACES study (Zill et al., 2003) is a nationally representative study of 2,800 children who entered Head Start in fall 2000. It found that 4-year-olds in Head Start classes that used High/Scope improved from fall to spring in letter and word identification skills and cooperative classroom behavior and decreased their behavior problems:

- On a scale of letter and word recognition, children in High/Scope classes registered a highly significant gain ($p < .01$) of 12.6 scale points, significantly more ($p < .05$) than children in classes using Creative Curriculum or other curricula.

- On teacher ratings of cooperative classroom behavior, children in High/Scope classes experienced a highly significant gain ($p < .01$) of half a standard deviation, significantly more ($p < .05$) than children in classes using Creative Curriculum or other curricula.

- On teacher ratings of total behavior problems, particularly problems involving hyperactive behavior, children in High/Scope classes dropped significantly ($p < .05$) during the year, significantly more ($p < .05$) than did children in classes using Creative Curriculum or other curricula.

Of the 91% of Head Start teachers who used one or more curriculum models, 39% used Creative Curriculum, 20% used High/Scope, and 41% used some other curriculum, such as High Reach, Scholastic, or Los Cantos Los Niños. The quality of Creative Curriculum and High/Scope classes was significantly higher than the quality of classes that used other curricula, particularly with respect to language. On the 7-point Early Childhood Environment Rating Scale (Harms, Clifford, & Cryer, 1998), with 5 identified as good, High/Scope classes averaged 5.04, Creative Curriculum classes averaged 5.02, and classes using other curricula averaged 4.55. On its language items, average scores were slightly higher, but the differences were about the same. On a quality composite, the average scores for High/Scope and Creative Curriculum were nearly half a standard deviation higher than the average scores for other curricula—clearly an educationally meaningful difference.

The High/Scope Training for Quality study (Epstein, 1993) also offers evidence for the effectiveness of the High/Scope preschool model as practiced throughout the U.S. Half of High/Scope-certified trainers in the study were in Head Start, 27% were in public schools, and 20% were in private child care agencies. They had a median 15 years of early childhood experience, 88% had completed college, and 85% had teacher-training responsibility—spending an average of 8 hours a week training teachers. At the time of the study, the High/Scope Registry listed 1,075 early childhood leaders in 34 states and 10 other countries who had successfully completed High/Scope's 7-week trainer certification program in the previous decade. The average trainer had trained 15 teaching teams, so an estimated 16,125 teaching teams, including 29% of all Head Start staff, had received High/Scope model training from these trainers. Since trainers regard 45% of these classrooms as examples of the High/Scope model, they would nominate an estimated 7,256 early childhood classrooms throughout the U.S. and around the world as examples of the High/Scope model. High/Scope classrooms were rated significantly better than comparison classrooms in terms of classroom environment, daily routine, adult-child interaction, and overall implementation. The children in High/Scope programs significantly outperformed the children in comparison programs in initiative, social relations, music and movement, and overall child development.

Didn't the High/Scope Perry Preschool program achieve a level of quality that cannot be duplicated in ordinary preschool programs?

This criticism is rooted in the fact that the High/Scope Perry Preschool program paid teachers public school salaries and added a 10% bonus because the program was a special one. There is no reason to think that such pay would have attracted teachers who were substantially better than other public school teachers, and in fact the teachers who worked in the program were hired locally by ordinary search and hiring procedures. Nevertheless, current child care and Head Start teacher salaries average only about half as much as average public school teacher salaries (National Institute for Early Education Research, 2003). More and more preschool programs, however, are hiring teachers at public school salaries. It has also been suggested that the quality of the Perry Preschool program was due, in part, to the charismatic leadership of the program's director, David Weikart (Schorr, 1989). While Weikart's leadership was certainly essential to the program's success, there is every reason to believe that any dedicated preschool program director could exercise similar leadership with respect to assuring the quality of the programs under his or her supervision. Such leaders insist on program quality and fidelity to a validated educational model and strive to provide program staff with all the resources and encouragement they need to achieve them, including adequate salaries.

Although the program had a strong effect on children's intellectual performance, didn't it fade out over time?

It is true that the High/Scope Perry Preschool program had a statistically significant effect on children's IQs during and up to a year after the program, but not after that (as shown in Table 3.3, p. 61). This pattern has been found in numerous other studies, such as those in the Consortium for Longitudinal Studies (1983). The pattern raises two questions: How far does it generalize? What does it mean?

For some time, the pattern of children's intellectual performance found in this study was taken to represent all outcomes of this and similar programs. It was concluded that these programs had strong effects that faded out over time. However, all of the subsequent findings of program effects in this study (effects on school achievement, high school graduation, adult earnings, and crime prevention) disprove this conclusion. Indeed, so many studies have now found evidence of long-term effects of high-quality preschool programs that the opposite conclusion is practically indisputable: **High-quality preschool programs for young children living in poverty do have long-term effects.**

So what is the meaning of the fadeout of program effect on children's intellectual performance? More than anything else, it teaches us about the nature of multiage intelligence tests. Unlike most achievement tests that are age-specific, most intelligence tests, like the Stanford-Binet (Terman & Merrill, 1960), are designed to be used with individuals of a wide range of ages, from early childhood to adulthood. Also unlike achievement tests, intelligence tests are not designed to assess program effects, and so the way they function in this role was not, and is not, well understood. Multiage intelligence tests actually consist of a series of age-specific test batteries (the Stanford-Binet has six items per battery) designed to function with a specific age level, such as children 4 years old or children 4 years and 6 months of age. The preschool studies found effects at the ages during and 1–2 years after the program, but not subsequently. Children with preschool program experience got more items right on those age-specific batteries, but did not get more right on age-specific batteries designed for older children. It seems reasonable to conclude, then, that when used to assess preschool program outcomes, intelligence tests functioned more like achievement tests than intelligence tests, and indeed that is precisely the use to which they were put. Imagine if achievement tests for grades 4–8 were all combined into one grand multiage test of achievement. It would not be at all surprising if a really good grade 4 classroom improved children's achievement test scores on this test at grades 4 and 5, but not at grades 6, 7, and 8. That is precisely what happened in the temporary effects of high-quality preschool programs on children's intellectual performance.

To take this thinking to a theoretical level regarding children's intellectual performance, we might simply say that the preschool studies showed intellectual performance to be environmentally sensitive—it went up in educationally productive preschool settings and down in less educationally productive elementary school settings. Or, to put it in terms of program and no-program groups, it went up when the program group's experience was more educationally productive than that of the no-program group and returned to the same level as that of the no-program group when both found themselves in the same elementary school settings.

Was the preschool program's effect on intellectual performance critical to its success, and can this goal be replaced by another goal, such as mastery of early literacy skills and other content?

The causal model presented in this monograph identifies intellectual performance as the gateway from the preschool program to all subsequent program effects. However, the original hypothesis was that a good preschool program would increase children's intellectual performance permanently, not temporarily; and typically, after early childhood, intellectual performance does not change much (Terman & Merrill, 1960). Perhaps rather than identifying the gateway variable as early childhood intellectual performance, we should call it the preschool intellectual boost.

The High/Scope educational model was originally called the Cognitively Oriented Curriculum (Weikart et al., 1970) because it focused on cognitive, logical processes identified in Piaget's theory of education (Piaget & Inhelder, 1969)—such as representation, classification, and seriation. Tests of early childhood intellectual performance demonstrably tap these processes. So the High/Scope preschool classroom provides a preschool intellectual boost as measured by these tests. It also provides other experiences that facilitate these intellectual processes, such as planning and reviewing one's activities, exploring what one is curious about, and developing a sense of personal control over the events of one's life—what might be called intellectual performance, broadly defined.

It makes sense to combine or supplement this emphasis on intellectual processes with a focus on early literacy or mathematics skills found to predict later achievement, but it does not make sense to replace the first with the second. To do so runs the risk of sacrificing the known long-term effects on school achievement, high school graduation rates, lifetime earnings, and crime prevention.

Why did the High/Scope Perry Preschool Project affect males and females differently?

Males and females in this study differed substantially from each other on educational attainment and lifetime arrests.

Evidence of stronger program effects on females appears for regular high school graduation rate, repeating a grade, and treatment for mental impairment. Over 2½ times as many program females as no-program females graduated from regular high school (84% vs. 32%), whereas about the same percentages of program and no-program males graduated from regular high school (50% vs. 54%). Half as many program females as no-program females repeated a grade (21% vs. 41%), while slightly more program males than no-program males repeated a grade (47% vs. 39%). Less than one fourth as many program females as no-program females (8% vs. 36%) were treated for mental impairment, while only two thirds as many program males as no-program males were treated for mental impairment (20% vs. 33%).

Evidence indicates that the program effect on criminal arrests was stronger for males than for females, partly because males had more arrests: 69% of no-program males, but only 34% of no-program females, were arrested five or more times. The evident program effect in persons with five or more arrests was a reduction of about one third for males (45% vs. 69%) and for females (24% vs. 34%), but because the percentages were higher for males, the reduction in number of arrests was greater. The starkest gender difference was in arrests for drug crimes, for which less than half as many program males as no-program males were arrested (18% vs. 49%), while the percentages were about the same for program and no-program females (8% vs. 11%).

A possible explanation for this pattern is that teachers and school staff responded differently to girls and boys whose academic performance improved as a result of receiving the preschool program. As would be expected, educators responded to the preschool program's effect on girls' early academic performance by keeping them in regular classes rather than by having them repeat a grade or by assigning them to special classes for mental impairment. Girls who were not tracked into repeated grades or special classes were more likely to graduate from regular high school. On the other hand, boys in the program and no-program groups were retained in grade and assigned to special classes for mental impairment at about the same rate, despite better performance on intellectual tests by the group who had preschool. This may be because teachers and school staff focused primarily on classroom misconduct (more common in both groups of boys than in the girls) rather than on objective measures of academic performance such as intellectual tests. For this reason, the intellectual gains made in preschool by the male program group may not have translated as expected to gains in the high school graduation rate and in other long-term indicators of educational success.

Conclusions

The major conclusion of this midlife phase of the Perry Preschool research study is that **high-quality preschool programs for young children living in poverty contribute to their intellectual and social development in childhood and their school success, economic performance, and reduced commission of crime in adulthood.** This study confirms that these findings extend not only to young adults but also to adults in midlife. It confirms that the long-term effects are lifetime effects. The Perry Preschool study indicates that the return to the public on its initial investment in such programs is not only substantial but larger than previously estimated.

The study draws these conclusions about a 2-year preschool education program for 3- and 4-year-olds living in low-income families. Teachers had bachelor's degrees and certification in education, and each served 5–6 children. They used the High/Scope model of participatory education in daily 2½-hour classes and visited families weekly. In this model, teachers arranged the classroom and daily schedule to support children's self-initiated learning activities, led both small-group and large-group activities, and helped children engage in key experiences in child development. Teachers studied and received regular training and support in their use of this educational model.

The most basic implication of this study is that all young children living in low-income families should have access to preschool programs that have features that are reasonably similar to those of the High/Scope Perry Preschool Project. Findings from this long-term study and others reviewed in this report have motivated policymakers to invest more in preschool programs. But because policymakers practice the art of political compromise, these programs have seldom met the standard of reasonable similarity identified here. Recognizing this problem, more recent efforts, such as the Abbott court decision in New Jersey and the recent constitutional amendment in Florida, have sought to require key program standards from the beginning of a program. These are hopeful signs and models for the future.

The High/Scope Perry Preschool Project serves as a symbol of what government programs can achieve. The High/Scope Perry Preschool study also offers a challenge, a kind of policy gauntlet, for decision makers at local, state, and national levels. It demonstrates what can be done, and their challenge is to do it. The High/Scope Perry Preschool, the Abecedarian, and the Chicago programs described in this report all have significant benefits. Though they illuminate different aspects of the question of lasting effects of preschool education, they all reflect the same challenge of providing high-quality preschool programs that include low-income children so that these children get a fair chance to achieve their potential and contribute meaningfully to their families and to society.

References

Advisory Committee on Head Start Research and Evaluation. (1999, October). *Evaluating Head Start: A recommended framework for studying the impact of the Head Start program*. Washington, DC: U.S. Department of Health & Human Services.

American College Testing Program. (1976). *User's guide: Adult APL Survey*. Iowa City, IA: Author.

Anderson, D. A. (1999). The aggregate burden of crime. *Journal of Law and Economics, 42*, 611–642.

Angrist, J. D., Imbens, G. W., & Rubin, D. B. (1996). Identification of causal effects using instrumental variables. *Journal of the American Statistical Association, 91*, 444–472.

Anthony, J. C., & Helzer, J. E. (in press). Epidemiology of drug dependence. In M. T. Tsuang & M. Ehen (Eds.), *Harvard textbook in psychiatric epidemiology* (2nd ed.). New York: John Wiley and Sons.

Arbuckle, J. L. (1999). *Amos*. Chicago: SmallWaters Corp. Now available from SPSS.

Arthur, G. (1952). *The Arthur Adaptation of the Leiter International Performance Scale*. Beverly Hills, CA: Psychological Service Center Press.

Attanosio, O. P., & Hoynes, H. W. (2000). Differential mortality and wealth accumulation. *Journal of Human Resources, 35*, 1–29.

Bachman, J. G., & Johnston, J. (1978). *The Monitoring the Future Questionnaire*. Ann Arbor, MI: University of Michigan Institute for Social Research.

Bachman, J. G., O'Malley, P. M., & Johnston, J. (1978). *Adolescence to adulthood: Change and stability in the lives of young men: Vol. VI. Youth in transition*. Ann Arbor, MI: University of Michigan, Institute for Social Research.

Bachu, A, & O'Connell, M. (2001, October). Fertility of American women: June 2000. *Current Population Reports*. Washington, DC: U.S. Census Bureau. Retrieved December 4, 2003, from *http://www.census.gov/prod/2001pubs/p20-543rv.pdf*.

Barnes, H. V. (1991). *Predicting long-term outcomes from early elementary classroom measures in a sample of high-risk black children*. Unpublished doctoral dissertation, University of Michigan, Ann Arbor.

Barnett, W. S. (1985a). Benefit-cost analysis of the Perry Preschool program and its policy implications. *Education Evaluation and Policy Analysis, 4*, 333–342.

Barnett, W. S. (1985b). *The Perry Preschool program and its long-term effects: A benefit-cost analysis*. Ypsilanti, MI: High/Scope Press.

Barnett, W. S. (1992). Benefits of compensatory preschool education. *The Journal of Human Resources, 27*(2), 279–312.

Barnett, W. S. (1993). Benefit-cost analysis of preschool education: Findings from a 25-year follow-up. *American Journal of Orthopsychiatry, 63*(4), 500–508.

Barnett, W. S. (1995). Long-term effects of early childhood programs on cognitive and school outcomes. *The Future of Children, 5*(3), 25–50.

Barnett, W. S. (1996). *Lives in the balance: Age-27 benefit-cost analysis of the High/Scope Perry Preschool program* (Monographs of the High/Scope Educational Research Foundation, 11). Ypsilanti, MI: High/Scope Press.

Barnett, W. S. (2002). Early childhood education. In A. Molnar (Ed.), *School reform proposals: The research evidence* (pp. 1–26). Greenwich, CT: Information Age Publishing.

Barnett, W. S. (2004). Does Head Start have lasting cognitive effects? In E. Zigler & S. Styfco (Eds.), *The Head Start debates* (pp. 221–249). New Haven, CT: Yale University Press.

Barnett, W. S., Belfield, C. R., & Nores, M. (2004). *The High/Scope Perry Preschool program: A cost-benefit analysis using data from the age-40 follow-up* (Working Paper). Ypsilanti, MI: High/Scope Educational Research Foundation.

Barnett, W. S., Belfield, C. R., Nores, M., & Schweinhart, L. S. (in press). *A cost-benefit analysis of the High/Scope Perry Preschool program using data from the age 40 follow-up* (Monographs of the High/Scope Educational Research Foundation, 15). Ypsilanti, MI: High/Scope Press.

Barnett, W. S., Brown, K., & Shore, R. (2004). The universal vs. targeted debate: Should the United States have preschool for all? *Policy Matters, 6.* New Brunswick, NJ: National Institute for Early Education Research, Rutgers University.

Barnett, W. S., Robin, K. B., Hustedt, J. T., & Schulman, K. L. (2003). *The state of preschool: 2003 state preschool yearbook.* New Brunswick, NJ: National Institute for Early Education Research. Retrieved July 9, 2004, from *http://nieer.org/yearbook/.*

Barnett, W. S., Young, J., & Schweinhart, L. J., (1998). How preschool education influences long-term cognitive development and school success. In W. S. Barnett & S. S. Boocock, (Eds.), *Early care and education for children in poverty: Promises, programs, and long-term results* (pp 167–184). Albany, NY: State University of New York Press.

Berrueta-Clement, J. R., Schweinhart, L. J., Barnett, W. S., Epstein, A. S., & Weikart, D. P. (1984). *Changed lives: The effects of the Perry Preschool program on youths through age 19* (Monographs of the High/Scope Educational Research Foundation, 8). Ypsilanti, MI: High/Scope Press.

Berrueta-Clement, J. R., Schweinhart, L. J., & Weikart, D. P. (1983). Lasting effects of preschool education on children from low-income families in the United States. In R. Sornson (Ed.), *Preventing school failure: The relationship between preschool and primary education* (pp. 110–120). Ottawa, Ontario: International Development Research Centre.

Blank, R., & Ellwood, D. T. (2002). Poverty and welfare: The Clinton legacy for America's poor. In J. Frankel & P. Orszag (Eds.), *American economic policy in the 1990s.* Cambridge, MA: MIT Press.

Bloom, B. S. (1964). *Stability and change in human characteristics.* New York: Wiley.

Brame, R., & Piquero, A. R. (2003). Selective attrition and the age-crime relationship. *Journal of Quantitative Criminology, 19,* 107–127.

Brearly, M., & Hitchfield, E. (1966). *A guide to reading Piaget.* New York: Schocken Books.

Bronfenbrenner, U. (1974). *A report on longitudinal programs: Vol. 2. Is early intervention effective?* (DHEW Publication No. (OHD) 74–24). Washington, DC: U.S. Department of Health, Education, and Welfare.

Brunswick, A. F., & Messeri, P. (1985). Drugs, life style, and health: A longitudinal study of urban black youth. *American Journal of Public Health, 76*(1), 52–57. See also listing at Murray Research Center, *http://www.radcliffe.edu/documents/murray/0845StudyDescription.pdf.*

Bureau of Justice Statistics (BJS). (2001). *Justice expenditure and employment extracts* (NCJ 202792). Washington, DC: U.S. Department of Justice.

Bureau of Justice Statistics (BJS). (2002a). *Criminal victimization in the United States.* Washington, DC: U.S. Department of Justice.

Bureau of Justice Statistics (BJS). (2002b). *Sourcebook of criminal justice statistics* (30th ed.). Washington, DC: U.S. Department of Justice.

Bureau of Labor Statistics (BLS). (2002). *Current Population Survey March 2002.* Retrieved December 8, 2004, from *http//www.bls.gov/cps/ads/sdata.htm.*

Campbell, F. A., Breitmayer, B., & Ramey, C. T. (1986). Disadvantaged single teenage mothers and their children: Consequences of free educational day care. *Family Relations, 35,* 63–68.

Campbell, F. A., & Ramey, C. T. (1995). Cognitive and school outcomes for high-risk African American students at middle adolescence: Positive effects of early intervention. *American Educational Research Journal, 32,* 743–772.

Campbell, F. A., Ramey, C. T., Pungello, E. P., Sparling, J., & Miller-Johnson, S. (2002). Early childhood education: Young adult outcomes from the Abecedarian project. *Applied Developmental Science, 6,* 42–57.

Carneiro, P., & Heckman, J. J. (2003). Human capital policy. In J. J. Heckman & A. B. Krueger (Eds.), *Inequality in America: What role for human capital policies?* Cambridge, MA: MIT Press.

Clarke, S. H., & Campbell, F. A. (1998). Can intervention early prevent crime later? The Abecedarian project compared with other programs. *Early Childhood Research Quarterly, 13,* 319–343.

Cohen, M. A. (1998). The monetary value of saving a high-risk youth. *Journal of Quantitative Criminology, 14,* 5–33.

Cohen, M. A., Rust, R. T., Steen S., & Tidd, S. T. (2004). Willingness-to-pay for crime control programs. *Criminology, 42,* 89–109.

Consortium for Longitudinal Studies. (1983). *As the twig is bent . . . lasting effects of preschool programs.* Hillsdale, NJ: Erlbaum.

Conyers, L. M., Reynolds, A. J., & Ou, S-R. (2003). The effect of early childhood education on subsequent special education services: Findings from the Chicago Child-Parent Centers. *Educational Evaluation and Policy Analysis, 25,* 75–96.

Cost, Quality, & Child Outcomes Study Team. (1995). *Cost, quality, and child outcomes in child care centers* (2nd ed.) [Public Report]. Denver: Economics Department, University of Colorado at Denver.

Currie, J. (2000, April). Early childhood intervention programs: What do we know? Chicago: Joint Center for Poverty Research. Retrieved from *http://www.brook.edu/es/research/projects/cr/doc/currie20000401.pdf.* (ERIC Document Reproduction Service No. ED 451 915)

Currie, J., & Thomas, D. (1999). Does Head Start help Hispanic children? *Journal of Public Economics, 74,* 235–262.

Cutler, D. M. (2002). Equality, efficiency, and market fundamentals: The dynamics of international medical-care reform. *Journal of Economic Literature, 40,* 881–906.

Dahlberg, G., Moss, P., & Pence, A. (1999). *Beyond quality in early childhood education and care: Postmodern perspectives.* London: RoutledgeFalmer.

Dalaker, J. (2001, September). Poverty in the United States: 2000. *Current Population Reports—Consumer income.* Washington, DC: U.S. Census Bureau (P60-214). Retrieved June 17, 2003, from *http://landview.census.gov/hhes/poverty/poverty00/table5.html.*

Datta, L. (1976). The impact of the Westinghouse/Ohio evaluation on the development of Project Head Start: An examination of the immediate and longer-term effects and how they came about. In C. Abt (Ed.), *The evaluation of social programs* (pp. 129–181). Beverly Hills, CA: Sage Publications, Inc.

Day, J. C., & Newburger, E. C. (2002, July). The big payoff: Educational attainment and synthetic estimates of work-life earnings. *Current Population Reports, Special Studies.* Washington, DC: U.S. Government Printing Office. Retrieved May 31, 2004, from *http://www.census.gov/prod/2002pubs/p23-210.pdf.*

Deutsch, M. (1962). *The Institute for Developmental Studies annual report and descriptive statement.* New York: New York University.

Disaster Center, The. (2004). United States crime index rates per 100,000 inhabitants. Retrieved August 9, 2004, from *http://www.disastercenter.com/crime/uscrime.htm.*

Dodge, D. T., Colker, L., & Heroman, C. (2002). *The Creative Curriculum for preschool.* Washington, DC: Teaching Strategies, Inc.

Duncan, G. J. (1992, May 19). E-mail communication.

Dunn, L. M. (1965). *Peabody Picture Vocabulary Test manual.* Minneapolis, MN: American Guidance Service.

Economagic.com. (2004). *Gross domestic product price deflator over time.* Retrieved May 28, 2004, from *http://www.economagic.com/em-cgi/data.exe/fedstl/gdpdef+1.*

Education Commission of the States. (2003). State-funded prekindergarten programs. Retrieved November, 20, 2003, from *http://www.ecs.org/ecsmain.asp?page=/html/ProjectbySubject.asp?issueID=37.*

Elliott, D. S., Ageton, S. S., & Canter, R. J. (2002). An integrated theoretical perspective on delinquent behavior. In F. T. Cullen & R. Agnew (Eds.), *Criminological theory: Past to present, essential readings* (2nd ed.) (pp. 324–334). Los Angeles: Roxbury.

Ellwood, D. T., & Jencks, C. (2004). The spread of single-parent families in the United States since 1960. In D. P. Moynihan, L. Rainwater, & T. Smeeding (Eds.), *The future of the family.* New York: Russell Sage, 2004. Retrieved August 12, 2004, from *http://ksgnotes1. harvard.edu/research/wpaper.nsf/rwp/RWP04-008/$File/rwp04_008_jencks_ellwood_ rev_2_June04.pdf.*

Epstein, A. S. (1993). *Training for quality: Improving early childhood programs through systematic inservice training.* Ypsilanti, MI: High/Scope Press.

Epstein, A. S. (1999). Pathways to quality in Head Start, public school, and private nonprofit early childhood programs. *Journal of Research in Childhood Education, 13*(2), 101–119.

Epstein, A. S., & Neill, P. (1995–1996). *Evaluation of the High/Scope Georgia Lead Teacher Training Program.* Ypsilanti, MI: High/Scope Educational Research Foundation.

Farnworth, M., Schweinhart, L. J., & Berrueta-Clement, J. R. (1985, Fall). Preschool intervention, school success and delinquency in a high-risk sample of youth. *American Educational Research Journal, 22,* 445–464.

Farrington, D. P. (2003). Developmental and life-course criminology: Key theoretical and empirical issues. *Criminology, 41,* 221–246.

Federal Bureau of Investigation (FBI). 2002. *Crime in the United States.* Washington, DC: Department of Justice. Retrieved August 19, 2004, from *http://www.fbi.gov/ucr/ucr. htm#cius.*

Federal Election Commission. (n.d.). *Voter registration and turnout 2000.* Retrieved August 23, 2004, from *http://www.fec.gov/pages/2000turnout/reg&to00.htm.*

Federal Election Commission (n.d.). *Voter registration and turnout by age, gender & race 1998.* Retrieved August 23, 2004, from *http://www.fed.gov/pages/98demog.htm.*

Federal Register. (2004, February 13). *2004 Health and Human Services poverty guidelines for the 48 contiguous states and DC, 69*(30), 7336–7338.

Fisher, G. M. (1992, Winter). The development and history of the poverty thresholds, *Social Security Bulletin, 55*(4), 3–14. Summary retrieved online October 14, 2003, from *http:// aspe.os.dhhs.gov/poverty/papers/hptgssiv.htm.*

Fitz-Gibbon, C. T., & Morris, L. L. (1987). *How to analyze data.* Newbury Park, CA: Sage.

Flavell, J. (1965). *The developmental psychology of Jean Piaget.* New York: Van Nostrand.

Freeberg, N. E. (1974). *Development of assessment measure for use with youth-work training program enrollees, phase 2: Longitudinal validation* (Final Report, U.S. Department of Labor, Document No. ETS PR-74-1). Princeton, NJ: Educational Testing Services.

Frey, B. S., & Stutzer, A. (2002). *Happiness and economics.* Princeton, NJ: Princeton University Press.

Froebel, F. (1826, 2004). *Education of man.* Honolulu: University Press of the Pacific.

Fullerton, D. (1991). Reconciling recent estimates of the marginal welfare cost of taxation. *American Economic Review, 81,* 302–308.

Garces, E., Thomas, D., & Currie, J. (2000, December). *Longer-term effects of Head Start* (Working Paper 8054). Cambridge, MA: National Bureau of Economic Research. Retrieved July 14, 2004, from *http://www.nber.org/papers/w8054.*

Gilliam, W. S., & Zigler, E. F. (2001). A critical meta-analysis of all evaluations of state-funded preschool from 1977 to 1998: Implications for policy, service delivery, and program implementation. *Early Childhood Research Quarterly, 15,* 441–473.

Gilliam, W. S., & Zigler, E. F. (2004). *State efforts to evaluate the effects of prekindergarten: 1977 to 2003.* New Brunswick, NJ: National Institute for Early Education Research. Retrieved July 9, 2004 from *http://nieer.org/resources/research/StatePreKMeta.pdf.*

Goodson, B. D., Layzer, J. I., St. Pierre, R. G., Bernstein, L. S., & Lopez, M. (2000). Effectiveness of a comprehensive, five-year family support program for low-income families: Findings from the Comprehensive Child Development Program. *Early Childhood Research Quarterly, 15,* 5–39.

Gormley, W., Gayer, T., Phillips, D., & Dawson, B. (2004). *The effects of Oklahoma's universal pre-k program on school readiness.* Washington, DC: CROCUS, Georgetown University.

Gray, S. W., Ramsey, B. K., & Klaus R. A. (1982). *From 3 to 20: The Early Training Project.* Baltimore, MD: University Park Press.

Grossman, H. (Ed.). (1973). *Manual on terminology and classification in mental retardation* (3rd ed.). Washington, DC: American Association on Mental Deficiency.

Hanushek, E. A. (1998). Conclusions and controversies about the effectiveness of schools. *Federal Reserve Bank of New York Economic Policy Review, 4,* 1–22.

Harms, T., Clifford, R. M., & Cryer, D. (1998). *Early Childhood Environment Rating Scale* (Rev. ed.). New York: Teachers College Press.

Head Start Bureau. (2003). *Head Start Program Fact Sheet, 2003.* Washington, DC: Administration for Children and Families. Retrieved November 20, 2003, from *http:// www.acf.hhs.gov/programs/hsb/research/2003.htm.*

Head Start Child Outcomes Framework. (2003). *Head Start Bulletin, 76.* Washington, DC: Administration for Children and Families, U. S. Department of Health and Human Services). Retrieved January 5, 2004, from *http://www.headstartinfo.org/publications/hsbulletin76/hsb76_09.htm.*

Head Start Quality Research Consortium. (1995–2000). *Fall 1998 and spring 1999 parent interviews.* See *http://www.acf.hhs.gov/programs/core/ongoing_research/qrc/qrc.html.*

Hodgson, T. A. (1992). Cigarette smoking and lifetime medical expenditures. *Milbank Quarterly, 70,* 81–125.

Hohmann, M., Banet, B., & Weikart, D. P. (1979). *Young children in action: A manual for preschool educators.* Ypsilanti, MI: High/Scope Press.

Hohmann, M., & Weikart, D. P. (1995). *Educating young children: Active learning practices for preschool and child care programs* (1st ed.). Ypsilanti, MI: High/Scope Press.

Hohmann, M., & Weikart, D. P. (2002). *Educating young children: Active learning practices for preschool and child care programs* (2nd ed.). Ypsilanti, MI: High/Scope Press.

Howe, M. (1953). *The Negro in Ypsilanti.* Unpublished master's thesis. Eastern Michigan University, Ypsilanti, MI.

Hoxby, C. M. (1999). Where should federal education initiatives be directed? In M. H. Klosters (Ed.), *Financing college tuition: Government policies and educational priorities* (pp. 28–52). Washington, DC: AEI Press.

Hunt, J. M. (1961). *Intelligence and experience.* New York: Ronald Press.

Husten, C., Jackson, K., & Lee, C. (2004). Cigarette smoking among adults—United States, 2002. *Morbidity and Mortality Weekly Report, 53*(20):427–431. Retrieved August 30, 2004, from *http://www.cdc.gov/mmwr/preview/mmwrhtml/mm5320a2.htm.*

Kağitçibaşi, Ç., Sunar, D., & Bekman, S. (2001). Long-term effects of early intervention: Turkish low-income mothers and children. *Applied Developmental Psychology, 22,* 333–361.

Kakalik, J. S., Furry, W. S., Thomas, M. A., & Carney, M. F. (1981). *The cost of special education.* Santa Monica, CA: Rand Corporation.

Karoly, L. A., Greenwood, P. W., Everingham, S. S., Houbé, J., Kilburn, M. R., Rydell, C. P., et al. (1998). *Investing in our children: What we know and don't know about the costs and benefits of early childhood interventions.* Washington, DC: Rand Corporation. Available at *http://www.rand.org/publications/MR/MR898/.*

Kaufman, A. S., & Kaufman, N. L. (1994). *Kaufman Functional Skills Test.* Circle Pines, MN: American Guidance Service, Inc.

Kennedy, W., Van de Riet, V., & White, J. (1963). Normative sample of intelligence. *Monographs of the Society for Research in Child Development, 28*(6, Serial No. 90).

Kirk, S. A. (1958). *Early education of the mentally retarded.* Urbana, IL: University of Illinois Press.

Kline, R. B. (1998). *Principles and practice of structural equation modeling.* New York: Guilford Press.

Levin, H. M., & McEwan, P. J. (2002a). *Cost-effectiveness analysis* (2nd ed.). New York: Russell Sage.

Levin, H. M., & McEwan, P. J. (2002b). *Cost-effectiveness and educational policy.* Larchmont, NJ: AEFA Handbook: Eye on Education.

Locurto, C. (1991). Beyond IQ in preschool programs? *Intelligence, 15,* 295–312.

Love, J. M., Kisker, E. E., Ross, C. M., Schochet, P. Z., Brooks-Gunn, J., Paulsell, D., et al. (2002). *Building their futures: How early Head Start programs are enhancing the lives of infants and toddlers in low-income families: Vol. 1, Final technical report.* Washington, DC: U.S. Department of Health & Human Services. Retrieved July16, 2004, from *http://www.acf.dhhs.gov/programs/core/ongoing_research/ehs/impacts_vol1/impacts_vol1.pdf.*

Lucas, J. W., Schiller, J. S., Benson, V. (2004). *Summary health statistics for U.S. adults: National Health Interview Survey, 2001.* Washington, DC: National Center for Health Statistics Vital Health Stat, 10(218).

MacArthur Foundation Research Network on Successful Midlife Development. (1997). MIDI—The Midlife Development Inventory. Obtained from Director Gilbert Brim, Vero Beach, FL.

Massé, L. N., & Barnett, W. S. (2002). A benefit-cost analysis of the Abecedarian early childhood intervention. In H. Levin, & P. McEwan (Eds.), *Cost-effectiveness analysis in education: Methods, findings and potential. 2002 Yearbook of the American Education Finance Association.* Retrieved July 28, 2004, from *http://nieer.org/resources/research/ AbecedarianStudy.pdf.*

McCarthy, J. J., & Kirk, S. A. (1961). *Examiner's manual: Illinois Test of Psycholinguistic Abilities, experimental version.* Urbana, IL: University of Illinois, Institute for Research on Exceptional Children.

McKey, R. H., Condelli, L., Ganson, H., Barrett, B. J. McDonkey, C., & Plantz, M. C. (1985). *The impact of Head Start on children, families, and communities* (final report of the Head Start Evaluation, Synthesis, and Utilization Project). Washington, DC.: CSR, Inc

Michigan Department of Corrections. (2004). *Offender tracking information system.* Retrieved May 27, 2004, from *http://www.michigan.gov/corrections/0,1607,7-119-1409—,00.html.*

Michigan Family Independence Agency (FIA). (2003). *Michigan Family Independence Agency information packet, Policy Analysis and Program Evaluation Division.* Retrieved August 19, 2004, from *www.michigan.gov/documents/FIA-InformationPacket0503_ 67749_7.PDF.*

Miller, T. R., Cohen, M. A., & Wiersema, B. (1996). *Victim costs and consequences: A new look* (National Institute of Justice Research Report). Washington, DC: National Institute of Justice. (NCJ-155282)

Mrozek, J. R., & Taylor, L. O. (2002). What determines the value of life? A meta-analysis. *Journal of Policy Analysis and Management, 21,* 253–270.

MSIS. (2001). *MSIS statistical reports for federal fiscal years 1999, 2000 and 2001: Michigan, Centers for Medicare and Medicaid Services.* Retrieved August 19, 2004, from *http:// www.cms.hhs.gov/medicaid/msis/01mi.pdf.*

National Center for Education Statistics, U.S. Department of Education. (2002a). *Digest of educational statistics.* Retrieved August 19, 2004, from *http://nces.ed.gov/programs/ digest/.*

National Center for Education Statistics, U.S. Department of Education. (2002b, August). *Statistics of state school systems; revenues and expenditures for public elementary and secondary education; and common core of data surveys.* Retrieved September 2, 2004, from *http://nces.ed.gov/programs/digest/d02/tables/PDF/table166.pdf.*

National Center for Health Statistics. (1998). *Survival rates by gender.* Retrieved December 8, 2004, from *http://www.cdc.gov/nchs/hus.htm.*

National Center for Health Statistics. (2004a). *Alcohol use.* Retrieved June 23, 2004, from *http://www.cdc.gov/nchs/fastats/alcohol.htm.*

National Center for Health Statistics. (2004b). *Illegal drug use.* Retrieved June 23, 2004, from *http://www.cdc.gov/nchs/fastats/druguse.htm.*

National Child Care Information Center. (2004a). *Child care workforce qualifications.* Retrieved July 11, 2004, from *http://www.nccic.org/poptopics/qualifications.html.*

National Child Care Information Center. (2004b). *Early childhood workforce salaries. Retrieved July 11, 2004, from http://www.nccic.org/poptopics/salaries.html.*

National Institute of Diabetes and Digestive and Kidney Diseases, Weight-control Information Network. (2003). *Statistics related to overweight and obesity.* Retrieved August 30, 2004, from *http://www.niddk.nih.gov/health/nutrit/pubs/statobes.htm.*

National Institute on Drug Abuse. (2003). *Drug use among racial/ethnic minorities, revised.* Retrieved on August 30, 2004, from *http://165.112.78.61/pubs/minorities.*

National Institute for Early Education Research. (2003). *NIEER fact sheet on Head Start teachers.* Retrieved July 1, 2004, from *http://nieer.org/resources/facts/index. php?FastFactID=12.*

National Prekindergarten Center. (2003). *Prekindergarten policy framework.* Chapel Hill, NC: FPG Child Development Institute, University of North Carolina.

O'Brien, R. W., D'Elio, M. A., Vaden-Kiernan, M., Magee, C., Younoszai, T., Keane, M. J., et al. (2002, January). *A descriptive study of Head Start families* (FACES Technical Report I). Washington, DC: Administration on Children, Youth, and Families, U.S. Department of Health and Human Services. Retrieved May 28, 2004, from *http://www.acf.hhs.gov/ programs/core/ongoing_research/faces/technical_report/technical_report.pdf.*

Oden, S., Schweinhart, L. J., & Weikart, D. P. (2000). *Into adulthood: A study of the effects of Head Start.* Ypsilanti, MI: High/Scope Press. (ERIC Document Reproduction Service No. ED 444 730)

Office of Compensation and Working Conditions (OCWC). (2002). *Employer costs for employee compensation historical listing (annual), 1986–2001.* Washington, DC: U.S. Bureau of Labor Statistics.

Ogle, L., Sen, A., Pahlke, E., Jocelyn, L., Kastberg, D., Roey, S., et al. (2003). *International comparisons in fourth-grade reading literacy: Findings from the Progress in International Reading Literacy Study (PIRLS) of 2001.* U.S. Department of Education, NCES. Washington, DC: U.S. Government Printing Office. (NCES 2003 073)

Olds, D. L., Eckenrode, J., Henderson, C. R., Jr., Kitzman, H., Powers, J., Cole, R., Sidora, K., Morris, P., Pettitt, L. M., & Luckey, D. (1997). Long term effects of home visitation on material life course and child abuse and neglect: 15-year follow-up of a randomized trial. *The Journal of the American Medical Association, 278.* 637–643.

Olds, D. L., Henderson, C. R., Jr., Cole, R., Eckenrode, J., Kitzman, H., Luckey, D., Pettitt, L., Sidora, K., Morris, Pl, & Powers, J. (1998). Long-term effects of nurse home visitation on children's criminal and antisocial behavior: 15-year follow-up of a randomized trial. *The Journal of the American Medical Association, 280.* 1238–1244.

Olds, D. L., Henderson, C. R., Jr., Phelps, C., Kitzman, H., & Hanks, C. (1993). Effects of prenatal and infancy nurse home visitation on government spending. *Medical Care, 31.* 155–174.

Olmsted, P., & Montie, J. (Eds.). (2001). *What do early childhood settings look like? Structural characteristics of early childhood settings in 15 countries.* Ypsilanti, MI: High/Scope Press.

Piaget, J. (1960). *The psychology of intelligence.* Totowa, NJ: Littlefield, Adams.

Piaget, J. (1968). *Six psychological studies.* New York: Random House.

Piaget, J., & Inhelder, B. (1969). *The psychology of the child.* New York: Basic Books.

Piaget, J., Inhelder, B., & Szeminska, A. (1964). *The child's conception of geometry.* New York: W. W. Norton.

Planning and Evaluation Service. (1998). *Even Start: Evidence from the past and a look to the future.* Washington, DC: U.S. Department of Education. Available at *http://www.ed.gov/pubs/EvenStart/.* (ERIC Document Reproduction Service No. ED 427 890)

Proctor, B. D., & Dalaker, J. (2003, September). *Poverty in the United States: 2002* (P60-222). Washington, DC: U.S. Government Printing Office. Retrieved May 31, 2004, from *http://www.census.gov/prod/2003pubs/p60-222.pdf.*

Ramey, C. T., & Campbell, F. A. (1984). Preventive education for high-risk children: Cognitive consequences of the Carolina Abecedarian Project. *American Journal of Mental Deficiency, 88,* 515–523.

Rapsheets.com. (2003). Information retrieved January 23, 2003, from *http://www.rapsheets.com.*

Reynolds, A. J. (2000). *Success in early intervention: The Chicago Child-Parent Centers.* Lincoln, NE: University of Nebraska Press.

Reynolds, A. J., Temple, J. A., Robertson, D. L., & Mann, E. A. (2001). Long-term effects of an early childhood intervention on educational achievement and juvenile arrest: A 15-year follow-up of low-income children in public schools. *Journal of the American Medical Association, 285,* 2339–2346.

Reynolds, A. J., Temple, J. A., Robertson, D. L., Mann, E. A. (2002). Age 21 cost-benefit analysis of the Title I Chicago Child-Parent Centers. *Educational Evaluation and Policy Analysis, 4,* 267–303. Version retrieved July 28, 2004, from *http://www.ssc.wisc.edu/irp/pubs/dp124502.pdf.*

Ruopp, R., Travers, J., Glantz, F., & Coelen, C. (1979). *Children at the center: Summary findings and their implications* (Final report of the National Day Care Study, Vol. 1). Cambridge, MA: Abt Associates.

Scanzoni, J. H. (1971). *The Black family on modern society: Patterns of stability and security.* Chicago: University of Chicago Press.

Schorr, L. B. (1989). *Within our reach: Breaking the cycle of disadvantage.* New York: Doubleday.

Schweinhart, L. J. (1987). Can preschool programs help prevent delinquency? In J. Q. Wilson & G. C. Loury (Eds.), *From children to citizens: Families, schools, and delinquency prevention* (pp. 135–153). New York: Springer-Verlag.

Schweinhart, L. J. (2001). Getting ready for school in preschool. In Sornson, B. (Ed.), *Preventing early learning failure* (pp. 110–120). Alexandria, VA: Association for Supervision and Curriculum Development.

Schweinhart, L. J. (2002a, Spring). How a preschool study has influenced public policy. *Interplay,* 40–44.

Schweinhart, L. J. (2002b, June). Right from the start. *American School Board Journal. 189*(6), 26–29.

Schweinhart, L. J. (2002c). The three types of early childhood programs in the U.S. In A. J. Reynolds, M. C. Wang, & H. J. Walberg (Eds.), *Early childhood programs for a new century (Issues in children's and families' lives series* pp. 241–154). Washington, DC: CWLA Press.

Schweinhart, L. J., Barnes, H. V., & Weikart, D. P. (1993). *Significant benefits: The High/Scope Perry Preschool study through age 27* (Monographs of the High/Scope Educational Research Foundation, 10). Ypsilanti, MI: High/Scope Press.

Schweinhart, L. J., Berrueta-Clement, J. R., Barnett, W. S., Epstein, A. S., & Weikart, D. P. (1985a, Summer). Effects of the Perry Preschool program on youths through age 19—A summary. *Topics in Early Childhood Special Education, 5,* 26–35.

Schweinhart, L. J., Berrueta-Clement, J. R., Barnett, W. S., Epstein, A. S., & Weikart, D. P. (1985b, April). The promise of early childhood education. *Phi Delta Kappan, 66,* 548–553.

Schweinhart, L. J., & Weikart, D. P. (1980). *Young children grow up: The effects of the Perry Preschool Program on youths through age 15* (Monographs of the High/Scope Educational Research Foundation, 7). Ypsilanti, MI: High/Scope Press.

Schweinhart, L. J., & Weikart, D. P. (1981a, December). Effects of the Perry Preschool program on youths through age 15. *Journal of the Division for Early Childhood, 4,* 29–39 Reston, VA: Council for Exceptional Children.

Schweinhart, L. J., & Weikart, D. P. (1981b). Perry Preschool effects nine years later: What do they mean? In M. J. Begab, H. C. Haywood, & H. L. Garber (Eds.), *Psychosocial influences in retarded performance: Vol. 2, Strategies for improving competence* (pp. 113–126). Baltimore: University Park Press.

Schweinhart, L. J., & Weikart, D. P. (1983). The effects of the Perry Preschool program on youths through age 15—A summary. In Consortium for Longitudinal Studies, *As the twig is bent . . . Lasting effects of preschool programs* (pp. 71–102). Hillsdale, NJ: Lawrence Erlbaum Associates.

Schweinhart, L. J., & Weikart, D. P. (1988a). Early childhood education for at-risk four-year-olds? Yes. *American Psychologist, 43,* 665–667. (Response to Formal schooling for four-year-olds? No, by E. F. Zigler, 1987, *American Psychologist, 42,* 254–260.)

Schweinhart, L. J., & Weikart, D. P. (1988b). Education for young children living in poverty. Child-initiated learning or teacher-directed instruction? *Elementary School Journal, 89,* 213–225.

Schweinhart, L. J., & Weikart, D. P. (1988c). The High/Scope Perry Preschool program. In R. H. Price, E. L. Cowen, R. P. Lorion, & J. Ramos-McKay (Eds.), *Fourteen ounces of prevention: A casebook for practitioners* (pp. 53–65). Washington, DC: American Psychological Association.

Schweinhart, L. J., & Weikart, D. P. (1989, Spring). Head Start's high potential. *Policy Review,* pp. 85-86. (Response to False start? The fleeting gains of Head Start, by E. Borden & K. W. O'Beirne, *Policy Review,* Winter, 1989.)

Schweinhart, L. J., & Weikart, D. P. (1991). (Response to "Beyond IQ in preschool programs?" (by C. Locurto, 1991. *Intelligence, 15,* 313–315.)

Schweinhart, L. J., & Weikart, D. P. (1992). The High/Scope Perry Preschool study, similar studies, and implications for public policy in the U.S. In D. Stegelin (Ed.), *Early childhood education: Policy issues for the 1990s* (pp. 67–88). Norwood, NJ: Ablex.

Schweinhart, L. J., & Weikart, D. P. (1993, November). Success by empowerment: The High/Scope Perry Preschool study through age 27. *Young Children, 48*(7), 54–58.

Schweinhart, L. J., & Weikart, D. P. (1995). The High/Scope Perry Preschool study through age 27. In R. R. Ross, D. H. Antonowicz, & G. K. Dhaliwal, *Going straight: Effective delinquency prevention & offender rehabilitation* (pp. 57–75). Ottawa, Canada: Air Training & Publications.

Schweinhart, L. J., & Weikart, D. P. (1997a). The High/Scope Preschool Curriculum Comparison study through age 23. *Early Childhood Research Quarterly, 12,* 117–143.

Schweinhart, L. J., & Weikart, D. P. (1997b). *Lasting differences: The High/Scope Preschool Curriculum Comparison study through age 23* (Monographs of the High/Scope Educational Research Foundation, 12). Ypsilanti, MI: High/Scope Press.

Schweinhart, L. J., & Weikart, D. P. (1998). Why curriculum matters in early childhood education. *Educational Leadership, 55*(6), 57–60.

Sears, P. S., & Dowley, E. M. (1963). Research on teaching in the nursery school. In N. L. Gage (Ed.), *Handbook of research on teaching.* Chicago: Rand McNally.

Shonkoff, J., & Phillips, D. A. (2000). *From neurons to neighborhoods: The science of early childhood development.* Washington, DC: National Academy of Sciences Press.

Shore, R. (1997). *Rethinking the brain: New insights into early development.* New York: Families and Work Institute.

Siegel, J. (1998). *Stocks for the long run* (2nd ed.). NY: McGraw-Hill.

Skeels, H. M. (1966). Adult status of children with contrasting early life experiences. *Monographs of the Society for Research in Child Development, 31* (3, Serial No. 105).

Skeels, H. M., & Dye, H. G. (1939). A study of the effects of differential stimulation on mentally retarded children. *Proceedings of the American Association of Mental Deficiency, 44,* 114–136.

Smart Start Evaluation Team. (1999, September). *A six-county study of the effects of Smart Start child care on kindergarten entry skills* (Report to North Carolina Dept. of Health and Human Services). Chapel Hill, NC: Frank Porter Graham Child Development Center. Available at *http://www.fpg.unc.edu/%7Esmartstart/reports/six-county.pdf.* (ERIC Document Reproduction Service No. ED 433 154)

Smilansky, S. (1968). *The effects of sociodramatic play on disadvantaged preschool children.* New York: John Wiley.

Smith, T., Kleiner, A., Parsad, B., Ferris, E., & Greene, B. (2003, March). *Prekindergarten in U.S. public schools, 2000–2001: Statistical analysis report.* Washington, DC: National Center for Education Statistics. (NCES 2003-019) Retrieved November 20, 2003, from *http://nces.ed.gov/pubs2003/2003019.pdf.*

Snyder, J. J., Reid, J. B., & Patterson, G. R. (2003). A social learning model of child and adolescent antisocial behavior. In B. B. Lahey, T. E. Moffitt, & A. Caspi (Eds.), *Causes of conduct disorder and juvenile delinquency* (pp. 27–48). New York: Guilford Press.

Solon, G. (1992, June). Intergenerational income mobility in the United States," *American Economic Review, 82,* 393–408.

Solon, G. (1999). Intergenerational mobility in the labor market. In O. Ashenfelter & D. Card (Eds.), *Handbook of Labor Economics* (Vol. 3A, pp. 1761–1800). Amsterdam: North Holland.

Sparling, J., & Lewis, I. (2000–2003). *Learningames, The Abecedarian Curriculum* (5 volumes). Chapel Hill, NC: MindNurture Press, Inc.

Stephan, J. (1999). *State prison expenditures, 1996.* Washington, DC: U.S. Department of Justice.

Stoney, L., & Greenberg, M. (1996). The financing of child care: Current and emerging trends. [Special issue on financing child care]. *The Future of Children, 6*(2), 83–102.

Stossel, S. (2004). *Sarge: The life and times of Sargent Shriver.* Washington, DC: Smithsonian Institution Press.

Terman, L. M., & Merrill, M. A. (1960). *Stanford-Binet Intelligence Scale Form L-M: Manual for the third revision.* Boston, MA: Houghton-Mifflin.

Tiegs, E. W., & Clark, W. W. (1963). *California Achievement Tests: Complete battery* (1957 ed.). Monterey Park, CA: California Test Bureau (McGraw-Hill).

Tiegs, E. W., & Clark, W. W. (1971). *California Achievement Tests* (1970 ed.). Monterey Park, CA: California Test Bureau (McGraw-Hill).

Tobias, T. N., Baker, M. W., & Fairfield, B. A. (1973). *The history of Ypsilanti—150 years.* Ypsilanti, MI: Ypsilanti Sesquicentennial Committee.

U.S. Administration for Children and Families. (2001). *Program performance standards for operation of Head Start programs by grantees and delegate agencies.* Retrieved July 11, 2004, from *http://www.acf.hhs.gov/programs/hsb/performance/1304A.htm.*

U. S. Administration for Children and Families. (2004a). *Head Start program fact sheet for FY2002 and FY 2003.* Retrieved July 11, 2004, from *http://www.acf.hhs.gov/programs/ hsb/research/2003.htm* and *http://www.acf.hhs.gov/programs/hsb/research/2004.htm.*

U. S. Administration for Children and Families. (2004b). *Income guidelines for participation in Head Start programs.* Information retrieved from *http://www.acf.hhs.gov/programs/ hsb/about/incomeguidelines/index.htm* on May 28, 2004.

U.S. Census Bureau. (1998). *Tabulations derived from the June 1977 Current Population Survey; Current Population Reports* (Series P70-9, table 1; Series P70-20, table 1, Part A and Part B; Series P70-30, table 1; Series P70-53, table 1; and table 1 of this report). Retrieved December 4, 2003, from *http://www.census.gov/population/socdemo/child/ p70-62/tableA.txt.*

U.S. Census Bureau (2000). *American factfinder.* Retrieved June 4, 2004, from *http://fact-finder.census.gov.*

U.S. Census Bureau. (2002). *Current Population Survey.* Washington, D.C.: Bureau of Labor Statistics.

U.S. Census Bureau. (2003a). *Educational attainment in the United States: March 2002, Detailed tables* (PPL-169). Retrieved June 20, 2004, from *http://www.census.gov/ population/www/socdemo/education/ppl-169.html.*

U.S. Census Bureau, Housing and Household Economic Statistics Division. (2003b). *Transitions into and out of poverty, by selected characteristics: 1996–1997* (Table 5). Retrieved May 31, 2004, from *http://www.census.gov/hhes/www/sipp96/table059697. html.*

U.S. General Accounting Office. (1997). *Head Start: Research provides little information on impact of current program.* Washington, DC: U.S. General Accounting Office. Available at *http://www.gao.gov* (search for HEHS-97-59). (ERIC Document Reproduction Service No. ED 407 167)

Vinter, R. D., Sarri, R. S., Vorwaller, D. J., & Schafer, W. E. (1966). *Pupil Behavior Inventory: A manual of administration and scoring.* Ann Arbor, MI: Campus Publishers.

Weber, C. U., Foster, P. W., & Weikart, D. P. (1978). *An economic analysis of the Ypsilanti Perry Preschool Project* (Monographs of the High/Scope Educational Research Foundation, 5). Ypsilanti, MI: High/Scope Press.

Wechsler, D. (1974). *Manual for the Wechsler Intelligence Scale for Children* (Rev. ed.). New York: Psychological Corporation.

Weikart, D. P. (Ed.). (1967). *Preschool intervention: Preliminary results of the Perry Preschool Project.* Ann Arbor, MI: Campus Publishers.

Weikart, D. P. (1988). A perspective in High/Scope's early education research. *Early Childhood Development and Care, 33,* 29–40. Great Britain: Gordon and Breach.

Weikart, D. P. (1989). Early childhood education and primary prevention: Prevention in human services. *The National Mental Health Association, 6*(2), 285–306.

Weikart, D. P. (1996). High-quality preschool programs found to improve adult status. In I. Frones, C. Jenks, I. Rissini, & S. Stephens (Eds.), *Childhood: A Global Journal of Child Research, 3* (pp. 117–120). London/Thousand Oaks/New Delhi: Sage Publications.

Weikart, D. P. (1998). Changing early childhood development through educational intervention. *Preventive Medicine, 27,* 233–237.

Weikart, D. P. (2002). The origin and development of preschool intervention projects. In E. Phelps, F. F. Furstenberg, Jr., & A. Colby, *Looking at lives: American longitudinal studies of the twentieth century* (pp. 245–264). New York: Russell Sage.

Weikart, D. P., Bond, J. T., & McNeil, J. T. (1978). *The Ypsilanti Perry Preschool Project: Preschool years and longitudinal results through fourth grade* (Monographs of the High/ Scope Educational Research Foundation, 4). Ypsilanti, MI: High/Scope Press.

Weikart, D. P., Deloria, D., Lawser, S., & Wiegerink, R. (1970). *Longitudinal results of the Ypsilanti Perry Preschool Project* (Monographs of the High/Scope Educational Research Foundation, 1). Ypsilanti, MI: High/Scope Press.

Weikart, D. P., Olmsted, P. P., & Montie, J. (Eds.) (2003). *A world of preschool experience: Observations in 15 countries.* Ypsilanti, MI: High/Scope Press.

Weikart, D. P., Rogers, L., Adcock, C., & McClelland, D. (1971). *The Cognitively Oriented Curriculum: A framework for preschool teachers.* Urbana, IL: University of Illinois.

Weikart, D. P., & Schweinhart, L. J. (1992). High/Scope preschool program outcomes. In J. McCord & R. E. Tremblay (Eds.), *Preventing antisocial behavior: Interventions from birth through adolescence* (pp. 67–86). New York: The Gilford Press.

Westinghouse Learning Corporation. (1969). *The impact of Head Start: An evaluation of the effects of Head Start on children's cognitive and affective development* (Vols. 1–2). Washington, DC: Clearinghouse for Federal, Scientific, and Technical Information.

White, S., Day, M. C., Freeman, P. K., Hantman, S. A., & Messenger, K. P. (1973). *Federal programs for young children: Review and recommendations.* Washington, DC: U. S. Government Printing Office. (Publication No. [OS] 74-101)

Whitebook, M., Phillips, D., & Howes, C. (1993). *National Child Care Staffing Study revisited: Four years in the life of center-based child care.* Oakland, CA: Child Care Employee Project. Retrieved July 11, 2004, from *http://www.ccw.org/pubs/nccssrevisit.pdf.*

Wolfe, B. L. (2002). Incentives and challenges of TANF design: A case study. *Journal of Policy Analyses and Management, 21,* 577–586.

Wolfe, B. L., & Zuvekas, S. (1997). Nonmarket outcomes of schooling. *International Journal of Educational Research, 27,* 491–502.

Xiang, Z., & Schweinhart, L. J. (2001). *Ready for success: Annual report of the Michigan School Readiness Program longitudinal evaluation.* Ypsilanti, MI: High/Scope Educational Research Foundation.

Yoshikawa, H. (1995, Winter). Long-term effects of early childhood programs on social outcomes and delinquency, *The Future of Children, 5*(3), 51–75. Retrieved December 7, 2004, from *http:www/futureofchildren.org/usr_doc/vol5no3art3.pdf.*

Zigler, E. F. (1987). Formal schooling for four-year-olds? No. *American Psychologist, 42,* 254–260.

Zigler, E. F., & Butterfield, E. C. (1968). Motivational aspects of changes in IQ test performance on culturally deprived nursery school children. *Child Development, 39,* 1–14.

Zill, N., Resnick, G., Kim, K., O'Donnell, K., Sorongon, A., McKey, R. H., et al. (May 2003). *Head Start FACES (2000): A whole child perspective on program performance—Fourth progress report.* Prepared for the Administration for Children and Families, U.S. Department of Health and Human Services (DHHS) under contract HHS-105-96-1912, Head Start Quality Research Consortium's Performance Measures Center. Retrieved July 11, 2004, from *http://www.acf.hhs.gov/programs/core/ongoing_research/faces/faces00_4thprogress/faces00_4thprogress.pdf.*

Invited Comments on *Lifetime Effects: The High/Scope Perry Preschool Study Through Age 40*

James J. Heckman

Distinguished Service Professor
University of Chicago, American Bar Foundation,
and University College, London

This report substantially bolsters the case for early
interventions in disadvantaged populations. More than
35 years after they received an enriched preschool program,
the Perry Preschool participants achieve much greater
success in social and economic life than their counterparts
who were randomly denied treatment.

The High/Scope Perry Preschool study is unique in the long-term follow-up of its participants. Children ages 3–4 were randomly assigned to the High/Scope intervention and followed at selected points of their lives until age 40. Since the Perry data are the centerpiece of the case for early intervention, the arrival of the age 40 report is an important event.

The results reported in this monograph largely confirm the findings of the previous age 27 report. As a group, children assigned to the treatment group continue to perform much better on a variety of socio-economic measures than those randomized out. Crime rates are lower for participants, schooling attainment rates are higher, earnings are higher, and pregnancy occurs later for the female participants. Cost-benefit analyses presented in the age 27 report, which are based on extrapolation of outcomes, now rest on a more secure foundation in the age 40 report, since more of the data missing at age 27 were available.

My commentary is intended to help make an already good thing better and to place this report in context. My hope is that these data are analyzed further, because some mysteries remain. The reporting style of the monograph relies too heavily on conventional statistical tests of significance on singular outcomes at one point in time. I suspect that an even stronger case for early intervention would emerge from an analysis of joint outcomes over different outcomes and over the entire life cycle of participants.

Noncognitive Skills

A main message of this analysis is that even though IQ was not permanently boosted by the Perry intervention, motivation, self-control, and the like were. That is why program participants' schooling levels and achievement test scores are higher and crime rates lower than their no-program counterparts.

This evidence is extremely important. Much of the emphasis in American educational policy is on improving cognition and using achievement tests to measure the success of interventions. But the Perry Preschool study tells us that improving social skills and strengthening the perseverance and motivation of children are major products of early interventions. More perseverance on the part of children and stronger motivation not only translate into higher achievement test scores but also into success in many dimensions of social life not currently measured by school accountability schemes.[1,2]

Issues of Data and Inference

Since the sample is small (123 initial participants) it is important to use the data as efficiently as possible. More use of the longitudinal (and family cluster) feature of the data could be made. Comparisons in this monograph are made cross-sectionally at ages 27 or 40 without analyzing the individual life cycle profiles that would be of fundamental interest for understanding human development processes. The reported evidence shows patterns of life cycle improvement in individual treatment group members versus control group members. It would be valuable in a continuation of this study to analyze individual growth profiles rather than group means over time. By presenting its evidence in the form of statistical tests applied one hypothesis at a time, this report understates the strength of the evidence. The general pattern (based on the reported means) suggests that on many outcome dimensions, and over time, the Perry intervention produces favorable outcomes. Thus, the outcomes as a whole should be analyzed rather than outcomes one by one. Part of this whole should consist of life cycle growth profiles (e.g., changes in schooling, wages, and the like for individuals).

Relying so heavily on statistical significance testing, outcome by outcome, is a very conservative method and eliminates a lot of valuable information on the pattern of favorable outcome results. Effects that are not statistically significant for one outcome, but are favorable, are not "zero." The evidence is more nuanced, and a better reporting style on a further analysis is needed to extract the full wealth of information contained in this study.

In testing whether or not a coin is fair, one can look at the number of times it comes up heads in a long trial. Nonparametric tests based on

---

[1] Heckman, Stixrud, and Urzua (2004) develop models of the effect of cognitive and noncognitive skills on socioeconomic outcomes and use these models to explain the Perry data.

[2] See Carneiro and Heckman (2003) and Heckman and Masterov (2004).

this principle have been in the statistical literature for more than 60 years. Exact small-sample methods are available to execute such tests that do not rely on the large-sample statistical theory used in this report and that account for the persistence of individual and family characteristics over time. These methods can be used to adjust for effective sample size by modeling correlation and dependence across outcomes. In Perry, there are many outcomes for each participant and each control group member. These outcomes consist of the same measure across time (e.g., education, earnings, or crime rates) and different outcome measures at the same time and over time. If the Perry treatment had no effect, then the long string of favorable outcomes that appears to characterize the experiment both over time and over many dimensions of social and economic performance would not be evident. It would be scientifically fruitful to perform more comprehensive small-sample joint tests and compute just how unlikely it would be for this *configuration* to arise from pure chance. If, on hundreds of trials and with different measures, the experimental results are favorable, as they seem to be, as a whole they are likely to be statistically significant, even if on any measure at any time the estimated effect is not.

A better longitudinal analysis would also correct for the dynamics of the life cycle in producing the subset of participants and nonparticipants able to make a transition. Thus, even though people start out much the same at ages 3 and 4, they experience different life cycle trajectories. At later ages, they face different opportunities. The influence of the past has to be reckoned with in measuring outcomes at a point in time. Treatment group members may have reported lower wages in the teen years than control group members because the treatment group people were going to school and working at part-time jobs. Their children will be younger than control group children because they delayed childbearing. The current cross-section analysis frame that focuses on analyzing outcomes one age at a time should be bolstered by an event history analysis that recognizes the way people "at risk" for (i.e., able to experience) an event are different from the rest of the population and that these differences emerge over the life cycle.

It would also be useful to perform a more systematic analysis of missing data. Not only is there considerable nonresponse on many questions but data are systematically missing (e.g., wages for people in prison or out of the work force). Given the small sample sizes, a sensitivity analysis would be useful to determine what findings are robust to alternative treatments of missing data.

Intergenerational Multipliers

Although the data are fragmentary, they suggest but by no means firmly establish that in the next generation, the performance of the children of participants is better than that of nonparticipants (see Table 6.4, p. 115). The children of treatment group parents are more likely not to be enrolled in special education, to graduate from high school, and to not be arrested. This evidence should be more carefully documented to account for the delayed childbearing (and younger ages) of the participants' children. We know that older and more educated mothers produce children with better socioeconomic performance. The cost-benefit analysis should account for this benefit. It would bolster the already strong case for early intervention.

Health Outcomes

Some of the health outcomes may appear to look perverse (e.g., higher blood pressure for participants, more overweight males, more asthma) although these effects are not statistically significantly different from zero. Since more of the program participants are working, the perverse effects may simply be due to the fact that working people are more likely to be subject to stress and the like.

Gender Differences

The heavy reliance on statistical significance tests leads the authors to report gender differences selectively. Even though some differences are not statistically significant, they are interpretively important and appear to reveal a pattern. The current report is tantalizing. It shows a reversal of employment effects by gender at ages 27 and 40, but provides no explanation for it.

The main effect of the program appears to be on the schooling of women, their employment (at age 27, but not at age 40), and on teenage childbearing. For men, the main effect is on crime and (inexplicably) employment at age 40. Is the employment effect exclusive of prisoners who were treated as "not employed" in the analysis? Once more, event history analysis accounting for people eligible for the event being analyzed may account for the anomaly.

There is an emerging body of literature on gender and child development. This study could contribute greatly to it by systematically reporting differences by gender whether or not they are statistically significant. I suspect that the pattern of outcomes for women as a whole versus men as a whole (across many outcome measures and over time) is statistically significant.

Cost-Benefit Study

I found parts of the cost-benefit study speculative:

1. The opportunity cost of funds is set too low. Fullerton's 15% is generally considered too low, the more commonly used measure, 50%, is more widely accepted (Browning, 1983). Use of these welfare cost numbers will reduce the benefit/cost ratio.

2. The earnings extrapolations and interpolations based on the Current Population Study data are unwise. The Perry children are of low initial ability. The National Longitudinal Survey of Youth (Bureau of Labor Statistics, 2001) data have information on ability, and the children in that study are in the age range

(and calendar year range) of the Perry children. Interpolation from NLSY data correcting for ability would give more convincing earnings streams. The Panel Study of Income Dynamics can be used for extrapolation to older ages and has some (limited) ability tests.

3. Adding intergenerational effects would boost measured returns and be of interest, as noted earlier. More educated women make better mothers and delay childbearing. I suspect that a proper accounting of the benefits of better parents on the next generation would greatly improve the estimated returns, especially if the crime, earnings, and parenting of study participants' children are taken into account. Such an enhancement of the cost-benefit study could draw on a large body of evidence on such effects from nonexperimental studies reported in Heckman and Masterov (2004).

Linking Up With Other Data

Perry's lessons will be of much greater generality if the experimental data are embedded in and enrich large-scale, nonexperimental studies and are also compared with other experimental studies. This will enhance what can be learned from both types of studies. My hope is that such embedding will be undertaken in the future.

Summary

This report provides valuable new evidence on the effectiveness of early interventions. Arguably, the evidence reported here understates the strength of the evidence in support of early interventions.

References

Browning, E. K. (1987). On the marginal welfare cost of taxation. *American Economic Review 77*(1), 11–23.

Bureau of Labor Statistics (2001). *NLSY Handbook 2001.* Washington, DC: U.S. Department of Labor.

Carneiro, P., & Heckman J. (2003). Human capital policy. In J. Heckman & A. Krueger (Eds.), *Inequality in America: What role for human capital policies?* Cambridge, MA: MIT Press.

Heckman, J., & Masterov, D. (2004, September). *The productivity argument for investing in young children* (Committee for Economic Development Working Paper 5). Retrieved December 8, 2004, from *http://www.ced.org/projects/kids.shtm/#working.*

Heckman, J., Stixrud, J., & Urzua, S. (2004). *The effects of cognitive and noncognitive skills on labor and behavioral outcomes.* Unpublished manuscript, University of Chicago, Economics Department (forthcoming *Journal of Labor Economics).*

Life Begins at 40!

Diana T. Slaughter-Defoe

Constance E. Clayton
Professor in Urban Education
Graduate School of Education
University of Pennsylvania

Life begins at 40! That is, it does if in the previous 39 years you have been sufficiently supported to lay the foundation for success. This is the profound message of this important research report on a longitudinal study of over 100 African Americans who generously shared their lives with us so that we might learn if a high-quality preschool experience can lead to a better adult life in this new millennium.

Educated in the Committee on Human Development at the University of Chicago, I have always been interested in reading about growth, development, and change in human lives. Further, I have had a special interest in those interventions in the earliest years that can influence the quality of a life cycle. Finally, urban children, parenting, and the resultant consequences for the children's educational development and learning have been a special interest of mine for many years. This longitudinal study, to my knowledge the only one that has followed a group of African Americans for nearly 40 years, has brought together all these special interests! It is exemplary in design and rigorous in method, including data analyses. Given the scientific rigor, I plan to use my comments to point to issues raised for me about poverty and human development by this important corpus of work that, without a doubt, establishes the preeminent legacy to the early childhood education field of David Weikart and his very special colleagues.

In addition to the Executive Summary, Chapter 10 provides an excellent overview of the design of the study, its major findings, and the authors' perspective on how these findings do and do not relate to other early educational initiatives that serve similar sample populations today (e.g., Head Start). The big picture is that the High/Scope Perry Preschool Project participants surpassed control group participants in this randomized control group study on educational attainment, indices of employment and financial well-being, and in being least likely to be involved with either the criminal justice system or with welfare and social services. Chapter 10 indicates that the authors firmly believe that the educational focus of the High/Scope Perry Preschool Project, coupled with visits to families over a 2-year period during which the preschool child (aged 3–5) was enrolled, are the essential program ingredients required to produce differences between the experiences of their program participants and others in either the control group or in other preschool program variants, e.g., a direct instruction/teacher-centered program, or a traditional, socially supportive nursery school program without a strong educational component. The authors also strongly believe that quality in preschool curricula requires well-educated teachers (bachelor's degree or better), small class sizes (averaging 8 childen per teacher), and regular parental contacts (biweekly). Few Head Start or other preschool programs currently meet these stringent requirements for high-quality programs—though the authors are convinced that many could. And yet, given these results, I think few programs can afford *not* to meet them—whether federal, state, or privately operated—if the goal of the program is to make a favorable impact on the potentially adverse effects of poverty on human development.

Nonetheless, what we know today is that different children and family members obtain different benefits from standard program curricula. From the study report, we cannot determine how different participants sampled the elements of the total program (i.e., the actual "dosages") experienced by each participant; thus, like the authors, without additional data we are compelled to assume the cumulative, integrative effects of all aspects of the High/Scope Perry Preschool Project on all participants. We also have to assume that all interveners implemented their responsibilities to the program equally well. Today, we know there is likely to be variability along both of these dimensions—dosage and degree of program implementation—and we are more likely to include indices to assess these aspects of the programs in our research. Fortunately for Schweinhart and his colleagues, they had few "no differences" between program and control group participants to explain; however, I think this information would have been useful to better understand obtained male-female differences in longitudinal program outcomes.

Special attention was directed to Chapter 7, which focuses on the economic public policy implications of the research. I consulted with a doctoral student[1] in this area at the University of Pennsylvania about the findings reported in that chapter. We were both impressed with what we learned from our independent reading of the chapter entitled "Lifetime Cost-Benefit Analysis." Authors Barnett, Belfield, and Nores describe how they monetized the impact of the High/Scope Perry Preschool Project and calculated the lifetime present value of the program's costs and benefits. This method aggregates all of the program effects, both from the individual and societal levels, and estimates the aggregate benefit of $258,888 per program participant, in constant 2000 dollars discounted at 3%, versus a $15,166 program cost per participant.

We strongly felt the study, which tracks both program and control groups to age 40, is an improvement on Barnett's 1996 cost-benefit analysis, which examined the groups through age 27. Estimates are still used to predict costs and benefits for the 41–65 year time frame. The current study also validates the prediction methodology used for the earlier study, since the actual costs and benefits from ages 28–40 were quite consistent with the predicted levels. In this analysis, almost 80% of the return of the program is to the general public, with most of the societal benefits (86%) resulting from crime reduction. Crime costs are estimated separately as

---

[1] Personal communication, October 15, 2004. Many thanks to S. Nemeroff.

costs to victims, the criminal justice system, and incarceration and probation costs. Overall, 93% of the public return of the program was due to
males, with crime costs for male program participants only 59% of the
crime cost for the male control group participants.

The doctoral student I consulted felt that the positive returns of
the program were robust even under various sensitivity simulations that
varied both the discount rate and the cost estimation assumptions. Under
all sensitivity scenarios, male participants contributed positively to the
return of the program. We both felt that, quite possibly, benefits are even
higher than estimated, considering that the analyses only focused on
five key indicators: crime savings, higher earnings, education savings,
increased tax revenue due to higher earnings, and welfare savings. For
example, the program impacts on health, mortality rates, and intergenerational effects were not monetized nor included in the present cost-benefit
analysis.

This leads to a more general comment. Many persons who will read
this report will be concerned about the long-term social supports to the
well-being of the children who initially participated in the preschool
program. Those children are now adults, many of whom are responsible for rearing children of their own. However, as a policy report, this
document is clearly designed to appeal to those governmental and social
policymakers who are concerned less about the humanity of the program
participants and more about their "nuisance" value or the potential they
have for disruptive, undesirable costs and consequences for society. In
Chapter 8, for example, the structural equation model discussion depicts
a careful selection and tracking of sociopsychological variables across the
37-year time frame that are individually, rather than ecologically, focused;
that have considerable "face validity" among nonpsychologists; and
that stress what even the most conservative communities in American
society would value and consider indicative of lifelong success: higher
educational attainment, higher financial earnings, and lower number of
crime-related arrests and convictions. No Freudian "lieben und arbeiten"
(love and work) for these program participants—in today's contemporary
society they must achieve that on their own time without the support of
U.S. tax dollars!

I mention this because I know that the report's authors are well
aware of the broad and sweeping importance of developmentally appropriate practices to the teachers and caregivers who served these adults
years ago in the Perry Preschool Project. These caregivers highly valued the children's development and strongly supported the children's
parents in being an integral part of that process. Probably few of the
caregivers at the time were especially concerned with the fiscal and
material well-being of the youngsters or their future educational credentials. Rather, the 1960s caregivers of the Perry Preschool Project children
were more likely to be concerned that the children come to appreciate, enjoy, and love learning for its own sake, to value education as a
vehicle for the development of critical thinking skills, and to become the
kind of persons who are generally respectful and caring of others' well-
being—persons who would, by definition, never self-consciously pursue
victimization nor harm of fellow citizens. Chapters 8–9 do not present
much data on these points. For example, from this report I do not know

much of the personal attitudes and values of the original High/Scope Perry Preschool Project teachers. Thanks to the comparative curricula study reported in Chapter 10, however, I am inclined to believe with the authors that explicit, individualized educational programming was of enduring value, regardless of the more lofty goals and mission that many of these "sixties" teachers and teacher aides undoubtedly held for their children. However, given this line of thinking, I could not help but wonder what values and qualities program participants presently hold for their own children, in contrast to those held by control participants for their children. Conversely, from this perspective, it is even more remarkable that the program participants became "successful adults" in the more generic or universal sense of the term.

Predictably, the eight case studies in Chapter 9 provide important descriptive information on the life courses of study participants with reference to education, employment and earnings, and criminal records. However, the studies also nicely sketch family, health, and community factors influencing participants. To the extent that this could be determined from reports to their interviewer, it seems that after the preschool program ended, even the program participants had evidence of serious life challenges in the form of continuing poverty, exposure to drugs in the communities in which they lived, and the multiple family and social problems that can spiral out of control without help. I wish it had been possible to ascertain how their obvious resiliencies enabled them to overcome those challenges. For example, participants did not emphasize the importance of particular elementary or high school teachers; they did speak of their own commitment to schooling but, except for family of origin, they did not stress enduring friendships, networks, or associations (including the church or spirituality) in their lives across time. From a social and institutional perspective, it almost seemed as if, after the preschool program, they and their families were essentially loners.

No wonder this excellent program had such a penetrating and long-term influence. As the author of Chapter 9 states: "The life courses of the 8 case study participants have been remarkably stable over time. Individuals who were successful early in life continue to be successful at midlife, and individuals who encountered failure in school and work or engaged in criminal activity early on continued to follow that pattern" (pp. 189–190). A longitudinal case study of the first group of 1965 Head Start children obtained similar findings (Slaughter-Defoe & Rubin, 2001). We found preschool and kindergarten teachers were able to predict remarkably well which children would be more or less successful in school by the conclusion of the youths' high school experience.

It should not be this way, and it did not have to be this way with those involved in the High/Scope Perry Preschool study either. Over time, other groups and institutions (e.g., schools, churches, community centers, youth groups and clubs, political organizations and groups) could have supported control group participants, thus reducing the gaps, and even potentially blurring the early differences between them and program participants. However, the researchers found that, since preschool, the individuals appeared to have gained little else from the extra-familial associations they subsequently had in our society. Although I learned from these important case studies and thoroughly enjoyed reading them, it saddened me to realize and once again appreciate how alone those who are impoverished can be at critical developmental and transitional points in their own lives. We as a society must commit to doing better at providing community supports for marginalized and poor individuals who do not have the social capital and resources needed to create enduring positive and supportive community ties.

If it is really true that "life begins at 40," then my best hope for all the participants is that they live long enough to see both themselves and their children enjoy a better quality of life. Based on the presented data, I close by expressing my deep appreciation to the High/Scope Perry Preschool Project staff for giving their program participants a tremendous "head start" in that regard.

References

Slaughter-Defoe, D., & Rubin, H. (2001). A longitudinal case study: Implications for early intervention and urban educational problems. *Educational Psychologist, 36*(1), 31–44.